RESISTING EQUALITY

The Citizens' Council,
1954–1989

STEPHANIE R. ROLPH

LOUISIANA STATE UNIVERSITY PRESS
BATON ROUGE

Published by Louisiana State University Press
Copyright © 2018 by Louisiana State University Press
All rights reserved
Manufactured in the United States of America
First printing

DESIGNER: Michelle A. Neustrom
TYPEFACES: Chaparral Pro, text; Cervo Neue, display
PRINTER AND BINDER: Sheridan Books, Inc.

LIBRARY OF CONGRESS CATALOGING-IN-PUBLICATION DATA

Names: Rolph, Stephanie Renee, author.
Title: Resisting equality : the Citizens' Council, 1954–1989 / Stephanie R. Rolph.
Other titles: Making the modern South.
Description: Baton Rouge : Louisiana State University Press, [2018] | Series:
    Making the modern South | Includes bibliographical references and index.
Identifiers: LCCN 2017037460 | ISBN 978-0-8071-6915-5 (cloth : alk. paper) |
    ISBN 978-0-8071-6916-2 (pdf) | ISBN 978-0-8071-6917-9 (epub)
Subjects: LCSH: Association of Citizens' Councils of Mississippi. | Citizens'
    Councils of America. | Mississippi—Race relations. | Mississippi—Politics
    and government—1951–
Classification: LCC HS2330.C483 R65 2018 | DDC 323.1196/073076209045—dc23
LC record available at https://lccn.loc.gov/2017037460

To Marc

CONTENTS

ACKNOWLEDGMENTS / ix

Introduction / 1

1 Born into Defiance / 13

2 Nurtured in Fear, 1954–1957 / 31

3 From the Capital City to the Nation's Capital, 1958–1960 / 69

4 The Center Weakens, 1961–1962 / 98

5 Abandoning the Harvest, Plowing New Fields, 1963–1964 / 125

6 Flight and White Reunion: The Citizens' Council after 1964 / 155

Conclusion / 186

NOTES / 191

BIBLIOGRAPHY / 223

INDEX / 231

ACKNOWLEDGMENTS

I have often replied to questions about the timeline of this project with laments about the length of its gestation. Its development over the past several years has mirrored the follies and shortsightedness of a young scholar traveling from graduate school into her career. Along the way, I have been fortunate to have crossed paths with fellow scholars in a variety of fields who helped this project grow from a narrowly focused dissertation into a proper contribution.

Connie Lester saw the earliest and roughest versions of my assessment of the Citizens' Council and nearly every iteration of it since. My gratitude to her as a mentor extends beyond her guidance to me as a senior scholar and encompasses my personal admiration for her strength, resilience, and generosity. Alan I. Marcus adopted me as his student in the last throes of my graduate school days when my fears of concluding the project and submitting versions of it for publication threatened to stall my completion indefinitely. He expected more than I ever thought was reasonable. He was right. Mark Goodman took me under his wing early and often and helped me cultivate my curiosities about conservative media venues like *Forum*.

The graduate program at Mississippi State University provided opportunities for research and support that directly impacted my collision with the Citizens' Council. In particular, the Citizens' Council *Forum* radio collection in the Mitchell Memorial Library Special Collections Department provided a lifeline of insight into the Council's ideology, its political alliances, and the longevity of its cause. The archivists there, Mattie Abraham and Betty Self, welcomed me every day for fifteen months and provided much needed distractions when transcribing became monotonous. I have special appreciation for Mattie, who patiently loaded and unloaded every reel for me, multiple times a day, for months. Without her commitment, *Forum* would not have been transcribed. Along similar lines, Leigh McWhite at the University of Mississippi's Archives and Special Collections has consistently suggested productive leads and guided me through connections I would never have considered. Archivists and staff members at the Mississippi Department of Archives and History always met me with warmth and expertise. Anne Webster, Clinton Bagley, Julia Young, and Joyce Dixon-Lawson supported my searches and accommodated last-minute requests as the project went through final revisions.

Mississippi State brought me together with lifelong friends. Andra Knecht and Jeffrey Howell made for excellent office mates, colleagues, and friends. They provided laughs and reassurance when research stalled and job prospects seemed dim. Derek Cronin and Joel Barnes made Friday night poker games a worthwhile (and sometimes lucrative) distraction for me. As I transitioned out of the program, I was fortunate to meet Jason Ward, Anne Marshall, Jim Giesen, and Alison Greene as they began their careers at Mississippi State. They each embraced and encouraged my work and have remained valued friends as I have experienced my own transitions into early career. Their accomplishments have stood as models for my own aspirations.

The faculty and administration at Millsaps College have helped shepherd this project through additional research summers and the last-minute questions I had about the Citizens' Council and its allies. In particular, my dean, Keith Dunn, has provided support and encouragement by reminding me that my value to Millsaps is rooted in my contributions as a scholar. Emlee Nicholson, Suzanne Marrs, Jeanne Middleton-Hairston, Marlys Vaughn, Louwanda Evans, Amy Forbes, and Bill Storey have each provided advice, encouragement, and entertainment when my balance seemed irretrievably lost. Madeline Iles and Anna Morgan Leonards have been apt pupils who have made their own contributions to the field, which demand recognition and provide hope that southern history is vibrant and necessary.

In the summer of 2010, as I prepared to begin my appointment at Millsaps, Martha Swain invited me to join a group that has shaped my identity as a scholar in ways that I cannot articulate fully. The Delta Women

Writers required me to produce compelling scholarship, and their demands for quality work opened up opportunities that have been critical to my work. Our group has transitioned since my entry in 2010, but I have been grateful for nearly a decade of advice and mentorship from Emily Clark, Elizabeth Jacoway, Martha Swain, Elizabeth Payne, Beverly Bond, Anne Marshall, Cherisse Jones-Branch, Susan O'Donovan, Deirdre Cooper Owens, Karen Leathem, Janet Allured, Gail Murray, Pam Tyler, Sarah Wilkerson-Freeman, Shennette Garrett-Scott, Sylvia Frey, Sheila Skemp, Rebecca Tuuri, and Story Matkin-Rawn.

I cannot say enough about Randal Hall and his encouragement to me as I made final revisions to my *Journal of Southern History* article. His gentle prodding and positive feedback helped me pull a particular portion of this project into a field that I was unfamiliar with, and my work with the *JSH* has raised a number of new opportunities for me to think about the transnational networks of white supremacy of which the Citizens' Council was a member.

Years ago, David Goldfield initially identified my interest in the Council as worthwhile, before the dissertation had reached conclusion. It is hard to imagine this project without his wise suggestions for additional research and analysis. I am indebted to him for his close reading and his encouragement as we prepared the manuscript for final submission. Rand Dotson at LSU Press was patient and understanding as I familiarized myself with the "process," and I am grateful to the expertise of this press for their insights into both detail and big-picture considerations.

The daily reality of this project cannot be adequately captured. Lots of people have provided an environment where I could grow into academe without making it my whole life. Pat Oden, Brian Clanton, and Kristen McCoy have humored me throughout the life of this book and have never doubted its publication. They have also reminded me that there are other things to talk about. Betty and Raymond Moore and Melissa and Michael Rolph have been generous in their support and their childcare, voicing just the right amount of questions about the project's status. Larry Oden will not be able to witness the completion of this very long project, but in a number of ways his support enabled it to happen. Campbell and Scarlett have grown up alongside this book. Their questions and excitement as it has neared completion have assured me. Marc Rolph knew me before he knew about the Citizens' Council. I cannot imagine a better partner. He had no stake in this project other than my passion, but he endured the heaviest burden in its completion—me.

RESISTING EQUALITY

INTRODUCTION

In March 1967, Lola Lee Bruington of Pensacola, Florida, received a letter of inquiry from historian Neil McMillen about the Citizens' Council movement in Florida. With reluctance, she responded but surrendered few details, noting that the organization had found some difficulty in maintaining unified action across the state. In Florida, she lamented, the greatest obstacle to consensus within white resistance movements was politics. Internal splits emanated from the state's 1960 gubernatorial election, making the Council movement in the state an outpost of more centralized Council movements, like those in Georgia, Louisiana, and Mississippi. The "hard core" of resistance, a designation with which she identified, remained extant in the state, unlikely to surrender but "easily . . . destroyed." The tone of Bruington's response to McMillen was intentionally cryptic, and her letter concluded with an invitation to talk face to face about his questions. "There is much one does not put in writing," she explained, "and IF you use ONLY what has been printed, you know little re Citizens [*sic*] Councils."[1]

Forty-three years later, a different memory of the Citizens' Council surfaced and drew national attention when Mississippi governor and Yazoo City native Haley Barbour recalled his memories of the organization in an interview with the *Weekly Standard*:

> You heard of the Citizens Councils? Up north they think it was like the KKK. Where I come from it was an organization of town leaders. In Yazoo City they passed a resolution that said anybody who started a chapter of the Klan would get their ass run out of town. If you had a job, you'd lose it. If you had a store, they'd see nobody shopped there. We didn't have a problem with the Klan in Yazoo City.[2]

1

Bruington's and Barbour's reflections on the Council differ in their descriptions, but both locate the organization within a struggle for dominance among white people. For Bruington, existing political institutions and allegiances marginalized the Council's radical principles of "hard core resistance," forcing the organization to work in the shadows of racial moderation. Barbour, on the other hand, described the Council's work as the antidote to Klan violence, a moderating force for whites that maintained stability in the face of disruption. Decades separate their descriptions of the Citizens' Council, but in both cases, the organization's significance rested on its relevance among whites.

The Citizens' Council was born on July 11, 1954, in Indianola, Mississippi, within two months of the *Brown v. Board of Education* desegregation decision. It officially dissolved in 1989 when it shut the doors on its brick-and-mortar headquarters in Jackson, Mississippi. In the first decade of what would be a thirty-five-year tenure, Council leaders and supporters organized in opposition to the civil rights movement and reacted to increasing federal support of that movement by directing their efforts toward unifying their principles with the priorities of the existing white power structure. The alliances the Council sought were local, statewide, regional, national, and global, and the trajectory of the organization's activities, campaigns, and partnerships never deviated from that objective. In many cases, the Council's efforts toward local unity resulted in multilevel racial terrorism that manifested in economic intimidation as well as information-sharing among whites that encouraged violence against noncompliant blacks. But when viewed within the context of state politics, regional resistance frameworks, and national partnerships it becomes clear that the Council's success depended on white coalition-building that prioritized the fortification of white supremacy within existing institutions in lieu of directly addressing black demands for equality. It is that prioritization that enabled the Council to move into new territories when the fight to maintain legal segregation and disfranchisement failed.

In the twenty years that followed the statewide desegregation of Mississippi's public school system in 1970, the Council found new avenues for activism that provided comfortable dwellings in the developing landscape of post–civil rights America. While much of the Council's energies in the 1970s and 1980s went toward its monthly publication, *The Citizen,* the organization continued to leave deep footprints through its commitment to privatized, segregated education in Mississippi.[3] But Council administrators were also interested in and involved with the maintenance of white minority rule in Rhodesia and South Africa, a position that the Council occupied well into the 1980s.[4] The Council also provided enthusiastic support, through fund-raising events and publications, for George Wallace's presidential campaigns in 1964, 1968, and 1972, and became an outspoken supporter of using white southern resistance as a way to realign the priorities of the existing two-party system.[5]

The Council's post–civil rights activities suggest another look at the organization's origins, ideology, and activities over the course of thirty-five years. Historians have, for the most part, ignored the Council's later years, preferring to link the organization to the civil rights struggle (roughly 1954–1965). Doing so restricts our understanding of Council activism to its ultimate failure and eliminates any prospects for complexity. A longer look suggests that the Council's unwavering commitment to white supremacy ensured its continued relevance. The organization certainly migrated toward issue-specific campaigns but, intentionally or not, it cultivated ideology over political positions. That strategy outlasted the civil rights movement and enabled the Council to tap into existing and evolving networks of resistance, conservatism, and global politics. The consistency of its position and the shifting political allegiances that followed the civil rights movement ultimately saw success in its convergence with mainstream political ideology in the 1980s. It did so without significant adjustments to its founding principles of "states' rights and racial integrity."

This book takes a second look at the Citizens' Council, one that builds on Neil McMillen's profile of the organization and its sister movements, *The Citizens' Council: Organized Resistance to the Second Reconstruction, 1954–64.* When McMillen began his research in the late 1960s, the organization was debilitated in its influence over state politics, but nearly twenty years away from total collapse. His interviews with Council stalwarts like William J. Simmons, Robert Patterson, Louis Hollis, and Medford Evans chronicled their reflections on the movement's significance, even as their work was ongoing. In 1971, when the book saw its first publication, it received two book reviews from Council administrators George Shannon and John J. Synon, who published their evaluation of McMillen's work in the February 1972 issue of *The Citizen*. Beyond Shannon's comments about the poor proofreading, "monotonous" prose, and two instances of bad grammar, Synon found McMillen's treatment typical of the "left-wing carpetbaggers of our academic fraternity." The historian's offenses ranged from his short residence in "Dixie" (six years in 1972) to his exploitation of the Council's hospitality through numerous interviews and access to organizational records. McMillen's receipt of research support from the Woodrow Wilson Foundation and his use of archives from the Southern Regional Council and Anti-Defamation League made his work even more suspect in Shannon and Synon's estimation.[6]

George Shannon, who at the time was the managing editor of *The Citizen*, probably came closer to identifying the Council's true objection to McMillen's profile of the organization when he complained that the book read more like an obituary than a profile. He feared that while McMillen's account would serve as little more than an "irritant" to individuals who participated in the organization's work, its bias could "mislead" future generations about the civil rights movement.[7] In fact, despite Shannon's prediction, *The Citizens' Council* has withstood more than three decades of burgeoning scholarship on organized white resistance to the civil rights movement, and maintained central relevance in the historiography of both the civil rights movement and its opposition.

In the book's second edition, released in 1994, McMillen cogently identified a racial "reconfiguration" in American culture and politics since the collapse of the organized white resistance movement. Despite the dismantling of the overt and legally enshrined racism of the past, footprints of prejudice remained and even thrived in contemporary society. "Race remains," McMillen reflected in his preface, "the American obsession, our great national divide."[8] This study takes McMillen's reflections on "the American obsession" as its central question by following the Council's commitment to white supremacy from its birth in 1954 to the shuttering of its doors in 1989. That inquiry has yielded substantial evidence that the Council's sustained and unapologetic advocacy for white supremacy won the organization a variety of allies within Mississippi, across the country, and around the globe.

Placing the Council within a context of sympathetic partners, from its founding moments to its demise, provides a more accurate picture of how white supremacy converged with mainstream political thought in the years following landmark civil rights legislation. It also indicates the incredible adaptability that white supremacy contained. If the Council began as an organization committed to maintaining a legal system built on notions of white power and black inferiority at a time when that position was increasingly unpopular, it is critical to understand how that same ideology contributed to the conservative ascendancy that developed in the 1970s and 1980s. This examination of the history of the Citizens' Council suggests that such a convergence was not the result of a transformation within the organization, but rather a renewed embrace of white supremacy by the rest of the nation. For that reason, it is critical to provide a reexamination of the years that have received the most scholarly attention, 1954–1964, to complicate the Council's reputation as a local terrorist organization. It is more accurate to delineate the various levels of Council power between its local chapters and its statewide associations. The former acted more or less independently and relied on existing communities of white citizens that coalesced around the threat of black activism in their towns, cities, and counties. That coalescence often took the form of economic and physical intimidation as a means of discouraging black challenges to white authority. In contrast, the objectives of the Association of Citizens' Councils of Mississippi (ACCM) and the Citizens' Councils of America (CCA) tended to take the shape of propaganda (both in print and radio/television formats) and state-wide influence over elected officials. The CCA was the arm of the Council movement that cultivated its ideology and pursued partnerships with like-minded organizations. It maintained visible distance from the civil rights movement, preferring to focus on maintaining unity within the white power structure instead. The CCA and its leadership outlasted most of its local chapters because of the partnerships it forged and the ideology it cultivated. It became part of a national movement that included a variety of conservative and radical right organizations who observed the post–civil rights years as an alarming departure from traditional American values.

Historians of organized resistance to civil rights activism in the Deep

South can now claim a deep and nuanced field of scholarship that engages the complex ideologies, politics, cultures, and regions that nurtured white southern rebellion in the civil rights era. The route that white southerners traveled from segregation's defense into conservatism has become more visible in the process. The focus on conservatism, however, threatens to become the southern historian's "Lost Cause," an explanation that is a product of retroactive interpretation. Given what historians began to understand in the 1980s about the diverse coalitions that comprised conservative political power and the realization that the South was a critical piece of that formation, new questions about the ultimate fate of white resistance appeared. Such interpretations privilege white resistance, tracking its various locations over the course of several decades but all in the pursuit of finding conservatism as their end point.[9]

This study flips the lens, prioritizing the contexts within which the Citizens' Council acted. The period of time in which the organization existed included massive shifts in global priorities, political alignments, economics, and race consciousness. White resistance movements formed alongside all of those transformations and absorbed their meanings in ways that deeply informed their embrace of white supremacy in the postwar era. The organization was also the product of a long history of white southern resistance which provided both familiarity and resilience despite the increasing marginalization of the white South's position. Its connection with past movements and the embrace of national priorities led the Council to seek white allies instead of engaging directly with black activists. Its alliances with state and local government are well known and accurately described in McMillen's work, but less is known about the network of white supremacy that existed outside of Mississippi, the South, and even the United States. In essence, the Council movement went well beyond racial terrorism at the local level and sought to "white out" the civil rights movement through a reinvigoration of ideology and white activism. Using this perspective, it becomes clear that white supremacy was reborn in the civil rights era, not irreparably weakened.

A study like this is possible because of the breadth of insightful scholarship that has preceded it. Beyond the work done on conservatism in the United States in general and white resistance in particular, the evolution of civil rights scholarship has widened the chronological margins of black activism as well as its national borders. Scholars have convincingly established the transnational impact of black nationalism and decolonization on the American civil rights movement, recognizing that global transformations in the twentieth century directly influenced the ideologies of black civil rights leaders in the United States and vice versa. These leaders saw themselves acting within a global environment that united their struggles with people of color in other countries.[10]

There is evidence that white Americans saw themselves in similar ways. American history follows a trajectory of race-making and remaking, one that has consistently engaged in renewed forms of oppression as existing forms became anathema. In his comparative study of white supremacy in the American South and South Africa, historian George Fredrickson described white supremacy as the product of "historically conditioned tendencies" that regularly recycle and reassert dominance over nonwhite people. The consistent application of white dominance that he refers to has, historically, required fluidity as conditions shifted and acceptable approaches to oppression changed.[11] It seems logical to approach white resistance with this framework in mind. There were moments when the Citizens' Council was a marginal outlier of white adjustment to new racial norms, but those moments did not necessarily follow a linear progression. Historians are correct to point out that the Council's influence was never more powerful than it was in the months following the *Brown* decision. But it is misleading to gauge its influence based solely on its membership or general popularity. The Council's ideology survived through a series of partnerships and alliances, and those relationships developed through a recalibration of what Grace Elizabeth Hale has called "common whiteness."[12] The presence of race-based slavery in the colonial and antebellum South bonded whites of every class despite the myriad differences that separated them. The post-Reconstruction South saw new forms of common whiteness that sublimated economic, educational, and class disparities in the name of white superiority.[13] In many ways, the Council's mission and modus operandi mimicked historical models of white crisis and unification. What separates the Council movement from the race-baiting of demagogues like James K. Vardaman or Ben Tillman, however, was its desire to unify with whites outside of the South and even outside of the United States.

This study focuses most of its attention on the Citizens' Council movement in Mississippi as a way to better contextualize the breadth of those aspirations. While multiple other Councils and Council-like organizations dotted the landscape of the American South in the post-*Brown* years, Mississippi was its birthplace and its burial site. The headquarters for the Citizens' Councils of America resided in Jackson, and all of the organization's national and international campaigns emanated from its office there. It was the Council movement in Mississippi that oversaw the most ambitious aspirations of organized resistance, and it is within that location that this book seeks to understand those alliances. It is, however, prudent to explore organized resistance in other states to fully contextualize the Council's significance and comparative success in Mississippi. Scholars of sister organizations in other southern states readily concede that it was in Mississippi that the deepest impact of organized defiance existed. This work sheds some light on why that was the case by illuminating various formulas of political power, grassroots activism, and elite dominance that worked toward or against Council success in different southern states.

Each chapter that follows emphasizes a particular context within which white supremacy, as it existed within the Citizens' Council movement, operated. The chapters are organized chronologically in order to best understand the consistencies and adjustments that developing events demanded. Within each context, white supremacy was the central tenet, but particular influences impacted its articulation at specific times. In every circumstance, the Council sought sympathetic white allies who could strengthen its efforts and help create a network of activism that could more effectively resist change.

Chapter One examines the contours of conservatism and white southern resistance prior to the *Brown* decision. The sweeping changes that accompanied economic crisis, national war mobilization, the onset of the Cold War, and the growing visibility and frequency of black challenges to legal forms of exclusion prepared a rich field in which white southern resistance could reach maturity. From a national standpoint, the distaste for totalitarianism, first through the confrontation with fascism and later with communism, cultivated a body of conservative literature that increasingly associated centralized government with tyranny. Conservative media sources adapted that intellectual framework to more accessible, issue-based ideologies that promised to reach wider audiences. The Supreme Court's decision in *Brown v. Board of Education* in May 1954, however, provided a rallying issue that enlivened fears of federal interference by threatening state-sanctioned white supremacy. Existing networks of local black activism in Mississippi made that threat even more powerful, especially in light of white equivocation on the future of public schools. In the months immediately following *Brown*, the appearance of the Citizens' Council enabled rapid mobilization of organized resistance in the state. Its formation sought to silence moderation by prioritizing white unity over long-standing white divisions in the state. That model would carry the organization into greater success as threats multiplied around it.

Chapter Two scrutinizes the first two years of Council organization in Mississippi, a process that not only suggested leaders' desire for Council supremacy among competing resistance organizations but sparked a campaign for national significance. The comparative sluggishness of similar organizations in other states highlights the unique formula of grassroots support that the Mississippi Council enjoyed. The Mississippi movement also benefited from the committed leadership of William J. Simmons, a figure who remained at the center of the organization's work until its official end in 1989. Simmons's entry into Council leadership coincided with growing ambitions toward national significance, most visibly through the activation of the organization's publicity arm, the Educational Fund of the Citizens' Council. But those years also saw the beginning of contentious relationships with other entities in the state, especially the Mississippi State Sovereignty Commission, a state agency charged with functions similar to those of the Council but with the benefit of state funding.

Chapter Three details the height of Council popularity. Ross Barnett's election to governor in 1959 connected the Council to the highest echelon of power in Mississippi, an achievement that gave the organization access to state funding through the Mississippi State Sovereignty Commission, not for local Council activities, but for its weekly radio and television broadcast, *Forum,* a venue meant to bring the segregationist message to the rest of the country. Just as collusion between the Council and state government reached fruition, however, civil rights activism in Mississippi became more visible, challenging local Councils throughout the state to maintain their power at a time when Council administrators had begun shifting their gaze toward Washington, DC.

Chapter Four examines the collision between increasing Council demands for support and challenges from black activists throughout the state. It was during the years 1960–1962 that visible fractures between the Citizens' Council and the white power structure became clear. This critical period in the organization's history brings to light more differences between the Mississippi movement and its sister organizations in other states, many of whom saw significant drops in support both at the grassroots level and from political elites. The Mississippi Council experienced similar challenges, but its cultivation of wider networks of alliance pulled its priorities into new fields of national activism and opened up investments that provided more permanent spaces for its work to thrive.

Chapter Five examines the years 1963–1964, which were defined by increasing violence in the Council's home state. These years also ushered in the successful passage of the Civil Rights Act of 1964, the first of two significant pieces of sweeping civil rights legislation that cut at the core of Council resistance. Other organizations, however, surfaced in those years, and their existence provides evidence that the Council's footprint went deeper than its own initiatives suggest. The culture of defiance in Mississippi continued to thrive, pointing toward a recalibration of white resistance that no longer needed Council oversight to survive. The organization, in turn, continued to cultivate national networks of white alliance even as its influence in Mississippi withered.

The defeats of 1964 and 1965 forced the Citizens' Council to reconsider its investments if the organization was to continue. Chapter Six travels from 1965 to the Council's end in 1989, a period of time that saw a reinvigoration of white resistance on a national level. Because this period included a severe decline in local activities, including the end of production of *Forum,* an examination of the Council's monthly publication, *The Citizen,* provides useful insight into the political intersections of white southern resistance with political realignments at the national level. The Council's work in these years also suggests a relative abandonment of defiance in favor of flight, both ideological and geographical, from the changes the Council had for so long tried to stop.

To echo Lola Lee Bruington's warning to Neil McMillen, there is much we will never know about the Council's inner workings. This study in no way seeks to dilute the local terrorisms that the organization encouraged and orchestrated, but more attention is given to the corporate structure and ideology of the Citizens' Council than in its reputation among black activists and white moderates in Mississippi. Their impressions of the organization have great bearing on particular moments in the Council's history, and where that is true, those relationships have been explained. In particular, white moderates' relationship to the Council was a reflection of the organization's perceived power. As the Council's fortunes rose, moderate voices that cautioned against open defiance quieted. As the Council's popularity sank, moderates were more audible in their defense of practical solutions that sought to preserve white power within the boundaries of federal mandates. Each chapter shows those relationships and identities as evolving within specific moments of the civil rights movement and after. Much of what follows, however, tracks the Council and its leaders through their own words, ambitions, and perceptions in a rapidly changing nation and world.[14]

Readers will note that there is still much to find in the search for the Citizens' Council's footprint. This study does not aspire to complete that search. Rather, a new look at this infamous organization should raise compelling questions about how historians approach the phenomenon of organized white resistance during the civil rights movement and after, and the necessity of locating these individuals and organizations within their proper contexts. An entire body of scholarship is needed to track the network of alliances that came together amidst the challenges of the civil rights movement. In particular, it is imperative that scholars explore white supremacist organizations and other fringe movements during this period with gravity. Diminishing visibility should not imply conversion among their members. More importantly, their designation as "fringe" or "radical" should not imply irrelevance. Rather, we should consider the various paths they travel as maps to a diverse collection of sympathetic ideologies which, in particular moments of American history, come together to form movements that turn the historical lens to new coalitions of power and influence. To that end, while the book's conclusion coincides with the end of the Citizens' Council as an organization, my hope is that the reader will not track the arc of the organization's demise but find in these pages evidence of its survival.

CHAPTER 1

BORN INTO DEFIANCE

There is going to be a tremendous upsurge of conservatism during the
next four, eight, and twelve years. And as this moves like a tidal wave, we
will be carried to victory. Conservatism is on the march now for the first
time in thirty years—and we are part of the conservative movement.
—LOUIS HOLLIS, CITIZENS' COUNCIL ADMINISTRATOR

Either we will all stay white together, or we will be integrated county
by county and state by state." That statement appeared in the Citizens' Council's first official pamphlet in November 1954, a moment when
white unity in Mississippi seemed split over the future of the state's public school system.[1] Four months had passed since the founding of the
Council's first chapter in Indianola, Mississippi, and its first official publication signified a shift from its shadowy beginnings at the local level
to statewide activism, a move that marked the organization's realization
that local intimidation tactics would not be sufficient to resist changes
to the state's racial practices. For Council leaders, white moderates in the
state posed a greater threat to segregation than black activist organizations like the National Association for the Advancement of Colored People (NAACP). Consequently, white unity was their central objective, and
that focus led them to decades of partnerships and through an evolution
of white supremacy that traveled an arc from overt racial terrorism to
race-neutral conservatism.

In the organization's beginnings the Council's message was little more
than a naked endorsement of white supremacy that reflected its early
provincialism. Upon its founding, the Council proposed that white leaders in each community patrol local black activism using economic intimidation to discourage it. As the Council movement became public,
however, the role of ideology and the cultivation of resistance vernacular

became increasingly important as a way to unify whites across the state. But the Council model was not new or unique. Conservative opposition to the New Deal, criticisms of federal power, and the Dixiecrat revolt in 1948 signaled a groundswell of resistance from both the intellectual elite and the grassroots. Increasing evidence of black activism and the announcement of *Brown v. Board of Education* in May 1954 crystallized those fears and activated white reaction. When the Citizens' Council emerged as a potential solution in October 1954, it did so in a prepared environment that contained familiar ideology and potential colleagues. What distinguished the Council movement from peer organizations that predated *Brown*, however, was its ability to translate conservative ideas into a language of defiance for local whites in predominantly black counties and towns. Resistance to desegregation mandates in these communities was assured, but the Council's presence and propaganda tied that resistance to lofty principles of constitutional integrity and local control. Council-guided resistance, then, manifested as more than violence and intimidation tactics. From its earliest moments, its leaders articulated ideals that would long outlast the issues that initiated the organization's formation.

The ideas that shaped Council-led resistance existed decades before the Supreme Court's announcement of *Brown*. Conservative intellectuals began to draw attention in the 1930s for their opposition to the New Deal and their advocacy for isolationism during World War II. While most Americans celebrated the end of the war, conservative ideologues wondered if recent socialist victories in Western Europe would prove contagious in the United States, given the federal government's rapid expansion under Franklin Roosevelt's administration.[2] In a slightly different way, white southerners witnessed the bureaucratic expansion with similar alarm. As the federal government offered economic assistance through work programs and other forms of federal aid, threats to the South's racial hierarchy seemed imminent. The convergence of those two frames of resistance helped forge an alliance that would link white resistance to the civil rights movement and create a philosophy that could preserve white power even if its current manifestations, segregation and disfranchisement, did not survive.

Conservative intellectuals writing in the 1930s and 1940s remained relatively unknown outside of their own circles. Albert Jay Nock, Friedrich A. Hayek, Peter Viereck, Bernard Iddings Bell, and others wrote extensively about their philosophy instead of their politics, a choice that rendered grassroots activism unlikely. Their approach emphasized ideology over policy, a deliberate prioritization that rejected progressive ideals as a guide for social improvement.[3] In particular, they disapproved of the wave of social welfare measures and government regulation that preceded World War I and reappeared in some form during the New Deal. In short, conservative intellectuals did not believe the government was obliged to improve the daily lives of its citizens. The conservative movement that began to grow in opposition to the New Deal identified the progressive philosophy as wholly destructive and linked its approach to the totalitarian regimes that initiated World War II.[4] As early as 1935, Albert Jay Nock, an inspiration for many of the conservative writers who gained popularity in the 1950s and 1960s, wrote that the differences among fascism, communism, and socialism were nearly imperceptible. It was more accurate, he argued, to discuss what they shared: a firm allegiance to the state as the ultimate source of authority and wisdom alongside an "equivalent depletion of social power."[5] The state itself was "antisocial," he continued, and moved "grudgingly towards any purpose that accrues to society's advantage." The nature of state power, he argued, was forever bent toward accumulating more power.[6]

Nine years later, in 1944, Friedrich A. Hayek's *The Road to Serfdom* issued similar warnings. Hayek's experiences as a witness to the creeping totalitarianism in Europe during the 1930s alarmed him in its assault on individual liberty. An Austrian economist, Hayek's work pointed to the danger of centralized power, especially regarding economic policy.[7] The emphasis on outcomes of equality and social justice, he argued, often distracted citizens from the means by which governments could achieve them. Speaking specifically of socialism (although Hayek, like Nock, identified little to distinguish isms from each other), Hayek explained that the achievement of its end required the total abolition of individual production, private ownership, and entrepreneurship. In their place would appear a central planning body, one that could hope to represent no more than a minority of its citizens.[8] Done for moral purposes to achieve equitable ends, such moves were not within the purview of the state, a body that should only act to establish long-standing laws that could persist in changing times, always protecting the individual in pursuit of his own path.[9]

In 1949, Peter Viereck, a poet and political philosopher who taught at Mount Holyoke, moved closer to defining conservatism as the solution to the fears that Nock, Hayek, and others identified as endemic to both Europe and the United States. In *Conservatism Revisited,* Viereck described conservatism as "self restraint; preservation through reform . . . balance . . . nostalgia" and "unbroken historical continuity." At its "fire-center" was what Viereck identified as an "emotional élan . . . a reverence for the dignity of the individual soul."[10] His remarks described a cyclical movement of ideas and progress, one that was organically grown in the traditions of man as an individual. Viereck's conservatism stood in contrast to what he identified as "rationalist liberalism," a position that embraced "abstract blueprints" instead of concrete solutions. The liberal impulse, he asserted, defined freedom without embodying it.[11]

Economy and state growth were not the only institutional threats that postwar conservative intellectuals identified, however. Education, in their estimation, was especially vulnerable to state control and indoctrination. In 1952, Bernard Iddings Bell published his warning against federally supported school systems, an issue that white southerners would find especially helpful in articulating their opposition to *Brown's* ruling in 1954. In *Crowd Culture,* Bell described the public school system in the United States as a "large-scale government monopoly." Increasing standardization and conformity, he explained, would inevitably weaken individualism and dissent while lowering the expectations for achievement. The mediocrity that resulted, he explained, "frets and frustrates the more able while it flatters the incompetent."[12]

Certain threads of conservatism remained sequestered within academe and circulated only through disciplinary journals, but in the years between 1945 and 1954, conservative publications for popular audiences multiplied. Publications like *The Freeman, American Mercury, Human Events,* and *Facts Forum* articulated the fears of their readers regarding the reach of the federal government, communism, and social justice.

Unlike previous writings that plotted the philosophy of conservatism but disconnected from issues, these publications foregrounded current events as platforms for ideological debate.[13]

It was within the pages of these publications that most conservative intellectuals honed their craft. Men like Albert Jay Nock, Frank Meyer, Friedrich Hayek, and Frank Chodorov developed a following through their commentaries and reflections on current events. In the process they contributed to the popularization of conservative philosophy among white Americans across the country. The priority that these publications gave to limited government and local control challenged what their contributors saw as the Left's obsession with morality and justice as guiding principles. Instead, the writers who shaped conservative media in the postwar, pre-*Brown* years offered concrete approaches to governance that promised to survive shifting circumstances and eliminate complexity. To put a finer point on their contribution, conservative intellectuals offered stability in the midst of sweeping global and national changes. That alternative became more meaningful as the Cold War escalated and the challenge to white supremacy became more visible.[14]

Magazines like *Human Events, American Mercury,* and later, *National Review,* represented an appeal to wider audiences, but Dan Smoot's *Facts Forum* went one step further by encouraging its readers to participate in opinion-making and ideological debate. Each month, the newspaper featured a survey question, asking readers to send in their answers for publication in the following issue. It also headlined a question that guest writers answered from both a pro and con position, an approach meant to underscore the newspaper's commitment to balanced reporting and encourage more local participation in political debates. To further that objective, editors urged their readers to organize local "Forums" and "become salesmen for . . . basic American qualities."[15]

In addition to its print work, *Facts Forum* extended into more modern media venues in its radio and television broadcasts. In October 1953, the *State of the Nation* television and radio series began, a program that profiled state governors in an interview format. The *Facts Forum Washington* broadcasts hosted political figures as its guests, providing a free format for senators and members of Congress to articulate their positions on specific issues and win public support in the process. In addition to those two programs, Dan Smoot hosted a weekly radio broadcast that focused on the "pro and con arguments of . . . vital problems facing America."[16] These broadcasts reached a number of cities throughout the nation in the 1950s. In March 1953, the program premiered on WJPR, a Greenville, Mississippi, radio station. One year later, two other Mississippi cities, Meridian and Jackson, had picked up the broadcasts.[17] In November 1953, the program achieved national exposure when its public affairs program, *Answers for America,* appeared on the American Broadcasting Company (ABC) network in prime time.[18]

Facts Forum served as a blueprint for conservative white activism, not only in delineating the steps to effective organizing, but also in the accessibility it gave to conservative ideology. The requests for reader participation alongside articles by conservative intellectuals like Ludwig von Mises, William F. Buckley Jr., and James Burnham made an intriguing formula that helped transform conservative philosophy into daily conversations about politics. It also forged alliances among white Americans who might have little else in common outside of their support for conservatism. H. L. Hunt, an oil tycoon from Texas known for his libertarian leanings, was its chief investor, although by 1953 *Facts Forum* claimed several regular contributors.[19] Hunt's support points to the financial underpinnings that an operation like *Facts Forum* required. More importantly, it suggests an early alliance between members of the financial elite and diverse coalitions of white readers, many of whom were transitioning from working-class roots to middle-class status.

Facts Forum went further to ensure its appeal to a diverse audience of white Americans by giving space to southern segregationists like Georgia's governor Herman Talmadge, Mississippi senator James Eastland, and John Birch member and future Citizens' Council administrator Medford Evans, who became managing editor of the publication in 1954. In its February 1955 issue, the debate question chosen for the pro/con debate asked, "Do you think that this recent segregation decision was good for America?" The affirmative answer to the question revealed the way in which *Facts Forum* could claim balanced debate, yet drive home its conservative message. In its support of the *Brown* decision, the pro-desegregation statement managed to amplify all of the consequences that white conservatives and segregationists predicted when explaining their opposition to the decision. The tone of the editorial was glib in its appraisal, describing the ruling as evidence of "progressive American democracy's twentieth century victory over the forces of reaction, bigotry, and prejudice." With that designation elucidated in the opening remarks, the insights that followed drew attention to the misguided motivations of the court. The statement's author encouraged readers to recognize the true hero of the monumental decision, President Dwight D. Eisenhower, whose "quiet, determined, dedicated efforts . . . created the conditions—the national attitude, the national atmosphere—which made that school segregation decision possible." Eisenhower's actions were "unmotivated by fear of pressure of groups, with no thought of glory or political gain." His appointment of Chief Justice Earl Warren (a figure that segregationists and conservatives alike held in low esteem) was a sound decision. Warren was "a nice guy who deserved some kind of reward for supporting Ike politically," even though critics decried his lack of experience, a fact that the editorial's author found refreshing. "Where previous Chief Justices had found themselves tied down by judicial precedents and hedged about by narrow legalisms," the statement read, Warren was able to supersede the "lifeless letter of the law and interpret our Constitution as a living, dynamic instrument of government." This approach allowed for application of "twentieth century concepts of what freedom and equality mean."[20] The utopian tone that this argument embodied while flouting process, precedent, and tradition is obvious. It drove home the point that Warren's motivations grew out of a grasp for political gain and a complete and willful disregard for the Constitution and its limits. The emphasis on ends over means was something that conservative intellectuals like Hayek and Nock railed against in their writings.

What the pro statement insinuated through satire, the con statement made plain. Eschewing the relaxed, casual approach to process, the con argument began its answer with a clear condemnation of the court's overreach. "The Supreme Court's decision," the statement asserted, "is not a judicial interpretation. . . . It is a political decision, grounded not in law, but in Earl Warren's notions about psychiatry and sociology." Forced desegregation was likely to infringe upon the "only real land of opportunity for Negroes in the world—the South," by eliminating jobs and destroying long-standing relationships between blacks and whites there.

The court's interference in these relationships, the statement continued, sought to replace "Christian love" with political power, a disastrous approach to human relationships and a certain path to centralized authority at the expense of state sovereignty.[21]

As these editorials illustrate, publications like *Facts Forum* thrived by articulating escalating anxieties among white Americans. The access to conservative ideology that the publication provided nurtured fear and shaped it into a broader political discourse. *Facts Forum* took otherwise sterile conservative theories of power and translated them into a language that could be applied to contemporary issues of foreign policy, economy, and education. As that transformation happened, the relationship between conservative ideology and the defense of segregation crystallized. The parallel achievements of accessible conservative ideology and organized white rebellion in the South served the purposes of both movements. For the former, white southerners brought with them their numbers and an issue that embodied the central tenet of conservative fears: federal overreach. For the latter, as the conservative movement drew diverse groups into its following, it promised national legitimacy for the segregationist cause and an adaptable philosophy that easily accommodated white supremacy.

This convergence was not readily apparent in the years prior to *Brown,* however. White southern backlash to Roosevelt's New Deal policies began in 1936 and represented the persistent impulse among white southerners to prioritize regional distinctiveness over national consensus. In a similar vein, conservative intellectuals were not especially invested in activating a democratic base of support. Historian Richard H. King describes conservative thinkers as embodying "a certain distaste" for grassroots organization. In his profile on the ideology of southern conservatism, King distinguishes the southern strand as more "traditionalist" in nature, a designation that held at its center an embrace of natural hierarchy that prioritized responsibilities of leadership and deference over civil rights. Consequently, southern traditionalists exemplified deep suspicions about notions of progress that mirrored conservative intellectuals' opposition to "planned change," especially when government motivated it.[22]

The paranoia about government power among both southern traditionalists and their conservative peers reflected both groups' identification of a moment of historical trauma that directly shaped their evaluation of government interventions. Just as many conservative intellectuals in the 1930s and 1940s drew from their experiences with European forms of totalitarianism in the lead-up to World War II, white southerners rooted their distrust of federal mandates in what historian Glenn Feldman identified as "Reconstruction Syndrome." The experience of defeat in the Civil War and the aftermath of federal Reconstruction policies, he argued, initiated a myth of martyrdom exemplified in Lost Cause ideology. Born into the "psychological trauma" of loss, Feldman marks this impulse as a repetitive touchstone of white southern identity most visible when southern traditions of white supremacy seemed vulnerable to federal reform. White southern reaction, whether through the platforms of grassroots revolt or political posturing, tended to take the form of "anti-black, anti-federal government, anti-liberal, anti-Yankee, anti-outsider/foreigner, and pro-militarily patriotic beliefs."[23]

The loyalty with which white southerners, especially those from the Deep South, adhered to these suspicions overshadowed their allegiance to the Democratic Party. This impulse was most apparent in the 1948 presidential campaign. President Harry Truman's support for civil rights reform at the federal level and his desire to make the Federal Employment Practices Committee a permanent agency made southern support for his reelection problematic. Leaders of the Democratic National Convention in July 1948 faced an increasingly vocal states' rights wing of the party that intended to oppose both a civil rights platform and Truman's nomination. But opposition did not turn into widespread support for rebellion. Attempts to create a powerful, unified states' rights faction stalled at the convention, and when it became evident that their demands would not be taken seriously, delegates from Mississippi and Alabama left in protest.[24]

The States' Rights Democratic Party, more commonly known as the Dixiecrats, met in Birmingham a few days later, but found little upon which they could agree. As attendees brainstormed over strategy, the specter of race and its place in the rebellion mirrored the deep divides that persisted among white southerners. In essence, the Dixiecrat movement drew its most dedicated support from the Deep South, a fact that reflected the earliest days of secessionist fervor in 1860–1861. The party's nomination of South Carolina governor Strom Thurmond for president, and Mississippi governor Fielding Wright for vice president, confirmed this similarity and furthered the realization that much separated white southerners politically, and little united them outside of their support for white supremacy.[25]

Despite its supporters' hopes, the Dixiecrat revolt in 1948 failed to win enough votes in the election to suggest that the Deep South's membership within the Democratic Party was critical to victory. Instead, the rebellion uncovered deep divides among white southerners in their commitment to regional allegiance. The apparent irrelevance of southern support also accelerated the Democratic Party's embrace of a more liberal platform that left less and less space for white segregationists to occupy years before Nixon's Southern Strategy heralded the white South's official entry into the Republican Party.[26] In the aftermath of revolt, white southern leaders felt compelled to think more deliberately about their strategy, particularly the role of states' rights ideology in uniting their cause with white northerners. Their failure to abandon audible appeals to white supremacy, however, remained an obstacle between the regions, and leaders of white resistance chose white unification in the South as the most productive avenue for organization. The result was a renewed commitment to white supremacy and its continued protection within the political, economic, and social institutions that held it.[27]

Such efforts were most visible in the proliferation of resistance literature after the 1948 election. Publications began to appear throughout the South, each of them proselytizing a defense of their opposition to a variety of federal encroachments. By 1950, *The States' Righter,* the bimonthly newspaper of the States' Rights Party, boasted a $200,000 budget that came from subscriptions and membership fees.[28] In addition to formal party publications, other outlets appeared, using similar language to articulate their commitment to white supremacy. The American States' Rights Association in Alabama published a pamphlet in 1953 urging unification among white southerners "to preserve and defend our way of life." Citing an overarching commitment to state sovereignty, the pamphlet made clear that the most threatening issue facing white southerners was federal intervention on matters of race. Its five-point agenda included three points related to protecting segregation at the state and federal level. The remaining two objectives described tactics that would directly address the "public school problem" if the Supreme Court announced a desegregation decision. The pamphlet also recommended a multimedia onslaught to inform citizens about the activities of integration proponents, evidence of the growing influence that anticommunism had on white resistance rhetoric.[29] Other publications (many of them short-lived) included the Grass Roots League's "Research Bulletin No. 1" (South Carolina) and *The Dixiecrat,* a publication of the Dixiecrats Democratic Association of Louisiana.[30]

Early attempts to mobilize white resistance prior to the *Brown* decision magnified fears of sweeping changes to the system of segregation and disfranchisement that had defined southern politics, economy, and society since the end of Reconstruction. But aside from raising awareness, concrete objectives remained unclear. Southern Democrats in public office, whether at the state level or in Washington, were not equally discontent with the Democratic Party, and many remained reluctant to jeopardize their influence within the party structure over potential shifts in the party's position on civil rights. The rank and file of the Democratic Party relied on party leaders, many of whom enjoyed the privileges of seniority and its benefits in Congress, to obstruct changes to the party platform. Their leaders' loyalty to the party proved frustrating to grassroots organizers at home. Unity between an increasingly restless constituency and political leaders in the South was necessary to leverage an effective challenge to federal intervention, but, prior to *Brown,* it failed to come together in a significant way.[31]

In contrast, black southerners experienced a surge of organization in the decade preceding the Supreme Court's desegregation decision. Local branches of the NAACP began to appear throughout the South in the 1940s, shifting the organization's focus from elite leadership to self-sustaining activism at the local level. Black southern activism was crucial to the success of national civil rights campaigns. The clear-cut discriminations of southern segregation and disfranchisement provided a more promising platform for local action than the slow-paced federal court system could offer on its own. In addition to local unification, alliances with progressive organizations like the Southern Conference for Human Welfare and the Committee for Industrial Organization increased interest in voting and employment equity across racial lines and tied achievement of racial equality to other causes. Another affirmation for black activism came in 1944 with the announcement of *Smith v. Allwright,* the Supreme Court decision that declared white primaries unconstitutional.[32]

Black Mississippians were not isolated from this progress. At the end of World War II, voter registration drives increased throughout the state, evidence that black discontent was quickly turning into organized activism. The founding of a Mississippi chapter of the Progressive Voters' League in 1946 increased interest among black Mississippians for these campaigns by working within existing networks of black organizations like churches and civic groups. That same year, the State Conference of Branches of Mississippi's NAACP formed in response to the increasing number of branches in the state. By 1952, black voter rolls included 20,000 individuals statewide, revealing an increase of nearly 13,000 from 1948.[33]

Increasing black activism at the local level in Mississippi was only the most recent of challenges to the white power structure. Between 1940 and 1950, the black population in the state had shrunk by 300,000, evidence of Mississippi's contribution to the Great Migration, a period of black southern migration to the North that began in the 1920s.[34] The refusal to accept poverty and terror at home when more promising economic opportunities existed elsewhere was an early sign of activism and one that posed the greatest threat in areas of the state that were almost wholly dependent upon black labor. In 1953, Mississippi's Speaker of the House and Dixiecrat supporter, Walter Sillers Jr., a native of Rosedale in the Delta region of the state, expressed these concerns in a letter to Governor Hugh White. In it, Sillers's disillusionment with the labor crisis is laid bare:

> The farm labor in [the Delta] is becoming scarcer and scarcer each year. The negroes are leaving for the north. I don't know altogether what causes it except they do not want to farm any more and it is probably that when they go to these industrial centers of the north they get high

wages while they are employed and when they are laid off the government puts them on the unemployment payroll, so they are either assured of continued employment or they draw government money. Regardless of the cause, we are confronted with a serious situation, and if there is anything you can do to help get an industry, even though it may be a small one, for Rosedale, I shall appreciate it, likewise all of the citizens here.[35]

Reactions to black activism, as Sillers's letter suggests, often contained practical economic concerns. Those concerns were indivisible from the states' rights principles that defined the Dixiecrat platform. Sillers's membership in that movement and his plea to Governor White underscore the intersections of economic concerns with the crafted ideological defenses that defined organized white resistance. White economic dependence on black labor relied on the continued protection of legally enshrined white supremacy. Persistent economic, educational, and political discriminations, however, undermined the ability to keep black Mississippians in the state. The growing visibility of black activism after World War II, secured by support from the federal government, threatened to uproot the entire system. White defenders of segregation and disfranchisement, as a result, faced multiple concerns as their system came under the scrutiny of the federal government and their black citizens. Regional unity promised some defense against federal compulsion but might mean little if white northerners found no common ground with the South. If that common ground proved to exist, it promised little assistance in addressing the groundswell of local black discontent that seemed to be on the horizon and gaining momentum. In Mississippi, by 1953, it was local black challenges to segregated education that won the most attention from the state's power structure.

As early as 1941, the Mississippi Association of Teachers in Colored Schools (MATCS) began lobbying white political leaders to address salary issues, extend the school year for black students, provide more higher education options for black teachers, and equalize black facilities with those of their white counterparts. The all-white Mississippi Educators Association (MEA) concurred with many of MATCS's recommendations, as did the Delta Council, a group of white elites who supported equalization of schools as a way to stem out-migration patterns by making "separate but equal" truly equal. Looming Supreme Court decisions no doubt figured prominently in white support for equalization measures. In 1946 this diverse support for reform led to legislative approval of $3 million for salary improvement, facility construction and renovation, and expanded opportunities for black teacher training. The legislative measure, however, did not specifically require that funds go toward black schools. As a consequence, most of the money went to white schools and white teachers. Faced with diminishing options, the MATCS began collecting money for a salary equalization lawsuit in 1947. In February 1948, Gladys Noel Bates, a black teacher in Jackson, volunteered to be the plaintiff. Unfortunately, the federal court dismissed her case in 1950, claiming that she had not sufficiently pursued administrative redress before suing.[36]

Bates's suit failed, but continuing disparities seemed problematic in light of the possibility of a federal desegregation order. With that in mind, the state legislature approved two salary bills, in 1950 and 1952, that allocated funds based on the number of black teachers in each county. Later, under the leadership of Governor Hugh White in 1953, sweeping legislation to achieve true equalization passed during a special education session of the state legislature, but funding never materialized. The expectation that money allocated for reform would be moot if the Supreme Court's decision found segregation unconstitutional gave pause to state legislators and black educators alike. For the latter group, the prospect of federally sanctioned desegregation held more hope than equalization in a state where promises from white leaders remained unfulfilled.[37]

The hesitation that accompanied legislative improvements to black schools reflected, in part, the pitiful state of Mississippi's public education system. In a poor state with a limited tax base, the gross disparities between white and black facilities, teacher salaries, and training underscored the general dearth of educational funding. White schools fell far behind those of other states, and when faced with the possibility of increasing educational funding, white parents, school boards, and community leaders lobbied hard for their own children over equalization of black schools, widening the gap even further. White unity took precedence, and once again, did so at the expense of black Mississippians.[38]

The fears that the school equalization issue surfaced explain much about Mississippi's role as a leader in the organized resistance movement. White supremacy was the glue that held together a diverse coalition of whites who would otherwise be divided along economic lines. The state's comparative poverty, not only in the nation but among southern states, made the possibility of black equality appear to be a deliberate refusal to improve conditions for whites. Among threats of federal interference, local black activism, and white division, addressing the third threat seemed to hold the most promise for resolving the other two.

Organized white reaction to the *Brown v. Board of Education* desegregation decision followed this logic. In a unanimous decision, announced on May 17, 1954, the Supreme Court decreed that the practice of "separate but equal" violated the provisions of the Equal Protection Clause in the Fourteenth Amendment. In its decision, the court effectively overturned the precedent set in *Plessy v. Ferguson,* the court's 1896 decision that upheld segregation in public accommodations. In *Brown,* the court examined segregation in public education, reviewing policies and practices in four separate school districts. Recognizing the vastly different historical context in which the Fourteenth Amendment was ratified, and the status of the still evolving public school system in the South when the court announced *Plessy,* the 1954 court chose to evaluate *Brown* using the contemporary need for public education as its guide. In its majority opinion, authored by Chief Justice Earl Warren, the court described public education as "perhaps the most important function of state and local governments . . . the very foundation of good citizenship." With this in mind, any practice of segregation, regardless of its ability to achieve equality, instilled a sense of inferiority among black students at an early age. When operated under legal sanction, the court concluded, the effect was even more detrimental. For that reason, segregation could not continue within the system of public education.[39]

The court's decision was not wholly unanticipated by white southerners. But the succinct language of the decision and its rejection of historical precedent directly challenged the traditions that had so long guided white supremacy. One of the earliest and most influential voices to respond to the *Brown* decision was Thomas P. Brady, a native of Brookhaven, Mississippi, and a member of the States' Rights Party who served on its Executive Committee and directed its Speakers Bureau. In the latter position, he had coordinated speakers to draw publicity for the party in other states. These speakers often emphasized the party's opposition to four landmark civil rights reforms that Presidents Franklin Roosevelt and Harry Truman supported: antilynch legislation, poll tax abolition, the end of white primaries, and desegregation in hiring practices through the creation of the Federal Employment Practices Committee. In this capacity, Brady had a deep exposure to the rhetoric of civil rights opposition as it applied to the protection of states' rights. His 1954 book, *Black Monday*, a response to the *Brown* decision, quickly became a popular call to action among segregationists throughout the South.[40]

The book began as a speech that Brady delivered to the Greenwood, Mississippi, chapter of the Sons of the American Revolution but, upon his audience's recommendation, he expanded it into a book that coupled conservative ideology (especially the familiar language of states' rights) with local movement, challenging white southerners to begin acting on their own behalf in defense of their way of life.[41] *Black Monday* represented an attempt to combine scientific racism with political ideology. Brady's opening sections on natural racial hierarchies struck a familiar chord among an audience of white southerners outraged by the decision, but his use of historical evidence and judicial precedent offered an intellectual alternative to the argument in *Brown*. As the book proceeded, Brady's description of the communist menace transformed the defense of segregation into an issue of global significance that demanded moral action. The South, in this scenario, must take action to defend its way of life, protect the Negro, and stave off communist inroads upon American democracy.[42]

Brady's call to action concluded the book and provided a blueprint for white resistance. In it, he identified fifteen targets of activism, the first three pointing to communism and its subversive advocates in the fields of education and religion. The real impact of Brady's blueprint, however, was in his proposal for collusion among the states that the desegregation decision directly impacted. He described this organizational effort as a "movement for saving America from Socialism and Communism." He demanded that coordination among states within this association be secret but law-abiding. Information dispersal was a critical function of the effort. Left-wing organizations and the NAACP were, he argued, central culprits in the widespread misrepresentation of the South and its practices. In order to combat that message, the organization would have to run its own education campaign to correct these unjust accusations. "The people of this country," he demanded, must "be aroused and alerted to the imminent dangers which we face."[43]

If political activism and educational efforts failed to work, Brady offered a final alternative, an option that, he insisted, "no southern man wants to take." The economic dependency of the southern Negro upon the white man made it possible for an economic "cold war" to be levied as a way to discourage black support for the NAACP. Such a tactic, he warned, would render the southern Negro "destitute."[44] It was this tactic for which the Citizens' Council would become infamous, both in the midst of the civil rights movement and in historical literature.

Brady's incorporation of natural racial hierarchy with fears of communism and federal overreach represented the combination of influences that characterized the nascent resistance movement that developed in the years preceding *Brown*. In his evaluation of the desegregation decision, conservative opposition to federal interference merged with deeply held beliefs about white supremacy in a printed address that could easily circulate among grassroots organizations. *Black Monday* not only gave shape to white southerners' fears about black dominance, but it challenged them to resist in specific ways, using the very power that segregation and disfranchisement enshrined. The channels of resistance, in Brady's estimation, were accessible and should be exercised at the local level. The empowerment that such a blueprint provided to white southerners disillusioned by what they perceived as rapidly increasing power in Washington, DC, must not be overlooked. Brady's address served to remind them why their fears and opposition were well placed, and it encouraged them to vigorously defend their position in the areas where they continued to hold power—their hometowns.

This was the environment that birthed the Citizens' Council. The postwar evolution of conservative thought developed alongside white southern alienation within the United States Democratic Party. The appearance and growing popularity of conservative media outlets like *Facts Forum* enlivened conservative ideology by encouraging grassroots participation in contemporary debates. When the Supreme Court declared an end to "separate but equal" in 1954, it exemplified a threat to states' rights and white supremacy. *Black Monday* offered a solution to those threats by emphasizing that the power to resist was in the hands of every white citizen committed to protecting their way of life. The Supreme Court was distant and its decisions remote. The ability to silence local black activism, however, was well within reach. The Citizens' Council organized these efforts over the next several months, honing its reputation in Mississippi as an agent of racial terrorism. But its efforts quickly reached beyond local intimidations and into the circulation of propaganda that translated conservative ideology into a defiant call for grassroots activism. Those efforts are a reminder that the organization was born into intersecting movements preceding *Brown,* and those movements provided a variety of homes within which southern white resistance could thrive, in the midst of and long after the civil rights movement.

CHAPTER 2

NURTURED IN FEAR, 1954–1957

But I want to tell you that from my own observation in Mississippi, this organization concept and [the Citizens' Council] is far, far overemphasized in the national press and so forth. In other words, my observation convinces me that the social and political integrity of the white people in the state of Mississippi was so well organized on the political sense that none of this organizational business really made a whole lot of sense. I mean they just did this naturally. They didn't need to belong to any kind of an organization. . . . They were white Mississippians and they knew each other and they knew who they were and they knew [who] was dependable. When a situation of this kind came on there was just a spontaneous gathering. —SAM BOWERS, IN REFERENCE TO A LYNCHING HE WITNESSED IN LAUREL, MISSISSIPPI, IN 1939

Robert "Tut" Patterson, a Delta planter and World War II veteran, was deeply affected by the rhetoric of resistance that Judge Thomas Brady articulated in *Black Monday*. A native of Clarksdale, Patterson's Confederate heritage, rooted in his great-grandfather's service as a Confederate general and his grandmother's memories of "Black Reconstruction," deeply informed his identity as a white southerner. As a young man he attended Mississippi State College (now Mississippi State University) and served as captain of its football team before enlisting in World War II and serving for twenty-seven months in the European theater as part of the 82nd Airborne Division. When he returned, Patterson spent a brief amount of time in Tennessee before partnering with two fraternity brothers in managing a plantation in Sunflower County, home to Mississippi's outspoken segregationist senator, James O. Eastland.[1]

Later described by writer James Graham Cook as one of "Apartheid's Organization Men," Patterson took Brady's call for local organization to heart. "'I became obsessed [with *Black Monday*],'" he explained to Cook in 1962, "'I started agitating around town . . . and said we ought to get ourselves a little organization to see if we can't do something.'"[2] Less than two months after the Supreme Court's decision, he did just that. Patterson called the organization's inaugural meeting in Indianola on July 11, 1954. Fourteen men attended the first meeting, including Indianola's mayor and the local bank president. When the second meeting commenced, seventy men were in attendance, evidence of the network of white leadership these men represented.[3]

The Council's identity as a Delta-born organization is critical to understanding the first years of its existence. The organization's objectives in those first years reflected the threat that school desegregation and voting access represented in an area of the state where whites were in the minority. As Council chapters multiplied, the tactics used to maintain white unity in a predominantly black region came to define the Council's influence throughout the state. Council organizations exercised vigilance over potential challenges to white power, using their connections and economic leverage to discourage black activism and white ambivalence. As their influence grew, so did their ambition. When the organization began to look outward toward regional expansion and national recognition, the tactics cultivated in the rich soil of the Delta's counties created liabilities that exposed the conflict between achieving dominance in Mississippi and securing national relevance. Consequently, as early as 1957, the organization was operating on multiple fronts through different campaigns, all in the service of preserving white supremacy.

Situated in the northwestern area of the state between the Mississippi and Yazoo Rivers, the Delta counties became the state's agricultural powerhouse following the end of the Civil War. After slavery's end, black laborers experienced several years of economic independence in this area, largely due to the desperation of white landowners forced to offer fair wages to maintain productivity. As the region began to benefit from public investments in flood control and as its landowners became more integrated into the national economy through cotton production, however, the economic gains for whites began to rapidly outdistance those of their black neighbors. By the 1880s, dramatic increases in black migration to the area drove down wages, and a statewide commitment to a one-party, white-controlled political system reversed many of the gains achieved during the Reconstruction years. By the 1890s, the region's accumulated wealth and its connections to commercial interests outside of the South contributed to a powerful lobby in the state capital in Jackson.[4]

The Delta area also included the highest concentration of the state's black population. By 1890, the region's twelve counties averaged a black-to-white ratio of 7:1.[5] Their labor, as Walter Sillers indicated in his letter to Governor Hugh White, was critical to the area's economy. But their numbers remained a consistent concern among white leaders, who regularly used their economic influence and violence to keep their black neighbors disempowered.

The Delta's economic culture and its unique demographics produced a specific approach to maintaining white control that relied on cooperation among all whites, planter and nonplanter alike. The effectiveness of the region's Farm Bureau organization in putting down challenges in the 1930s from a biracial coalition of disgruntled tenants, exemplified the power of white cooperation. Surveillance and harassment of participants in the Southern Tenant Farmers Union matched the tactics for which the Council would earn its early reputation.[6] These successful alliances provided a ready-made model for resistance to *Brown*.

In its first few months, the Citizens' Council worked quietly, avoiding public announcements of meetings. Instead, founding members of the Council mobilized support through their personal connections, building a community of resistance from the ground up through white solidarity. This community-based networking yielded immediate results. Within six weeks, seventeen chapters existed in Mississippi, products of Council ambassadors who went from town to town, meeting with community leaders face-to-face about their objectives. This growth drew attention, even if the organization's exact intent remained obscure. "The Negro knows we are organizing," Herman Moore, one of the founding members, acknowledged, "but he does not know what we plan to do."[7]

What Council organizers planned to do was to remove "agitators and the like" from local communities through economic pressure. In his

months-long study of the white resistance movement in the South, reporter Paul Anthony noted the success Council leaders had in controlling
their respective communities. The white power structure, he explained,
was "deeply rooted" and "strongly entrenched" in the Mississippi Delta,
and its mobilization was critical to resisting desegregation.[8]

The Delta's leadership of the Council movement shaped the organization in important ways and mirrored the system over which the planter
elite had presided for so long in that area of the state. Surveillance and
local intimidation through white networks of cooperation defined the
earliest months of its existence. As a network of individual chapters
formed, however, the local control and pressure that the Council's founders envisioned began to give way to calls for more proactive state- and
even region-wide approaches that would unite white resistance into a
political force. The true catalyst for drawing the organization out of the
shadows, however, was the call for desegregation coming from black activists in the state.

When the *Brown* decision came on May 17, 1954, state leaders began
to move to slow down attempts to implement it. Governor Hugh White's
"voluntary segregation" initiative revealed the nature of white reaction
in Mississippi, a strategy that can best be described as active denial.
White believed that cooperation with black leaders throughout the state
would successfully lead to an understanding that maintaining segregation in the state's educational system was in the best interest of black
teachers and administrators. Under the recommendation of black ministers and educational leaders, White arranged for a meeting with nearly
one hundred black leaders on July 30, 1954. His advisors were confident
that cooperation was imminent, so much so that they extended an invitation to representatives from the state's NAACP branches to attend.[9]

White's advisors soon realized, however, that they had vastly over-
estimated black cooperation. In a meeting on July 29, it became clear
that black leaders fully expected Governor White to begin the process
of implementing the Supreme Court's decision. When black leaders announced this expectation to White the next day, his reaction and that of
other white attendees was nothing short of shock.[10]

In addition to black leaders' demands for *Brown*'s implementation,
white Mississippians seemed divided in their reaction. Long-standing

political divisions existed that were closely associated with the demographic diversity of the state. Enmity between the Delta and other, less prosperous areas of the state was a relic of the post-Reconstruction years in Mississippi, a time when the state struggled to establish its public school system and provide adequate funding for it. The 1890 constitution required funding allocations based on the number of educable children in each county. The Delta counties benefited from this requirement in their ability to count black children, most of whom did not attend school, and apply the money toward the improvement of white schools. In predominantly white counties, by contrast, the actual totals of students closely matched attendance, and white schools often suffered underfunding, to say nothing of the impact on black schools. This practice changed in 1900 through a voter referendum that tied funding to actual attendance, but in future funding measures for public schools, the Delta counties remained opposed to increasing taxes because they feared the improvement it might bring to black schools.[11]

Equalization measures met with much opposition throughout the state in the years preceding *Brown,* but whites in the Delta were exceptionally outspoken in their hostility. Desegregation posed an even greater threat. Robert Patterson identified this demographic reality and its effect on public schools as a central concern of the Council movement. "We were faced with integration," he explained years later, "in a town where there were twenty-one hundred Negro students and seven hundred white. . . . We just felt like integration would utterly destroy everything we valued."[12]

The Council movement and its concern with schools, then, was especially popular among whites who lived in predominantly black areas of the state. For these people, public school closure was a viable solution to resisting federal mandates. For whites in other areas, where wealth was less concentrated and the ratio of blacks to whites was more balanced, reaction to *Brown* was not as clear-cut. For them, access to education through the public school system was critical to social mobility. Without the resources to invest in private education, poorer areas of the state would be devastated by school closures. In short, white Mississippians' reaction to the desegregation order was not unified. After negotiations with black leaders over school equalization plans ended so abruptly in July, support for closure of the state's public schools soared among legislators, but won firm opposition from the state's educators. Since the proposal had to be in the form of a constitutional amendment, it required popular support from registered voters in the state. Without the endorsement of Mississippi's educators, its successful passage was unlikely. To complicate matters further, passage of the constitutional amendment to close the public schools was tied to funding for equalization. This meant that underfunded white schools risked losing much needed upgrades if they failed to support the closure amendment. Governor White made this point clear in his address to Mississippi educators in the spring of 1954, ultimately securing their public support.[13]

The formation of Friends of Segregated Public Schools (FSPS) in October 1954, two months prior to the December election for the proposed amendment, kept successful approval far from certain, however. FSPS supported segregated schools but felt that school closure was an extreme solution. The inevitable outcome of school closure, FSPS argued, was a siphoning off of public funds to support private schools, a measure that would benefit Delta whites the most since they were in the minority. School equalization for that area of the state, then, was a nonstarter because it required such an enormous investment to bring black schools up to par. The private school option, on the other hand, would ensure that Delta money would support Delta schools, circumventing the debate over allocations of funding across the state. As an added benefit, tuition-driven private education promised to reinforce existing class divisions between wealthier whites and their poorer neighbors.[14]

The tension between the Delta and poorer areas of the state was not wholly unfamiliar to the state's leaders, who saw these divisions up close in each legislative session. But in this case it resurfaced at a time when white unity was especially critical in the face of federal directives. It was the perfect entry for Council exposure. Support for the amendment was the first official public campaign that the Citizens' Council supervised, and it did so under the newly created Association of Citizens' Councils of Mississippi (ACCM). With headquarters in Winona, sixty miles east of the Council's birthplace, the state association sought to consolidate Council work within the state and cultivated a coordinated publicity strategy.[15]

The first official publication of the Association was its pamphlet, "The Citizens' Council." Using a question-and-answer format, the pamphlet explained the Council's function, its necessity, and its structure. The organization, the opening paragraph stated, was a "modern version of the old-time town meeting called to meet any crisis by expressing the will of the people." The crisis, in this case, was pressure from outside groups seeking to shame white people into feeling like bigots for taking pride in their whiteness. The message that ran throughout the pamphlet called repeatedly for white unity and action akin to the "courage and faith" of their ancestors during Reconstruction, when white men were "beaten, in poverty and degradation, unable to vote and under the heel of negro occupation troops." Without their resolve, it continued, the South would be "a land of mulattoes." Vowing to maintain "the highest type of leadership" in each community where a chapter existed, the Council recognized that the fight against desegregation required "every patriotic white Southerner, rich or poor, high or low" to turn back the tide of black domination once more. The race-baiting rhetoric that the pamphlet espoused and its threat of colorblind equality spoke directly to the "poor" and "low" white men who, presumably, had the most to lose.[16]

Further evidence of this rhetoric existed in the organization's assessment of the NAACP as the most threatening enemy to white supremacy. Defining the organization's acronym as the "National Association for the Agitation of Colored People," the pamphlet assured its readers that the NAACP enjoyed the support of "alien influences, bloc vote seeking politicians and left-wing do-gooders." Accusations of prejudice and bigotry directed at white southerners were only the tip of the iceberg, the pamphlet warned, and a distraction from the true motive behind racial agitation which was a "one world, one creed, one race philosophy fostered by ultra-idealists and international left-wingers." NAACP pressure tactics, as they were often labeled in Council literature, were working to eliminate the racial pride that had built up over centuries among the country's most esteemed leaders. The equalization of all people, regardless of their "aptitude or heritage," the pamphlet predicted, would inevitably lead to "atheism, communism and mongrelization" for the entire nation.[17]

The Council's defense of white supremacy would become less stark as its leaders began to cultivate ambitions outside of the state and the South, but the antiliberal, anti-intellectual message would grow to closely resemble the conservative ideology that came into maturity alongside the civil rights movement. In its first attempts to establish its message, the Council returned to the well-worn race-baiting tactics used for decades to erase economic and class divisions among whites at the expense of black Mississippians. These early years were the most successful in terms of membership numbers, a fact that speaks directly (if not singularly) to Council leaders' knowledge of their audience. The counties in which Council growth was the highest contained a higher percentage of black residents, 50 percent or higher. Its lowest numbers came from the southern part of the state, where the black population was less than 33 percent. Vilification of the NAACP and unapologetic statements of white pride thrived when and where the threat seemed most imminent.[18]

The Council's strategy in 1954 aimed to accomplish two things: to increase the number of Council chapters in the state and to mobilize votes for approval of the school closure amendment. Each objective depended on the other for success. In articulating its opposition to *Brown*, Council literature focused on awareness of outsiders seeking to enforce the decision. Council membership was critical to monitoring such efforts. For school closure, however, the threat of local black activism was recognized as more pressing. Shortly after the state association's formation, Council administrator Fred Jones sent a letter to members describing the school closure issue as one that pitted black Mississippians against whites, effectively eliminating any possibility for white equivocation. Jones reminded his readers that since *Brown*'s announcement the attitudes of blacks in the state had "completely changed," a fact made evident when black leaders met with Governor White and "demanded a surrender," a reference to the July meeting where black leaders refused to accept the equalization measure in exchange for "voluntary segregation." Without community organization and proper white leadership through the founding of more Council chapters, Jones predicted, black pressure would escalate.[19]

By December, the Council's approach became more urgent in light of the coming election. In a letter written to "ALL MISSISSIPPIANS," Robert Patterson, now executive secretary of the ACCM, wrote a letter fully endorsing the affirmative vote on the school amendment. In it, he warned that "the eyes of the world are on Mississippi." Failure to pass it would be "most embarrassing" to the legislature, a group of men working tirelessly to maintain segregated schools in the state. Such a display would open the door wider for federal interference, especially in the field of education. Failure to support this protection was tantamount to denying the validity of states' rights doctrine. He warned of well-intentioned opposition to the amendment among "innocent, kind, misguided, well-intentioned people who are playing right into the hands of the mongrelizers."[20]

Patterson's plea discouraged any thoughtful consideration on the issue, urging whites in the state to ask themselves whether or not they supported segregation. If they did, a "yes" vote was the only option. Included with Patterson's letter was an information packet explaining the amendment's language and what voting "yes" meant, including a list of people and organizations for and against the amendment. The Council's message was clear. Under the "Against" column were two Mississippi journalists who were outspoken opponents of the Council, Oliver Emmerich and Hodding Carter. Also listed were the NAACP, "Northern CIO leaders" and the American Federation of Labor, groups that white Mississippians would know better as communist sympathizers and outside agitators. Among the supporters of the amendment were the state's top leaders, including an overwhelming majority of members of the State Senate and the House, the lieutenant governor, both US senators, the Mississippi Education Association (a reluctant endorsement), and the Mississippi Farm Bureau Association.[21]

The packet of information that the Council provided was meant to be distributed to various civic organizations and local associations. In addition to the list of endorsements, its contents distilled the proposed amendment and its possible consequences into simple language that focused on protecting the interests of white children, maintaining state sovereignty, and supporting segregation's defenders in other states. The first point it made was that the amendment was not meant to abolish the schools, but was "for the sole purpose of saving our schools by keeping white schools white and negro schools negro." White Mississippians simply needed to decide whom they trusted to manage their schools: the federal government or their legislators. Forced integration, it continued, would "mean death" to Mississippi schools, and refusal to accept this outcome would represent unity, especially in support of other states that had already passed similar amendments (South Carolina, Georgia, and Louisiana).[22]

If this logic proved ineffective, the Council added the threat of alienation within the white community as a possible consequence. In his October letter to white Mississippians, Fred Jones described the Council's tactics this way: "We can accomplish our purposes largely with economic pressure in dealing with members of the Negro race who are not cooperating, and with members of the white race who fail to cooperate, we can apply social and political pressure."[23] The economic pressure tactics leveled at uncooperative blacks are the better-known of the two strategies, but Council leaders had greater anxiety about maintaining white support in the state, and they used the twin causes of segregation and states' rights ideology to secure it. It worked. White voters in the state overwhelmingly approved the amendment. Its successful passage pointed directly to the Council's influence. In the twenty-six counties that had a Citizens' Council chapter, support for school closure was overwhelming. Only fourteen counties voted the measure down and none of them were in the Delta.[24]

The victory was a watershed for Council organization, an opening salvo that exemplified the public relations strategy that would dominate the defense of segregation in Mississippi for more than a decade. While Council chapters acted locally to terrorize blacks from organizing or cooperating with civil rights campaigns, the strategy of the state organization was quite different. In its pursuit of white support, the ACCM depended upon marketing a message that would simplify the race question by discouraging ambivalent whites from thinking too much about it. Use of the well-worn warnings about federal interference and black dominance that had so deeply defined white southern regional identity following Reconstruction showed little indication that the desegregation issue was any different from previous challenges white southerners had faced in defending their unique traditions.

But the atmosphere in which this victory was born was quite different from previous moments of white defiance, even if the details of that difference were not quite clear to Council leaders and their supporters.

By 1954, organized black activism was stable, had national backing, and showed signs of growth. The approval of the school closure amendment impacted the NAACP's perception of the powerful opposition blacks faced in Mississippi. In December 1954, it appointed its first field secretary to the state, Medgar Evers, a native of Decatur, a graduate of Alcorn Agricultural and Mechanical College, and a World War II veteran. Evers's tenure would last less than a decade but included some of the worst violence in the state's history against black Mississippians, including his own murder at the hands of a member of the Greenwood Citizens' Council, Byron de la Beckwith.[25] Evers's presence in the state made him a witness to the Council's work and its impact on black participation in civil rights activities.

The Citizens' Council's ascendancy in Mississippi was not yet solidified by the end of 1954, but its role in securing approval of the school closure amendment and the increasing numbers of chapters across the state suggested that it was a movement that held great promise. The Council's visibility grew at a moment when white leaders in the state were forced to come to terms with the reality of grassroots civil rights activism, and the Council emerged as the guiding hand for managing it. Considering the differences among white Mississippians and the varying levels of challenge they faced regarding local civil rights activity, the Council's call for white unity depended upon an ideology that appealed to diverse interests in the state and could maintain longevity as circumstances changed. In 1954, Council leaders' embrace of white supremacy was not surprising, but their emphasis on elite white leadership reflected the need to draw in potential white supporters who needed reassurance that response to *Brown* and local challenges to the status quo would not erupt in a violent backlash. The Council's early literature met that challenge by describing organized resistance as a countermeasure against alien influences like communism and the NAACP, but also, even more threatening, the activism of local blacks. That description was in direct contrast to the first few months of Council organization when supervision of local black activism was the central concern. When the Council's existence became public, the management of its message became paramount.

The conflicting priorities that accompanied Council growth in 1955 and 1956 tested the compatibility of an elite white leadership dependent upon the allegiance of small farmers, wage workers, and other working-class whites more responsive to racial epithets and threats of violence, covert or otherwise. John Temple Graves II, a longtime columnist for the *Birmingham Post-Herald* and a frequent defender of the Council movement, warned his readers that diverse coalitions within the organization could prove problematic. The rapid growth of chapters across the South "is so immense now," he worried, "it begins, like the Democratic Party, to include all kind. If every Klansman takes command, or lunatics on the far right, all is lost."[26] Despite such warnings, in its first years of organization when growth was critical, the Council cultivated the fears of its working-class membership over the high-minded ideology of conservatism that it would more directly embrace when race-baiting was no longer practical. This tactic persisted in part as a way to pull in more members, but increasing black demands to implement *Brown* exacerbated the urgency of white organization and the use of local terrorism.

Within months of the *Brown v. Board of Education* decision, the NAACP claimed that over five hundred school districts across the South had already desegregated, and the organization was hopeful that further progress was inevitable. The Supreme Court's follow-up decision on May 31, 1955, however, recognized that local circumstances would likely dictate the timing of desegregation, and the court urged school districts to begin moving in that direction even if the process was protracted. In response, the NAACP worked quickly to assist community leaders in circulating school desegregation petitions. In Mississippi, the Vicksburg chapter of the NAACP filed the first petition in the state in July 1955. The next day, the *Vicksburg Evening Post* printed the names of all 140 signatories, a move intended to intimidate local blacks from participating in similar actions. Black Mississippians in Clarksdale, Jackson, and Natchez filed similar petitions and received the same treatment, leading some of the petitioners to withdraw their names.

The response was more pointed in Yazoo City, a town at the southern end of the Delta where the Citizens' Council had a strong presence. When local blacks submitted their petition, their names appeared in the local paper, and signs were placed throughout the city and the surrounding countryside to ensure that white planters and business owners were aware of who had signed. In his annual report to the state NAACP office,

Medgar Evers described a series of retaliatory actions from whites in Yazoo City. Signors lost their jobs and received threatening phone calls. Wholesale distributors denied deliveries to black store owners, two of whom went out of business as a result. Economic pressure spread so swiftly that some of the signors left town, never to return. The ones who remained withdrew their names, and shortly after the NAACP chapter submitted the petition to desegregate city schools, its Yazoo City chapter was defunct. One year later, Evers wrote, "Hundreds of Negroes in Mississippi, especially those living in the Delta, have suffered as a result of economic reprisals, which has created an ever constant fear among the Negro population in that section of the state. As a result," he reported, "branch membership and financial contributions are far below that of last year."[27] Organized civil rights campaigns in the city remained elusive for years to come.

The reports from Ruby Hurley, regional director of the NAACP, expanded on Evers's evaluations. The Delta was under the control of the Citizens' Council, according to Hurley. Their tactics were "brazen" and included phone calls and threatening letters, and in one case, involved parking a hearse in front of a signor's house. "Every effort in and out of the book," she explained, "is being used to discredit and demoralize our leadership. And there is no source for help within the State." Hurley's letters and reports described dangerous conditions in Brookhaven, Cleveland, and Belzoni, and in them she identified the network of white cooperation that connected members of the Citizens' Council with local law enforcement. She called for aggressive monitoring of newspapers and asked members to report all incidents. Council members should be identified, she explained, so the NAACP could "compile the same kind of information on them that they are compiling on our officers, members and petitioners."[28]

As the movement spread into other states, similar reports surfaced, making the Council indistinguishable from the Klan in its tactics. Police arrested members of the Seaboard White Citizens' Council in Miami, Florida, as they attempted to place a cross in front of a black home, and rumors of a plot to dynamite black homes and housing projects in the area circulated. Council-led campaigns against the National Urban League succeeded in shuttering League offices in Tallahassee, Richmond,

New Orleans, Jacksonville, and Norfolk. Administrators closed regional offices in Atlanta and Los Angeles, citing Council pressure as a major factor. Black business owners in South Carolina suffered disruptions in inventory delivery, and NAACP supporters experienced Council-led service boycotts in which black patrons were prevented from using credit or purchasing goods in white-owned stores.[29]

Public perception of the Council could not be divorced from the reputation that these incidents built. As chapters appeared across the South and white retaliation took the form of economic intimidation, the Citizens' Council moniker became shorthand for organized white resistance in the South. National awareness grew as well. The NAACP's surveillance of Council activity often appeared in black-owned newspapers outside of the South. National newspapers like the *New York Times* also included coverage of these incidents. Increased scrutiny over the wisdom of Council-led resistance resulted, and the criticism it yielded encouraged administrators in the organization to begin crafting their own public relations campaigns and revealed much higher ambitions than the maintenance of segregation and disfranchisement.

The first detailed critique of the Council came early, from the cradle of its founding in the Mississippi Delta. In March 1955, before the first school petition in Vicksburg became public, Hodding Carter, a Greenville native and editor of the *Delta Democrat-Times,* wrote a profile of the organization in *Look* magazine. Carter acknowledged that eight months into its existence, the Council had won its battles without violence. But he warned that the Council's dependency upon non-elite whites for support in combination with the tyranny it leveraged against white political leaders undermined the organization's ability to wage a clean fight. The organization's approach of embracing white supremacist rhetoric, he continued, made black domination seem like a reality and insinuated that violence was inevitable. As the Council movement grew, he warned, that message was sure to create an explosive backlash.[30]

A little over a month later, Carter's warning seemed prescient. The murder of Reverend George Lee in Belzoni, Mississippi, came after a reporter, Simeon Booker, began tracking Lee's voter registration drive. Belzoni was a small Delta town less than thirty miles from the location of the Council's first chapter. It was also one of the troubled areas that Ruby Hurley identified in her reports to the NAACP. With the help of Gus Courts, a grocery store owner, Lee spent months convincing his neighbors that the potential power of black votes in Humphreys, a predominantly black county, was worth the risk. Their efforts yielded ninety-four successful registrations.

George Lee presented a problem for Council members who relied on white economic power as an effective tool to discourage black activism at the local level. Lee was a successful business owner, and his economic independence rendered those tactics ineffective. Lee's murder on May 7, 1955, suggests that violence was among the options local Councils applied if economic intimidation failed. His business success, according to Mississippi's NAACP field secretary Medgar Evers, "made it difficult for the Councils to squeeze him economically, so their only alternative was to kill him." Council influence in the area ensured that his murderers would not face charges. Lee was shot in the face while driving, but local law enforcement and the state's leading newspaper declared Lee's death an automobile accident. Despite Lee's murder and continued threats on his life, Gus Courts refused to remove his own name from the list of registered voters in Humphreys County, remaining the lone holdout. In November, he too was shot. He survived the gunshots, but not Mississippi. He moved to Chicago shortly after.[31]

Despite the official report that connected Lee's death with a car accident, the Council's involvement with his murder seemed well known. A sociology professor and proponent of civil rights reforms, Dr. Ernst Borinski, wrote the *State Times* in the weeks following the murder urging the Citizens' Council to reconsider its tactics. The organization's call for respectable, nonviolent resistance in light of Lee's murder, he warned, echoed "sounds . . . heard from the honorable citizens of Nazi-Germany" who claimed opposition to violence but "stood helplessly by when more than 6 million innocent people were exterminated." Borinski, who resided in Jackson and taught at Tougaloo College, a private black institution, recognized the organization as a community leader, but not a positive one. Instead, he described Council chapters as "agencies of community discord and illegal and undemocratic community pressures."

Anyone who remained a member or a supporter of the organization, he concluded, was inherently responsible for continued violence against black citizens.[32]

Lee's murder also drew national attention to the Council, especially in black press outlets like *Ebony* and *Jet* magazines, both of which, after World War II, made a transition from a format based in popular culture news to focused coverage of civil rights. Simeon Booker's interest in Lee's registration campaign extended to his murder, and its coverage shined a light on the tactics used to protect Lee's murderers. Connections between local blacks and a sympathetic black readership in the North, many of whom had southern roots, also undermined the isolation that accompanied being black in rural Mississippi, where white terror was a simple and permanent reality.[33]

Press scrutiny continued to escalate as violence against hopeful black activists persisted. Three months after Lee's murder, on August 13, a group of white men surrounded and shot Lamar Smith in front of the courthouse in Lincoln County. Smith had been working to prepare local blacks for state elections. Through registration drives and information about absentee voting (a considerably safer tactic than showing up at the polls), Smith's success exceeded that of Reverend Lee and Gus Courts. When election results came in and the number of absentee ballots showed a sharp increase, Smith's fate was sealed. No one was ever convicted of his murder, but Mississippi newspapers insinuated a link between his murder and the voting drive he led, a bald warning of the consequences of challenging the white power structure.[34]

Lee, Courts, and Smith were all activists and presumably knew the risks they faced as native black Mississippians in areas where Council tactics were well known. Emmett Till's visit to the Mississippi Delta and his subsequent murder, in contrast, galled the nation. Fourteen years old and a native of Chicago, Till's alleged remarks to a white woman who later recanted left him mangled and dead at the hands of two white men who escaped conviction despite their confession to a national magazine after the trial. Till's murderers had no clear ties to the Citizens' Council, but the media scrutiny that the trial put on Mississippi and its stalwart resistance contradicted all Council claims to high-minded white leadership in the state, especially given the movement's growing popularity.

The permanent presence of reporters from all over the country during the trial drove home the fact that local control and white unity within the state were not enough to stem the tide rising against Mississippi as violence in the state escalated.

Amidst the violence that defined Mississippi in 1955, the Association of Citizens' Councils of Mississippi published its first annual report in August 1955, reminding readers of the successes the organization enjoyed during its first year. With a statewide membership of 60,000 and 253 chapters, the Council took credit for channeling resistance to integration into "lawful, coherent and proper modes" instead of violence. The local flavor of the organization remained intact despite its growth, and the Council attributed most of its success to that fact. While the newsletter made no mention of Lee, Smith, or Till, it broadly claimed that Council "investigations" had "severely checked" NAACP influence over "local negro sentiment."[35] Council founder Robert Patterson urged his readers to continue to seek cooperation with each other and to exert influence in their spheres of civic activity, especially the churches. In the wake of three murders, his message was unchanged. The fight to maintain segregation, according to Patterson, remained a "mortal conflict" that could signal the "twilight of this great white nation."[36]

As the ACCM looked forward to continued growth and impact, it announced imminent publication of a monthly newsletter slated to appear in print by September or October. The monthly paper signified the entrance of the Council's most recognizable administrator, William J. Simmons, a member of the Jackson Citizens' Council, who agreed to edit the Council paper without salary.[37] Simmons was a native of Jackson and a graduate of Central High School and Mississippi College, a Southern Baptist institution in Clinton, a few miles south of Jackson. Simmons became acquainted with Robert Patterson through the latter's letters to the editor published in the *Clarion-Ledger,* the state's most popular newspaper. Later described as "the single most significant obstacle to the realization of . . . racial equality" in the state, Simmons would emerge as the most visible leader in the Council movement. In contrast to Patterson's rural planter sensibilities, Simmons brought a business approach to the Council's work, eventually occupying a suite of offices in downtown Jackson where political leaders and local law enforcement could regularly be found. Where Patterson preferred his house in Itta Bena to his office in nearby Greenwood, Simmons was most comfortable in a suit with a secretary to answer his calls. Their collaboration evidenced another element of the Council's success. Patterson's familiarities with white dominance in the Mississippi Delta and Simmons's influence in Jackson combined to maintain white power at both the local and state level.

Well traveled and educated, Simmons brought the polish to the organization that it would need to extend its network beyond the small Delta towns of Mississippi. When James Graham Cook interviewed him in 1962, he was struck by Simmons's comparative sophistication. "In contrast with many lesser segregationists," he noticed, "Simmons almost never permits himself the luxury of using the word 'nigger' or speaking in insulting terms of Negroes."[38] That quality was poorly reflected in Simmons's supervision of the Council's publicity efforts, however. The organization's monthly newspaper, *The Citizens' Council* (later renamed *The Citizen*), contained pages of race-baiting articles, cartoons, and editorials about the menace of black equality, the collusions between communism and civil rights campaigns, and the effeminate leadership of white liberal politicians. Simmons, perhaps better than anyone else in the organization, understood the balance of interests that existed within the state. The differences between large planters in the Delta, commercial interests in Jackson, and a variety of working-class whites scattered throughout the state complicated simple categories of rural versus urban. Simmons's contributions were crucial to crafting an organization that would speak to the anxieties of whites across the state through the cultivation of its publicity campaigns.

The establishment of its own media source could not have come at a more opportune time. Coverage of the Council's tactics in national media outlets multiplied in the wake of the 1955 murders. In October, the same month the inaugural issue of the *The Citizens' Council* appeared, an investigative piece appeared in *The Nation* about the white resistance movement. Dan Wakefield, the article's author, described for his readers a climate in Mississippi of "distrust and fear that breeds unsolved murders and threats of more." Rumors of Council vengeance through economic terror and "communiques" with information about local activists abounded. Despite the absence of hard evidence linking Council communications with recent murders, Wakefield concluded that white unity in Mississippi was impenetrable, a fact he attributed to the Council's success in shoring up support from every sector of white society, especially those in the courts and local law enforcement. The loose chain of authority from individual chapters to the state headquarters (now in Jackson, the capital city) allowed local leaders to pursue any means they considered necessary without danger of interference. Wakefield's article concluded with the statement that the Council's success in silencing white dissent and punishing black challengers had made racism "respectable" and so widespread that citizens interested in joining could simply go to their local bank to sign up.[39]

The Council's intent to be a sophisticated organization with elite white leadership that provided alternatives to violence was not the impression that national media sources received. In the wake of brutal violence for which no one was held accountable, they consistently described the Citizens' Council movement in the state as a cause of violence, not stability. Its influence over the centers of power and increasing evidence of economic pressure on blacks who supported desegregation and voting rights were impossible to ignore. A month after Wakefield's article, James Desmond, writing for the New York *Daily News,* avoided the Citizens' Council moniker altogether, referring to the organization simply as "the New Klan."[40]

Council leaders and their members were well aware of the reputation the organization had in Mississippi, the South, and the nation. But in Mississippi, press coverage that insinuated the Council's influence and effective use of intimidation, even if it took the form of murder, could be used to draw in non-elite whites who might otherwise consider the organization too well bred for their taste. This audience was clearly the target of *The Citizens' Council,* the monthly newspaper that began publication in October. Rather than serving as a countermeasure to bad press, the newspaper was a siren call to racists. Its articles, editorials, and cartoons embraced the tenets of racial hierarchy and minstrelsy. Using a collection of news stories found around the nation and world, readers could see the consequences of racial equality through crime, poverty, and miscegenation. Threats of communist infiltration, rape of white women, and white servitude infected each of these stories and served as a persistent call to white action against white liberals and black activists. Such tactics proved Hodding Carter's description correct. If the Citizens' Council intended to provide an alternative to Klan violence, its tactics were counterproductive.

Despite the race-baiting baggage that marked the earliest years of Mississippi's Council movement, however, historians have been cautious about connecting the organization into Klan-like groups that were also mobilizing during the civil rights movement. Neil McMillen, in his regional study on the Citizens' Council and similar organizations across the South, focused his work on what he called "the most 'respectable' wing of the resistance movement." He detailed the work of organizations that sought respectability and restraint, and the Citizens' Council, in his estimation, was the most apt example.[41] The tension of maintaining peace and order while lobbying for popular support, however, remained challenging for Council leaders in Mississippi and other states where the Council had a presence. Considering the fact that Council membership swelled when civil rights challenges seemed most threatening and that membership tended to be heaviest where the black-to-white ratio was greatest, respectable resistance was unlikely if not impossible to expect. It is also important to point out that Klan activity was dormant in the 1950s and did not resurface in Mississippi until 1963.

The Council was the only organization in the state committed to maintaining white supremacy and intimidating black Mississippians from participating in civil rights activities. The efforts it made to distance itself from the KKK, then, were irrelevant. The Council had no competition. If a citizen was fearful that white supremacy was in danger, membership in his local chapter was the only option for alleviating powerlessness. For that reason, the movement contained a variety of people who held a diversity of positions on how to exorcise those fears. Those constituencies did not begin to sort themselves out into separate organizations for several more years. When they did, the Council's strength in the state diminished. An informant for the FBI who infiltrated the Klan in the 1960s, Delmar Dennis, underscored this fact in an interview in 1990. Asked about the relationship between the Klan and the Citizens' Council, Delmar pointed to "a lot of overlapping" between the two. "The Citizens Council was first," he explained. "The Klan didn't really take off until about '63 and there were a lot of people who went from the Citizens Council to the Klan because they felt the Citizens Council wasn't doing enough. . . . So there were a lot of people in both."[42]

Another factor to consider when balancing the Council's desire for public respectability against its need for grassroots support, is the role that established channels of power took or avoided in the months following the *Brown* decision. Several states worked through legislative channels to avoid implementation of the desegregation order, absent the kind of organized resistance that the Citizens' Council represented in Mississippi. Seven southern states created special committees, through their legislatures, to study the legal requirements of the decision, including Mississippi, Alabama, and South Carolina, all strongholds of defiance. But more moderate Upper South states like Virginia and North Carolina also pursued legislative and legal stopgaps in the wake of *Brown*.[43] In each case, however, the political maneuvering that establishing and directing these committees required was often beset by the dynamics at play in each state, the rivalries that existed among different geographical and economic constituencies, and the commitment elected leaders were willing to make toward silencing grassroots movements as a way to avoid radical backlash.[44]

In cases where political leaders were trying to find pragmatic and legal solutions to the desegregation mandate, grassroots groups like the Citizens' Council could become problematic by inflaming the very constituents that public leaders needed to keep in check to contain white violence. Historian George Lewis explains this conflict as evidence that resistance to desegregation took the form of several "quite separate conversations . . . that ran concurrently."[45]

Nowhere was the conflict clearer than in the volumes of publications that Council organizations printed and disseminated. Beginning with Brady's *Black Monday*, publications like *Arkansas Faith, States' Rights Advocate, The Citizens' Council,* and *The Virginian* targeted working-class whites through articles and cartoons aimed at the "lowest common denominator of base racial fears" as a way to unify otherwise disparate white constituencies.[46] As political figures in each state worked through the sometimes protracted process of consensus, these publications, and the organizations that created them, offered a solution to the powerlessness that white constituents, especially those in predominantly black counties and urban centers, felt in the absence of clear legislative solutions.

Given these practical constraints, 1955 and 1956 were critical years for organized white resistance. It is the period in which the Council movement across the South spread most rapidly. In some states, Council organization followed the Mississippi model, while in other cases Councils more accurately embodied the respectable resistance strategies the organization in Mississippi proclaimed but often set aside to garner grassroots support. No other state, however, organized as quickly as Mississippi. Even in Alabama, where the Council movement was born in an area of the state that closely resembled the Mississippi Delta, the first Council did not form until November 1954, one month after the state association in Mississippi organized. In truth, however, the absence of an immediate threat of desegregation constrained growth. When petitions began to circulate in 1955, followed by the beginning of the Montgomery Bus Boycott, Council membership in Alabama soared.[47]

Alabama exemplified the contradictions inherent in white coalition-building in the organized resistance movement. Shortly after Alabama Councils formed their own state association under the guidance of the Council's founder, Robert Patterson, the differences among Councils in different areas of the state became visible. The executive secretary of the North Alabama Citizens' Council (NACC), Asa Carter, came under some criticism for alleged anti-Semitism and radical statements asking for the resignation of the University of Alabama's president after the school admitted its first black student in 1956. Carter and the NACC represented an area of the state historically poor and populated by small, mostly white, farmers. Most of the Council's power, however, hailed from the south central part of Alabama, where blacks made up a majority of the population. Council leaders from this area, like Sam Engelhardt, coveted responsible action and alliances with political leaders in Montgomery as a means to resist desegregation. Carter's actions threatened to undermine that objective, and he eventually left the state association and established the Alabama Citizens' Council as an alternative. By 1957, the northern movement had a reputation akin to the Ku Klux Klan's. And even though Carter's organization was an outlier of the state's organized resistance movement, his reputation undermined popular support for the Council statewide.[48]

At the other end of the spectrum, the Virginia Defenders of State Sovereignty and Individual Liberties was the closest version of the Citizens' Council in that state. It drew prominent public officials into its ranks quickly, and deliberately avoided grassroots membership altogether through the installation of a member-driven nomination process. Virginia's resistance often took shape within its legislative halls and the office of its governors. And while the shuttering of nine public schools to avoid desegregation in 1956 suggests vibrant defiance, that defiance was a product of complex political machinations and personal rivalries, not local activism.[49]

Louisiana provided another example of the combinations of power that worked in pursuit of obstruction. Its first Council was not founded until April 1955, and its second did not appear until September of that year. The comparative lag in popularity was likely attributable to the activism of Louisiana's state legislature, a body that by 1964 had passed no less than 131 pieces of legislation or resolutions to prevent desegregation. As in Alabama, Council membership proliferated around moments of civil rights challenges. In New Orleans, for instance, growth followed news of a federal court's denial of a state law meant to halt desegregation of New Orleans schools, leading Council administrator Bill Simmons to designate the New Orleans Council the largest in the nation. By 1957, however, membership lists had already experienced dramatic drops throughout the state.[50]

Countless variations of resistance proliferated in other southern states, which exemplified the complexities of organized resistance in a region rife with differences. Alongside the challenges of unifying whites within the same state, the variety of Council organizations, and their differing levels of popularity and success, made regional cooperation among them unlikely. For groups that sought national support for desegregation, these disparities created insuperable difficulties. As early as 1950, G. A. K. Sutton, a Floridian and admirer of Senator James Eastland, suggested that if the South meant to reassert its influence, it would have to begin presenting itself in more national terms. In a letter to Eastland, Sutton argued that the Dixiecrat label had been misleading about the states' rights movement. Supporters needed a moniker that would appeal to "average northern liberal republicans and to conservative democrats throughout the nation."[51] Eastland concurred, and during the course of his campaign for reelection in the summer of 1955, he articulated his support for a public relations strategy that would bring together all resistance groups in the South and explain the South's position to the rest of the nation.

The response was overwhelming. Letters poured into Eastland's Washington office in support of the publicity strategy, many of them from leaders of white resistance organizations. Stanley Morse, president of the Grass Roots League in South Carolina, described Eastland's suggestion as "very much needed" but one that should be "very carefully, cleverly planned by experienced public relations experts" using all accessible media forms—TV, radio, paid advertising, and "brief, snappy literature."[52] Mississippi's Speaker of the House, Walter Sillers, understood this dilemma and described it in a letter to Alabama state senator J. B. Henderson. Sillers, an open supporter of the Council movement and an avowed segregationist, expressed hesitation in organizing behind a narrowly construed defense of the South. The movement and its spokesmen should, he argued, "also give the National Picture and what is happening to the whole country through judicial decree. . . . In my opinion our fight can only, and must be, won North, East, and West of the Mason and Dixon line."[53]

Eastland was a vocal supporter of the Citizens' Council movement, but his vision of a regional organization suggests that he considered the organization limited in its impact outside of Mississippi. His founding of the Federation for Constitutional Government (FCG) in December 1955 indicated a more ideological approach that tied the South's position to a concept he called "Americanism," a position that embraced "free enterprise" as its slogan and avoided party or ideological labels in an effort to connect with sympathizers outside of the South.[54]

The FCG differed from the Citizens' Council in its intent to maintain a selective group of business and civic leaders to the exclusion of the general public. That vision and the prioritization of free enterprise as the central objective tied the organization to right-to-work issues and business interests. Leaders of the FCG intended to lobby support from nonsouthern contributors using these issues as a bridge between the South and the rest of the country. When the FCG hosted its inaugural meeting in Memphis in March 1956, representatives from twelve states attended, but attempts to attract nonsoutherners were not successful. The list of attendees was more or less a collection of segregationist spokesmen from across the South. In addition to Senator Eastland, Senator Strom Thurmond of South Carolina attended, along with former governors Herman Talmadge of Georgia and Fielding Wright of Mississippi. Council representatives were also present, including Bill Simmons, Tom Brady, and Robert Patterson from the Mississippi movement, and Roy Harris from Georgia's States' Rights Council. The overlap between the FCG board and Council leaders, however, ensured divided loyalties, and the Federation's attempts to attract conservatives from outside of the South tended to draw interest from radical right organizations like the Committee for Constitutional Government and the National Economic Council.[55]

This frustration was a common one in 1956. The Council movement's popularity, especially the activism of grassroots support, infiltrated the political atmosphere in 1956 and forced the hands of elected officials who embraced segregation but preferred to protect it through existing channels of power. The grassroots appeal of Council publications across the South and the sharp, racist language it cultivated ran into direct opposition to moderate voices holding public office. Mississippi's own governor, James P. Coleman (1955–1959), was opposed to the Council's influence in his state and feared it would unleash violence among whites who absorbed threats of race war and black dominance as a call to arms. North Carolina governor Luther Hodges held a similar position. Hodges understood that desegregation was inevitable and resistance futile. At the same time, admitting defeat in the midst of organized defiance was political suicide. Arkansas's governor Orval Faubus, who had won election in 1954 on a platform of racial moderation, found that segregationist sentiment in his state was growing too rapidly to maintain that position. He moved quickly to reassure constituents of his commitment to segregation. Faubus's transformation was directly tied to Council-driven fervor in the eastern part of the state. Arkansas's progressive delegation in Washington followed suit. Senator William J. Fulbright and Congressmen Brooks Hays and James W. Trimble, all three well known for their comparatively liberal positions on race, closed ranks and cloaked themselves in segregation's defense.[56]

Council influence across the South left elected officials grasping for their constituents' faith in them to defy *Brown*. In March 1956, as proof of their commitment, nineteen US senators and eighty-two representatives, all of them from the South, put their names to the Southern Manifesto, a document that articulated white southern opposition to *Brown v. Board of Education*, defining it as an extra-constitutional act of power and pledging their defiance through all legal means available. Support was not universal among southern delegations, however. In states where Council support was never a serious threat to political power (Tennessee, Texas, North Carolina, and Florida), congressional delegations split in their support or opposition to signing the statement. In states where a Council presence was visible and growing (Mississippi, Alabama, Arkansas, Virginia, South Carolina, Louisiana, and Georgia), delegations unanimously supported the statement. In Arkansas's case, Governor Faubus urged members of his state's congressional delegation to put their name to the Southern Manifesto as a way to avoid a Council takeover in the state. His suggestion matches historian John Kyle Day's evaluation of the document. Day argues in his study of the Southern Manifesto and its impact that many of the men who put their name on the document did so "to dilute extremist behavior." Instead, Council leaders in various states saw the document as an endorsement of their organization's position and claimed its announcement as a personal victory.[57] Faubus would soon learn firsthand just how influential Council opposition could be when he faced a desegregation crisis of his own in Little Rock in 1957. His decision to move away from his previously moderate position after the leader of the Capital Citizens' Council, Robert E. Brown, accused him of weak leadership, exemplified the kind of political realignments that the Council's presence could force. After adopting a more defiant stance against the desegregation of Central High School, Faubus earned an unprecedented third term as governor in 1958.[58]

The growing popularity of the Citizens' Council, no matter how short-lived it would be in some places, made 1956 a unique moment in the civil rights movement. The awakening of grassroots activism that the organization managed to initiate undermined existing political alliances and weakened the moderate position. In the case of Eastland's Federation for Constitutional Government, the attempt to strike a balance between its unifying message of Americanism and the race issue alienated its objectives from white southerners who were singularly concerned about segregation. The Council's phenomenal success in 1955 and 1956, not just in numbers but in influence, suggested that its unapologetic, undiluted embrace of white supremacy worked.

But the regional model that the FCG proposed was not lost on Council administrators. A month after the FCG meeting in Memphis, the Citizens' Councils of America (CCA) formed and officially convened in Jackson in October 1956 for board elections. The organization had diverse representation (its president was Willie Rainach of the Association of Citizens' Councils of Louisiana), but its first headquarters were in Greenwood, Mississippi, in the heart of the Delta. Robert Patterson was CCA secretary, and *The Citizens' Council* was its official publication.[59] In a description of the new organization's purpose in the October 1956 issue, the newspaper described the CCA as a natural extension of the state associations. Its functions would mirror the relationship between individual chapters and their state associations, assisting the former in planning efforts and publicity. The CCA charter prohibited its board from directing individual chapters or controlling the actions of state associations, reflecting the kind of relationship the Council insisted exist between the states and the federal government.[60]

As the Council expanded its vision for activism, new legislative restrictions ensured that white power in Mississippi remained firmly in place. Despite gains made in the months following *Brown*, black voters found themselves purged from rolls in a "re-registration" effort that local white officials conducted after the legislature approved new requirements in 1955. The consequences of signing a petition or attempting to register to vote were clear to black Mississippians by 1956, and the outward manifestation of fear was so obvious that the national office of the NAACP expressed grave concerns about the wisdom of continuing a Mississippi-based campaign.[61]

An investigation by the Southern Regional Council in November 1956 confirmed that Council power in Mississippi was unmatched in other

Deep South states, even though growth was rapidly increasing throughout the region. The SRC's report estimated there were over 80,000 members throughout the state and predicted that the organization would continue to wield "considerable influence" in the state for years, especially in areas like the Delta where the Council's will was "all-powerful."[62]

The Council's relationship with elected officials in high office was also strengthening. By the spring of 1956, Senator Eastland was forwarding his mail to Robert Patterson to alleviate the correspondence requirements of his office in Washington.[63] Eastland's early support for the Council movement and the access he provided to the increasing volume of mail he received expanded the ACCM's mailing lists and provided a wider readership for Council literature.

Despite the Council's increasing influence and recognized success, anxiety persisted among its leaders. In 1956, the Jackson Citizens' Council unsuccessfully sought an alliance with black leaders in the city to convince black Jacksonians that segregation's preservation was in their best economic interest, evidence that white leaders recognized black discontent and that they feared it would develop into protest.[64] In March 1956, Mississippi's junior senator John Stennis predicted that the lull in civil rights activity should not insinuate success. The escalation in movement outside of Mississippi, he argued, was evidence that the crisis was likely to continue for years. Based on the likelihood of continued agitation, Stennis suggested the formation of a Citizens' Council chapter in his home county of Kemper in east central Mississippi. In his estimation, Council leadership would properly serve local officials in deterring local blacks' attempts to register to vote. Access to the ballot represented the "real danger" of successful civil rights activism because once blacks registered, "there is not a chance for us to control other phases of the problem."[65]

The threat of black political power resonated with Council leaders and white southerners in general. Anxiety was especially prevalent in rural areas of the South where access to the vote would effectively end white political dominance. In Mississippi, disfranchisement of black voters and the white primary system created a political climate that thrived on racial demagoguery and raw appeals to white supremacy. Black political power threatened to overturn the entire system. This fear was well placed, but not only because black power would come at the expense of white power in some areas of the state. The entry of black votes would change the way in which candidates for political office could campaign in front of non-elite white voters. Racist appeals would no longer be practical with black votes at stake. The Black Belt areas also stood to feel a more dramatic impact from school desegregation.[66] These concerns would persist throughout the 1960s and 1970s when black political power became a reality, seeding a flight to the Republican Party where race-baiting blurred into conservatism.

Council growth in the state persisted, in part, because of these anxieties. For the remainder of the decade, the civil rights movement seemed quiet in Mississippi, but this period helped Council leaders focus on strategy more than immediate threats. It also absorbed the principle behind the Federation for Constitutional Government—alliances with groups outside of the South held more promise in securing the racial status quo than unifying like-minded white Mississippians. Financial support for that kind of work was critical. In the fall of 1955, a series of correspondence circulated at all levels of the Council movement about securing financial donations and coordinating an active network of white resistance organizations in the South. Both of these initiatives were important to extending Council influence from local chapters and into the mainstream of national politics.

In pursuit of an effective fund-raising strategy, the Council took its cues from the NAACP. In November 1955, Robert Patterson forwarded information to Eastland that he had collected about the NAACP's Legal Defense and Education Fund. The Education Fund took the NAACP name but was a separate entity, designating donations to the Fund tax-exempt through its 501(c)(3) status. Patterson asked Eastland to request a copy of the code so they could create a similar fund for the Citizens' Council.[67] In December 1956, the Educational Fund of the Citizens' Councils (EFCC) was created to counter the NAACP's educational program, an initiative that Council literature described as a commitment to "prepare public opinion for the total 'integration' of negroes into white society." In anticipation of the IRS granting the Fund tax-exempt status, Council leaders designed the EFCC as a donation-driven initiative, a departure from previous Council funding initiatives which were heavily dependent upon dues and subscriptions to the monthly newspaper. If the EFCC existed as a nonprofit corporation, money could be funneled in without requiring chapter membership. This distinction was a significant shift for the Council and drew a clear line between local activities and national aspirations. It also would have enabled donations from outside organizations and sympathetic individuals from all over the country who found some value in the Council's work. The EFCC persisted even though it never achieved tax-exempt status from the IRS, a fact that later drove Council leaders to seek funding directly from the State of Mississippi, testing the limits of white support for Council influence in Mississippi.[68]

Upon its creation, the EFCC set to work designing a counterattack to what its administrators saw as a multimedia onslaught from the NAACP. Council leaders feared that on radio and television, and in movie theaters, the acclimation to integration was slowly wearing down the commitment to segregation. It was through those venues, then, that the Council had to articulate its message. In late April 1957, the Council began a weekly television broadcast called *Citizens' Council Forum*. The program broadcasted from the Jackson NBC affiliate, WLBT, every Monday night at 6:30 p.m. Fred Beard, the station manager, was a member of the Jackson Citizens' Council and provided complimentary studio time to the program. By November, *Forum* added radio broadcasts to its format, making the recordings available without cost to interested stations.[69]

Forum's host and producer was Richard "Dick" Morphew. Morphew spent his childhood in Birmingham, Alabama, and Kansas City, Missouri. A graduate of the University of Missouri's School of Journalism, he sought work in Los Angeles before taking on newspaper work in Tupelo, Mississippi, and then moving on to take a job at WLBT and its radio affiliate, WJDX, as news staff in 1954.[70]

Despite his close affiliation with the Council's media strategies, Morphew's ideology was difficult to detect. There is no evidence that he had a background in similar movements or that his contributions to the Council's propaganda campaigns were motivated by anything beyond salary. He wrote a handful of editorials for *The Citizen,* and he traveled frequently on Council business, but the passion with which his colleagues Robert Patterson and Bill Simmons worked seemed less detectable in Morphew.

In his role as *Forum* host, Morphew guided the scripted question-and-answer format for the various guests who visited. In its first broadcasts, the show's guests were local Council members and Mississippi politicians. State leaders included Lieutenant Governor Carroll Gartin, Attorney General Joe Patterson, Secretary of State Herbert Ladner, and State Auditor E. Boyd Golding. Other notable guests were Ellis Wright (president of the Jackson Citizens' Council), *Black Monday* author Tom Brady, and Council founder Robert Patterson.[71] Its introductory monologue described the program's affiliation with the ACCM and defined the Citizens' Council movement as "a means of promoting public opinion," since "informed people will not surrender their freedom."[72]

The first radio broadcast, in November 1957, represented the direction *Forum* programs would follow for the next nine years. It featured all four Mississippi congressmen (John Bell Williams, William Colmer, Jamie Whitten, and Arthur Winstead) and Congressman Martin Dies of Texas. While most of the guests were native sons, the acquisition of national political figures as guests would soon become the norm, especially if those guests had a companion issue that could underscore the Council's opposition to segregation. In the case of Martin Dies, his appearance on the show highlighted the links between communist infiltration and recent racial strife in the South. Dies's chairmanship of the House Un-American Activities Committee (HUAC) from 1938 to 1944 implied expertise about the detection of communist influences. During his visit, a precursor to a Council rally held in Jackson that evening, Dies urged southern unity against the "trend toward centralized government and the destruction of our states' rights." He also warned southern political leaders to move beyond sectionalism and "battle for the interests of America."[73]

The transition from local interests to national impact was not an easy one to make. Most of the Council's perquisites came from the local network of support it received. Its ability to produce a weekly television and radio program was wholly dependent upon the donation of studio space and broadcasting slots. The EFCC had articulated the need to broaden the audience for segregation's defense, but the practicality of doing that given a weak funding structure and the distance between local and state authority built into Council hierarchy was problematic. In response to a letter of inquiry about the ACCM's progress on this front, Robert Patterson curtly replied that the Council was committed to shoring up white southern support. "We never buy publicity," he explained, "when we can get it free." As it stood in 1957, relationships with state governments were paying dividends and, Patterson argued, providing white Mississippians with the "greatest bulwark" against integration possible.[74]

In Mississippi, that bulwark took the form of a state agency, the Mississippi State Sovereignty Commission (MSSC). The legislature approved the creation of the agency in March 1956, the same month that Council leaders attended the FCG organizational meeting in Memphis. Under the sponsorship of Speaker of the House Walter Sillers and fifty-seven other House members, the bill described the agency as a gatekeeper of sorts, charged with protecting the sovereignty of the state against federal encroachments. Included in its duties were public relations activities that would advertise the segregationist position to other states and regions.[75]

A number of legislators recognized the footprint of the Citizens' Council immediately. The open-ended funding structure, the committee of twelve appointees charged with supervising the agency, and the proposal of public relations work within the agency, read like a page from Citizens' Council literature. The EFCC was not officially in existence when Sillers and his colleagues introduced the bill for the MSSC, and the proposed agency looked like a state-sponsored funding vein for the Council's marketing strategy. Even the segregationist-run evening newspaper, the *Jackson Daily News,* interpreted the proposal as a "blank check" for the Council. Despite formal objections to the bill, it passed nine days after its introduction.[76]

The Council's influence over the creation of the state agency is not clear. The subsequent formation of the EFCC nine months later and its incorporation as a state-approved nonprofit agency suggests that, at the very least, Council leaders expected the agency to funnel money to Council activities. But the establishment of a publicity arm of the MSSC threatened to infringe upon Council-run marketing campaigns, forcing cooperation between the agency and the organization if the former was meant to absorb the public relations activities of the latter. The Jackson Citizens' Council, under the leadership of Bill Simmons, wholly endorsed the idea of a state agency when Governor-elect J. P. Coleman submitted it to the Legal Educational Advisory Committee (LEAC) in 1955, a committee of advisors charged with brainstorming the best ways to protect segregation in the state.[77] Council support in 1955, however, preceded the Council's difficult relationship with Coleman, who eschewed Council influence in favor of more moderate policies, an approach that leaders like Bill Simmons considered an unforgiveable offense. In truth, Coleman's support for the agency's creation sprang from his hopes that a state-directed effort would dilute the more confrontational tactics he associated with Council leadership.[78] The relationship between Coleman and the Council would continue to deteriorate over the course of the next four years.

The initiative behind its creation and its support from the state legislature matched the efforts of the Council movement in Mississippi, however. The MSSC is best known as a state-level surveillance agency monitoring civil rights activity in the state, but in its first two years, the bulk of agency activities reflected its role as a public relations agency. Hal DeCell served as MSSC's first public relations director, and under his leadership the agency followed a course to stem the bad publicity directed at the state in recent years. Senator Eastland and Speaker Sillers, both proponents of taking the segregationist message outside of the South, fully supported this focus, and within months DeCell was serving as a consultant on a civil rights documentary with the Newsfilm Project, an initiative within the Fund for the Republic, Inc. The Fund for the Republic had engaged in equalization efforts and provided funding support for the Southern Regional Council. The tolerance in Mississippi for an organization with those connections was at low tide in 1957, and though DeCell's representation of Mississippi's point of view was exactly the kind of work the MSSC envisioned for its publicity arm, the budget review for the expenses incurred from his travel to Los Angeles was closely scrutinized. The increasing amount of travel costs to bring journalists down to Mississippi also alarmed legislators and the state auditor's office, leading to DeCell's resignation in 1959.[79]

The MSSC had more troubles on the horizon. Tensions with the Citizens' Council erupted soon after the agency activated. The two entities split over the construction of a Veterans Administration (VA) hospital in Jackson, a federal project that would require integrated facilities. The Council wanted to obstruct the project for that reason, but the Sovereignty Commission disagreed. Reaction from lawmakers and local news-papers was harsh, leaving the MSSC to defend itself against charges of hypocrisy and betrayal of the principles upon which it was created. The real evidence of this reaction came in the form of a $100,000 budget reduction for the agency and a legislative proposal that would enable direct funding of the Citizens' Council. The latter proposal failed, but it would resurface under a new administration.[80] Despite their disagreements, cooperation between the two groups was critical, and by the end of 1957, there was evidence that both were attempting to present a united front. Lieutenant Governor Carroll Gartin, a defender of the VA land grant, described Council members in the state as being of "a very high caliber . . . outstanding citizens, and citizens dedicated to the preservation of segregation in this state.[81]

The rift between the Council and Governor Coleman, however, was a different matter. The Council's attempt to secure MSSC funding for travel expenses failed when Coleman refused to approve it. When Robert Patterson suggested to Coleman that the Sovereignty Commission "pick up the tab" for Judge Tom Brady's upcoming speaking engagement at the Commonwealth Club in California, Coleman responded by questioning the ethics of a sitting Mississippi judge (Brady was at that time serving as a Circuit Court judge) visiting "a far distant state." Explaining his position as "a widely accepted principle throughout the bench and bar," Coleman suggested that Brady "hold himself aloof from all activities, except that pertaining to the duties of his office." Taxpayer money, he concluded, would not be used in furtherance of such a violation.[82]

The legislative proposal to direct taxpayer money to the Citizens' Council was, in part, a reaction to Coleman's decision, as well as evidence of a crisis of faith among some legislators about whether the Sovereignty Commission was fulfilling its charge. The chronology of events from the VA land grant to the creation of the EFCC suggests that the latter was born in response to Coleman's lack of cooperation. Council leaders must have felt encouraged by the proposal to direct tax money to its activities. The creation of the EFCC would facilitate that process. With civil rights activity in the state somewhat dormant for the remainder of the decade and cooperation with the MSSC limited, the Council dove headlong into its own media onslaught.

There was increasing evidence that the Council's media campaign would find an audience outside of the South. As noted above, a number of national publications had featured the Council movement and its leaders in their pages. They had done so to illuminate the nature of white resistance and its similarities to the Klan, but the profiles struck a nerve among conservatives, who found quite a bit in common with segregation's defenders. Publications like *Facts Forum* and *Human Events* often represented the South's point of view by featuring southern leaders as guest writers and by addressing the civil rights question through editorials by conservative intellectuals.

One of those writers was libertarian Frank Chodorov. Chodorov's fame came from his outspoken opposition to the New Deal in the 1930s and from his isolationism during World War II. He served as editor of the conservative publication *The Freeman* until he was fired for his radical views and founded his own news sheet, *analysis,* which merged with *Human Events* in 1951.[83] Chodorov had developed a small but passionate following during his transition from *The Freeman* to the merger with *Human Events,* and when his article "Civil Rights Versus Natural Rights" appeared in the magazine in 1957, the crystallization of widespread white resistance had begun.

Chodorov's evaluation of the civil rights debate was directly in response to pending civil rights legislation in Congress. The Council's publicity campaign after 1956 took the same approach, framing the issue as one that pitted states' rights against federal encroachment. Implementation of *Brown,* by 1957, was indefinite given the myriad of legal challenges that Deep South states lodged in its wake. But the decision's principles opened the door to congressional legislation, a more threatening directive given that Council defenses rested upon the argument that the Supreme Court had stepped into legislative territory, therefore violating the separation of powers doctrine.

Chodorov's distinction between civil and natural rights suggested an answer to this dilemma. In his assessment, civil rights "agitators" were concerned less with individual protections than they were with the enlargement of the federal government. Examining antilynching legislation, legislated social equality, access to the vote, and economic parity separately, he determined that none of these issues was in line with the principle of natural rights. Natural rights, he insisted, accompanied an individual at birth. Government could neither bestow nor enforce such rights. Its function was negative in that it could only police the infringement of individual rights. In essence, he argued, "the Government is itself enjoined by this concept from using its monopoly of power to invade the God-given rights of the individual." Under this definition, voting was not a right, but a privilege with practical restrictions. Social equality infringed upon an individual's right to pursue happiness in his choice of companions. That choice extended into the business world where, Chodorov argued, hiring practices were a matter of "conscience and convenience, a natural prerogative." Even antilynching legislation at the federal level was problematic for him because it made the act of lynching an offense against the government instead of an individual.[84]

Chodorov's article put a philosophical spin on the states' rights argument, removing the stigma of race altogether. It also superseded the regional provincialism that news reports on the Council movement and other forms of white resistance insinuated. His formula for evaluating the legitimacy of civil rights legislation is only one example of the field from which segregationists could draw to distance themselves from the burdens of race and region. In November 1955, the same month the ACCM formed, William F. Buckley published the first issue of *National Review*. In his publisher's statement, Buckley described conservatives as "nonlicensed nonconformists . . . dangerous business in a liberal world." Buckley's magazine targeted the victims of liberal intellectualism, a movement he held responsible for a "parasitic bureaucracy" dependent upon the will of a "thousand different pressure groups." He described the magazine as a check on social engineers who were prisoners to their vision of scientific utopia and its impact on the educational system.[85]

Along these same lines, in 1956, Clinton Rossiter's *Conservatism in America* heralded a return of conservative values, an event that Rossiter described as "equally momentous" as the advent of television, the development of the H-bomb, or the announcement of *Brown v. Board of Education*. Rossiter's "philosophical" conservatism emphasized principles of order and skepticism of reform. It rejected the "liberal" obsession with change and experimentation in lieu of stability and social order.[86]

The collective articulation of conservative revolt in these publications and others offered an intellectual script for segregation's defense and provided the kind of model that would frame the Council's own media strategies. It also introduced the organization to higher aspirations. Tied to a racial past that sprang from two hundred years of slavery, white southerners' reluctance to acknowledge, let alone embrace, change made them guardians of history, a description that most conservatives championed in the 1950s. The regional identity that defined white resistance in the first years of organization easily intersected with an ideology that valued organic social hierarchy and distrust of government.[87]

By the end of 1957, the Council's growth within Mississippi fueled its ambitions but left its focus in flux. Leaders of the movement had their eyes on a number of moving targets. In addition to growing membership rolls in the state, it had to evaluate the benefits and liabilities of cooperation with other entities like the Sovereignty Commission, a state agency that could funnel money to the Council if their relationship was amicable, but could severely obstruct state support if it was contentious. J. P. Coleman's refusal to embrace the Council's message was a glaring reminder that white moderates in the state were not loyal allies and were likely to cooperate only as long as public opinion required it. Organized civil rights campaigns remained elusive in Mississippi, but gestures toward race-blind ideological alliances with groups outside of the South threatened to undermine Council support among rural whites in the state. In short, Council success depended upon a series of uneasy alliances that threatened to unravel if civil rights activity escalated, white moderates defected, or rural whites lost faith in the Council's ability to maintain an atmosphere of fear.

Council growth across the South evidenced similar concerns among other southern states. While states like Louisiana and Virginia were not exact models of the movement in Mississippi, the interactions of Black Belt elites with predominantly white areas of the state and relationships between grassroots organizing and political leaders played determinative roles in how resistance shaped up in each model. No state, however, experienced the rapid, long-sighted growth that the Mississippi Council exhibited. Its ability to embed its objectives into channels of state power, despite the distaste that leaders like J. P. Coleman had about the consequences of such collusions, prepared a field of influence that Councils in other states could not imitate. In 1959 the full realization of that influence became clear.

CHAPTER 3

FROM THE CAPITAL CITY TO THE NATION'S CAPITAL, 1958–1960

The fact remains that in the South the Citizens' Council takes and merits most of the credit for whatever success massive resistance, with all its implications, has had; and there is little or no disposition by anyone, politician or not, to argue the point. —HODDING CARTER III

John Salter arrived in Jackson in 1961, in the thick of a "Citizens' Council coup" begun in 1959 with the gubernatorial election of Ross Barnett. Salter was an activist and sociology professor who moved to Jackson as a faculty member at Tougaloo College, a private black institution at the north end of the capital city. His involvement with student activists and his status as an outsider brought him into direct confrontation with the stifling environment that Barnett's administration and its partnership with the Citizens' Council created. Despite the passion and commitment of the students he mentored and their impatience to begin direct action campaigns, Salter described Jackson as a virtual graveyard of failed attempts:

> Jackson was watched continually and sharply for any signs of "weakening." The same conformity that strangled the white community outside Jackson existed within the capital and it was known that the Citizens Council and the Sovereignty Commission had at least one watchdog citizen in every city block in the white sections. The same fear that strangled the black community elsewhere in Mississippi strangled it in Jackson—

and it was known that the Citizens Council and the Sovereignty Commission had their spies there, too.[1]

Much of the Citizens' Council's early reputation for terror in Mississippi grew out of its influence in small, rural communities of the state where blacks outnumbered whites. The center of power for the organization as a whole, however, was in Jackson, home of the Jackson Citizens' Council and, later, the Citizens' Councils of America. Access to legislators, state agencies, media outlets, and prominent business leaders made the Jackson Council the most powerful chapter in the state. But at the center of coordinated Council activity, Jackson's unique position as the seat of government and the largest city in the state misrepresented the situation in Mississippi as a whole, especially regarding white unity. The power struggles between the Sovereignty Commission and the Jackson Citizens' Council, the disagreements between the ACCM and the Coleman administration, and other divisions among white leaders affected the strategies of the state organization in ways that were not necessarily representative of other parts of the state where Council influence remained unchallenged. The Council's presence in Jackson also set it apart from its sister organizations in other states that continued to hold more influence in Black Belt areas where the movement began than in state capitals or urban areas. As the Council leveraged increasing influence in Jackson, it distanced itself from the grassroots model that was the norm in most areas of the state where Council chapters existed. In its place appeared an organization that aspired to national influence. Just as Council leaders made moves in that direction, however, the civil rights movement in Mississippi became more visible and the Council's reputation in Mississippi as an effective guardian of white supremacy began to wane.

Originally formed as the Jackson States' Rights Association, the Jackson Council officially changed its name and joined the Association of Citizens' Councils of Mississippi in May 1955.[2] Jackson was a microcosm of the extent and limit of Council influence. The concentrated wealth and political power that the state's biggest city held represented the model of Council organization that Tom Brady and Robert Patterson imagined in 1954. Members of the Jackson Citizens' Council (JCC) were elite, educated, and well positioned to influence Mississippi's political response to developing events. The Hederman brothers, owners of the state's highest-circulated newspaper, *The Clarion-Ledger,* and its evening counterpart, the *Jackson Daily News,* were some of the JCC's most prominent members. Their connections provided controlled publicity for the Council and helped circulate the names and addresses of local activists by printing them in their papers.[3] In addition to the deep pool of Council leaders who supervised the Jackson chapter, Bill Simmons, who would become the most recognizable Council administrator, entered the Council movement through the Jackson branch. His activism and leadership eventually moved the Citizens' Councils of America headquarters from the Delta to Jackson, where it remained until the CCA disbanded in 1989.

The JCC's reputation as the most formidable Council chapter in the state was a product of the environment within which it worked. In the 1950s, Jackson was home to five colleges and multiple religious denominations. It was, comparatively speaking, the most cosmopolitan of all of Mississippi's cities, and the small-town surveillance and intimidations that defined the Delta movement were less visible. But the subtlety did not imply absence. The JCC set its sights on silencing dissent, especially among whites, intimidating them into cooperation, or humiliating them into leaving. Its campaign against the president of Millsaps College, a private, four-year, Methodist-affiliated institution in Jackson, is evidence of this fact.

Since its founding in 1890, Millsaps easily stood out as a progressive institution, insulated from the whims of racist governors and legislators who often used the threat of defunding as a way to monitor and dictate the curriculum of state-run institutions like the University of Mississippi. From 1926 to 1969, for example, the College was the only institution of higher learning in the state whose faculty taught evolution, since state universities were prohibited by law from doing so. When a student group at the institution publicly endorsed antilynching legislation, Senator Theodore Bilbo, one of the state's most outspoken and unapologetic defenders of white supremacy, designated Millsaps students victims of left-wing propaganda.[4]

Along similar lines, Millsaps frequently collaborated with Tougaloo College, a black institution in Jackson, through a biracial discussion group that included both students and faculty from each school. Such events stayed under the radar prior to the Council movement, but post-*Brown* alliances within the white power structure made the continuance of these meetings untenable in the capital city. JCC president Ellis Wright Sr. had multiple children enrolled at Millsaps in 1958, making the institution a likely target for Council threats, but the tension erupted when the Millsaps College Christian Council, a student and faculty-led group on campus, hosted a series of speakers during the month of March. The series was open to the entire campus community and provided six different discussion topics to be explored under the leadership of different speakers over the course of four weeks. All of the topics represented pressing social issues, including nuclear armament, current theological trends, and the meaning of life. The most controversial, however, was a discussion series entitled, "The Christian and Race Relations."[5] The series' first speaker was Dr. Ernst Borinski, a German immigrant and sociology professor at Tougaloo and, according to Sovereignty Commission files, a "race agitator."[6]

Borinski's criticism of the Council movement in the wake of George Lee's murder undoubtedly helped put him on the organization's radar. His involvement with the series of talks at Millsaps ensured the Council's attention. Special alarm erupted in response to one particular speaker, Reverend Glenn Smiley, field secretary for the Fellowship of Reconciliation and a supporter of integration. The Council's connections to the state's media created a maelstrom of reaction, most of it focused on an evolving public debate between the college's president, Ellis Finger, and Jackson Citizens' Council president Ellis W. Wright, whose son John, a Millsaps student, attended Borinski's lecture and reported back to his father.[7] Wright responded swiftly, making public a letter he had sent to Finger in which he described his reaction as "appalled and shocked," a feeling made worse by "the astounding revelation that mixed groups of students from Millsaps and Tougaloo have been meeting for several years." Reminding Finger of his sustained financial support of the institution through fund-raising and tuition for his children, Wright described Millsaps's activities as "intolerable," especially in light of the "life and death struggle" to which the Citizens' Council was deeply committed. He demanded the college explain its position on the segregation issue.[8]

President Finger's response, in a statement to the college's stakeholders that quickly became public, is revelatory of the narrow position racial moderates in Jackson could occupy under Council scrutiny. His defense amounted to a plea for the preservation of academic freedom, even as he assured his critics that his administration would more closely supervise future invitations to prospective speakers. Putting distance between the college's position and that of its faculty (whom he held responsible for Smiley's scheduled visit), Finger described the series of lectures as an opportunity for students to experience a variety of viewpoints on controversial and complicated issues, a right to which all college students were entitled. Taking a page from the Council's political position, Finger reflected that, "In an age when we are alarmed at the increasing controls of government, we should be strengthening those institutions which support and preserve freedom of speech."[9]

The JCC's response came during its Sunday afternoon broadcast of *Forum*. The program's host, Dick Morphew, opened the show by reading a letter from Bill Simmons in which the Council administrator invited President Finger to be a guest on the following Sunday's broadcast. "I have read with interest your statement in this morning's papers," Simmons's letter began, "Although you do not say whether your administration supports segregation or integration, you seem concerned about freedom of speech and bondage. As an accommodation, may we offer you fifteen minutes of choice television time . . . to explain your position?"[10] Finger declined, and the attacks continued.

The next day, Tom Ethridge, a writer for the *Clarion-Ledger*'s "Mississippi Notebook" column, reminded his readers that Millsaps had, in the past, been quite eager to accept the financial support of white Mississippians. Its betrayal of those patrons, he argued, was a "slap in the face." The very building in which Dr. Borinski lectured about the antithetical relationship between Christianity and segregation, was a building constructed, Ethridge explained, "with funds contributed by thousands of 'un-Christian' Methodists and other segregationist infidels throughout our state." Ethridge himself, he continued, had been largely responsible for the publicity associated with the fund-raising campaign even though he was never a Millsaps student. The campaign's success, he explained, drew from the perception that Millsaps was a "Mississippi institution, serving the best interests of our state and people." The sponsorship of a "European refugee" and known integrationist was a deep betrayal of this trust.[11]

The backlash to the Millsaps lecture series extended well beyond the Jackson area and underscored the reach of Council influence. A revival in Durant was cancelled when its scheduled speaker, Reverend J. Noel Hinson, wrote a letter to President Finger, congratulating him on his stand for academic freedom. It is unclear how the letter became public, but by March 10, Hinson's letter to Finger appeared in the *Jackson Daily News,* making him an instant enemy among segregationist stalwarts.[12] Along the same lines, the campus newspaper editor at Mississippi State University, L. E. Miller, wrote an editorial in support of Millsaps's willingness to present different perspectives on the segregation issue. The student council fired him shortly after the editorial appeared, explaining that his remarks were "fanning the fires" of the race crisis. After failing to get the required two-thirds majority to ratify its decision, the student council was forced to reinstate him. But the vote was close: 1,150 to 934, in favor of his removal.[13]

The Council's demand that Millsaps publicly affirm its commitment to segregation did not go uncontested, however, especially among some members of the state's press. Council critic Hodding Carter, editor of the *Delta Democrat-Times,* pushed back. He compared Wright and his Council colleagues to Nazis, "thought-control policemen" that held inexplicable influence over too many southern institutions. Only days after the story broke, Carter described Wright's demands as "monstrous" and "intolerable." The right to free speech and the right to listen to different points of view, he argued, belonged to every American, and organizations like the Jackson Citizens' Council stood in direct violation of those fundamental rights.[14]

Hazel Brannon Smith, editor of *The Lexington Advertiser* and another critic of the Council's tactics, made similar statements, aligning Mississippi's culture of fear with "Godless Russia where Christianity is frowned upon and the individual counts for nothing."[15] In a letter to Jackson's *State Times,* L. G. Patterson described the Citizens' Council as a "mighty octopus," trapping Mississippians in its tentacles. "Free speech is not allowed here," he stated. "Democracy is out, it's dead, the Citizens Councils censor who can speak, who to Preach and who to teach. They control the politicians and the elections, just as the Communists do where they are in control."[16]

All of these challenges to Council influence rested upon First Amendment freedoms and their application in an educational setting. Each of the critics also defended segregation, a fact that uncovers the complexity of the moderate position in Mississippi and its sister states.[17] Few white Mississippians supported integration outright, but they flinched against heavy-handed scare tactics that sought to silence dissent completely. The Council's aggressive reaction, meant to reassure white unity in Jackson, threatened to undermine it.

Ultimately, Finger's statement in support of academic freedom was not enough to satisfy the Jackson Citizens' Council, especially after backlash to its position surfaced. Two weeks after the flare-up, the College's Board of Trustees issued its own statement in assurance of its continuing commitment to segregation, a direct answer to Ellis Wright's demand that Millsaps explain its position.[18] The Council's influence was intact, but its reputation was blemished. Battles at home were a constant irritant to Council leaders, especially those in Jackson. The Millsaps controversy drove home the point that the organization's successes were often products of terror campaigns, rather than organic victories.

The Millsaps incident and the backlash it created developed at a critical time for the Council. The Mississippi state legislature convened in 1958 for its biennial session and, given the successes of the previous year, Council leaders expected to see dramatic progress toward the tightening up of white defenses. The 1958 session opened with a slate of anti-integration bills awaiting introduction. Within the slate was a resolution enabling the investigation of NAACP activity within the state under the supervision of the General Legislative Investigating Committee. Members of both houses approved the concurrent resolution on March 3 and March 4, prior to the Millsaps controversy.[19] Its passage provided public leverage against both Millsaps and Tougaloo. On March 17, Jimmy Morrow, an attorney and legislator from Brandon, a suburb east of Jackson, appeared on *Forum* to discuss the possible investigation of NAACP members in the state. "All we want to know are the facts," Morrow explained. When questioned about Dr. Ernst Borinski's involvement with the NAACP, Morrow recalled that Borinski's name had unanimously come up as a viable subject for investigation only days before, when his visit to Millsaps had appeared as a story in local papers. In lieu of commenting too specifically on the committee's intentions toward the Tougaloo professor, Morrow summed up the situation for his listeners: "Any man that could get up before a school or student body in Mississippi and say that segregation is un-Christian and ungodly and that the nigras are not afraid, that the law is on their sides, certainly does not know . . . the people of Mississippi."[20]

The fear of traitors in their midst undoubtedly vexed Council members like Morrow, but the Millsaps/Tougaloo controversy provided an opportunity for publicity at a time when the state legislature was considering a bill that promised to provide some financial relief for the Councils. Publicity worked both ways, however. The more attention the Council won through public demands like that of Ellis Wright's, the more it risked emboldening its detractors. On March 17, 1958, the state senate took up consideration of a bill to allow county boards of supervisors to allocate tax money for support of local Council chapters. It passed the Senate with only two dissents two days after its introduction.[21] On the heels of the public battle over Millsaps, however, the press was primed to use the bill's introduction as a challenge to Council influence. Editors throughout the state continued to affirm their personal support of the Citizens' Council, but they questioned the wisdom of granting the organization access to public funds without proper restrictions.[22] The state's NAACP, under the leadership of its field secretary, Medgar Evers, joined the chorus of skeptical whites. Evers warned an audience of 1,200 that, should the bill pass, all Mississippians would effectively become members of the Citizens' Councils through the allocation of their tax money.[23]

In light of such criticism, a substitute bill emerged out of the House that diluted the language of the bill, removing the reference to direct contributions to organizations. The adjustment allowed city and county governments to hire organizations to aid in the "dissemination of information, advertising and education of persons . . . concerning the principles of the sovereign rights of the state and the preservation of constitutional government." It was a thin veil but enough to win House approval.[24]

Forum broadcasts during the bill's consideration were more focused upon Council activities and membership pleas than was typically the case. Local attorneys, women involved in the organization, and members from the Jackson Citizens' Council appeared in succession to discuss a variety of issues. But no matter what the focus of the broadcast, each program circled back to membership and the need for white unity in the state.[25] In a discussion about a recent lawsuit contesting voting requirements in Jefferson Davis County, *Forum*'s host, Dick Morphew, questioned two Jackson attorneys, Webb Overstreet Jr. and Russell Moore III, who were also members of the JCC legal advisory team, about the best way for regular citizens to help maintain the state's voting laws. The answer was unsurprising. "The only way you can effectively win any fight," Overstreet answered, "is to wholeheartedly join in and present a united front. . . . And to us, the only effective way to do it is belong to the Council."[26]

Women's work was also expanding within the organization. Under the directorship of Sara McCorkle, who appeared on *Forum*'s first program in 1958, women's activities and youth outreach became additional investments for the ACCM. McCorkle's work extended earlier campaigns of the United Daughters of the Confederacy to educate white schoolchildren about their history. In its Council form, these programs were more direct, emphasizing the dangers of integration and interracial relationships. McCorkle's identification of women's work as a natural focus of the Council movement embraced traditional notions of home education and women's influence. She was especially concerned with the subtle influences of toys and church literature upon children and their normalization of interracial families. In the course of her work, McCorkle visited civic clubs and public schools and appeared on a New Orleans–area Council television program. One of the greatest successes she claimed was the contribution of choice titles from the Council's recommended reading list to school libraries, including Theodore Bilbo's *Take Your Choice: Separation or Mongrelization* (1946), Stuart Omar Landry's *Cult of Equality* (1945), and Tom Brady's *Black Monday*.[27]

In addition to circulated reading lists and library donations, McCorkle helped supervise annual essay contests for which the EFCC awarded two $500 scholarships to high school students as well as local chapter awards of $50. In the first contest, held during the 1958–1959 school year, contestants chose from four essay topics with a suggested reference list: "Why I believe in social separation of the races of mankind"; "Subversion in racial unrest"; "Why the preservation of States Rights is important to every American"; and "Why separate schools should be maintained for the white and negro races." Through these efforts the Council promoted their message by encouraging young people in Mississippi to understand the tenets of scientific racism. McCorkle's purpose in spearheading this work was to foster familiarity among students with the idea that "amalgamation of the races" was the death knell of many civilizations in world history.[28] She detailed all of these activities in her visit to *Forum* at the beginning of 1958, shortly before the state legislature convened.

Despite calls for white unity and the articulation of the good work the Council was doing, the proposed bill to allow local appropriation of tax money faced certain defeat. Governor Coleman described the bill as the Council's attempt to punish him for "refus[ing] to set fire to everything in the state," promising that his support for it would only come if the Sovereignty Commission had final approval power over allocations.[29] Coleman saw the bill as a direct attack on the Sovereignty Commission, an organization created for information dispersal and publicity, arguably a competitor of the Citizens' Council but one with state funding. The agency's final approval of these funding streams, then, was an untenable change, and the amended bill died before it could be sent to committee.[30]

Voters in the state immediately flooded Coleman's office with gratitude and praise for his position on the tax bill. Those letters provide valuable insight into the Council's reputation in the state, even among its own members. Kirby Tyrone described the bill as "an unwarranted demand upon the taxpayers. Although I am," he admitted, "a member of the Citizens Council, I do not go along with everything some of the membership advocate." Ed Walker expressed sympathy for the Council's objectives but explained he decided not to renew his membership when he "realized that this organization was being used to further the political interests of individuals." One of the founding members of the Calhoun City chapter, W. W. Brown, objected to the bill because of its encroachment on local supervision: "The citizens should sponsor it . . . and finance it without getting our state government or political sub-divisions mixed up with it."[31]

Not everyone who praised Coleman's stand claimed membership in the Council, but many of them pointed to Council tactics as heavy-handed. G. W. Misch affirmed Coleman's stand as representative of "all thinking people" in the state and suggested that legislators supported the bill out of fear from "certain organized groups." Louis E. Dollarhide, a professor at Mississippi College, described legislators as "timid" and more than willing for Coleman "to take the punishment for them." The Citizens' Council was described in these constituents' letters as a collection of "extremists," "self-appointed arbiters of the race question," and "political dictators." One letter, from Ed. C. Sturdivant, commander of the Sons of Confederate Veterans Jefferson Davis Camp, was more pointed and entirely doubtful of the organization's purpose: "Actual public knowledge of [the Council's] actions consists largely of whispered great things to come, knowing nods about great things that are happening in the dark, and one reprehensible attack on a church-supported college."[32]

Despite the defeat that Coleman's veto represented, the tiered structure of Council activity ensured that the organization was always working on multiple fronts. As the ACCM's attempts to secure state funding lost support, the Jackson Council engaged in its own membership drive as a way to increase membership dues. Since the beginning of the year, the Jackson Citizens' Council had designed and administered a "freedom of choice" survey to white Jacksonians to gauge their knowledge and support of the Jackson chapter. The survey consisted of only twelve questions. The first ten focused on integration of local schools, residential integration, and the survey subjects' status as qualified, registered voters. The final two questions asked subjects about their affiliation with the Jackson Citizens' Council. Council members conducted the surveys in person, in their own neighborhoods. Each surveyor carried a pamphlet, "The Eight Ifs," to assist their neighbors in aligning support for segregation with membership in the Council. Among the "ifs" listed in the pamphlet were a commitment to fighting communism, opposition to miscegenation, and support for state sovereignty. The pamphlet and the personal interview format aimed at shaming people into joining the organization. The sixth "if" stated as much: "If you realize that *indif-*

ference, apathy, and the inclination of some to accept desegregation as 'inevitable' . . . *are our greatest enemies*. . . . Then, you should immediately join the Jackson Citizens' Council."[33]

When Louis Hollis, a survey supervisor and future executive director of the Citizens' Councils of America, appeared on *Forum* to discuss the results, his tone was optimistic. Reporting that 84 percent of survey subjects had indicated they were not members of the JCC, Hollis declared that 69 percent of them accepted on the spot, proving that "people will join once they're asked."[34] Survey results undoubtedly skewed toward support for the Council because of the intimate nature of the interviews. Outspoken opposition to the JCC threatened individuals' livelihoods and their relationships with their neighbors, and the JCC was more than willing to leverage those fears to its advantage. So was the state association. In November 1958, Robert Patterson urged individual chapters to begin membership drives, explaining, "If each local organization will bear its share of the burden of financing . . . your State Association, we will be well prepared for the struggle that lies ahead. . . . This means you and me and all of our friends and neighbors."[35]

The drive for financial support in the wake of legislative failure was not just a product of furthering the Council's reach, but necessary to fulfill the organization's growing ambitions. In May 1958 plans were underway for moving the Council's weekly radio and television broadcast, *Forum,* from Jackson to Washington, DC. The move represented an opportunity for the Council to take the local program to a wider audience by featuring national political figures and their perspectives on pressing issues. The Washington location was beneficial for its access to members of Congress, but it also represented a cost increase for the CCA. Mississippi congressman John Bell Williams offered his House Recording Studio privileges to the CCA, but travel to Washington surely extended the organization's financial responsibilities dramatically.[36]

Council leaders, in other words, had to sell the program to potential donors by justifying its value to the cause of segregation. *Forum's* host, Dick Morphew, described the location change as a more deliberate way to uncover northern sympathy for the southern position, a fact that congressional votes could not adequately represent. The influence of pressure groups, according to Morphew's assessment, misrepresented the true conscience of most congressmen. *Forum*'s platform, he hoped, would provide an opportunity for them to express their true conservative feelings and educate the American people accordingly.[37] Bill Simmons's message was similar to Morphew's. The Washington series was, he argued, intended to "reduce to concrete examples" the states' rights position, so that viewers everywhere could understand how violations of states' rights directly impacted them. National exposure promised to "broaden the base of our movement," he explained, "so that the school segregation issue is presented in perspective as one of a number of vital areas affected by the present collectivist trend."[38]

The Mississippi Council's interest in reaching a national audience aligned its objectives with Council movements in the Upper and Peripheral South, where partnerships with sympathetic moderates and whites outside of the South almost always trumped the desire for grassroots support at home. The movement in North Carolina, for example, reflected both the geographic proximity and economic dependencies the state had with northern states. The most visible Council organization in that state, the Patriots of North Carolina, was comparatively "sedate," according to Neil McMillen. It formed in September 1955 and its charter membership boasted business and political leaders. Another distinguishing component of the Patriots was that it formed in the piedmont region of the state, outside of the Black Belt, an area that had come to overshadow agricultural strongholds in North Carolina.[39] The state's diverse economy required its political leadership to avoid radical defiance in order to maintain its image with national investors, especially the federal government, upon whom it depended for a burgeoning military industry. For that reason, groups like the Patriots did little to challenge moderate leadership that sought to avoid association with more radical strands of the resistance movement. Such moderation, however, did not necessarily imply cooperation with federal mandates. By 1964, North Carolina had only desegregated a tiny fraction of its whites-only schools, with fewer than 1.5 percent of black pupils attending previously segregated institutions.[40]

In Tennessee, the Tennessee Federation for Constitutional Government, the state's only significant Council organization, reflected a similar model. In 1956, the Federation denounced violent protests accompanying the desegregation of schools in Clinton, a small town in the Cumberland Mountains. Donald Davidson, a Vanderbilt professor, former Agrarian, and the Federation's founder and president, organized the group in protest of the Supreme Court's decision in *Brown*, but with the intent of resisting through the proper legal channels. The Federation suffered in support, however, finding itself in a virtual no man's land of more radical movements in the western part of the state, and white indifference to the east, where the black population was much lower than in other parts of the state.[41]

Forum's move to Washington illustrated the brilliance of the Mississippi Council's hybrid model of grassroots activism and respectable national lobbying efforts. The transition to a national audience required some adjustments to the Council message, but for the most part the program maintained its format. In its new introduction, a narrator described *Forum* as "the American viewpoint with a southern accent." A recording of "Dixie" followed, and the narrator continued: "The Citizens' Councils are dedicated to states' rights and racial integrity, to individual liberty and to race relations based on common sense, not on the power politics of left-wing pressure groups. The Citizens' Councils are primarily a means of mobilizing public opinion. Informed people will not surrender their freedom."[42]

From May until August, Morphew and Simmons guided *Forum* through a trial period in Washington to understand the total costs involved in producing the series and to gauge interest among congressmen to participate. The Jackson Citizens' Council covered expenses related to this trial period and, in a letter to Senator James Eastland, Simmons estimated an annual cost of $50,000 to produce the program. Fund-raisers in the Jackson business community were underway, he explained, "where we are naturally in a better position to get results than in places where we are not so well established." Simmons estimated *Forum*'s current audience as "10 million or more regularly," with the program airing on eighty television and radio stations across the South.[43]

In coming years, Simmons's claims proved to be severely inflated, but *Forum* was quickly becoming the Citizens' Council's main priority. The move to Washington ushered in a more sophisticated public relations campaign that distanced the Citizens' Council from its birthplace.

As early as 1959, the CCA was in pursuit of outside donors to subsidize its broadcasts. Bill Simmons prepared a press packet explaining the program's focus to interested stations or civic groups. Describing the program as "completely non-partisan and non-sectional," he identified *Forum* as a conservative public affairs program meant to challenge "the one-sided stream of propaganda leveled at the South by most national news media."[44]

The accompanying costs of maintaining *Forum*, however, were daunting. Expenses grew dramatically once *Forum* moved to Washington. During a ten-month period, total costs for the program topped $20,000. Over $8,000 of that total went toward salaries and over $4,000 covered travel costs. How the Council met those expenses is unclear. The report references over $8,000 taken as an advance from the Jackson Citizens' Council, a fact that Simmons referenced in his letter to Eastland. Over $18,000, however, came from what Simmons labeled as "advance contributions" to the program. Some of these donations must have come from individual pledges of support in fund-raising events for the Council, but there is evidence to suggest that money came from other sources as well. In a letter to Eastland on March 13, 1959, Simmons referenced an upcoming meeting with "Mr. Weyher" about *Forum*. Harry F. Weyher, president of the Pioneer Fund from 1958 to 2002, is likely the "Mr. Weyher" whom Simmons referenced. The Pioneer Fund was an organization founded in 1937 to pursue race-related genetic research in support of eugenics. Weyher's interest in *Forum* was not surprising. In 1959, the Council was still heavily engaging in racist vitriol through its literature and *Forum* guests. The enclosures that accompanied the letter to Eastland (financial reports, a form letter to interested broadcasters, and a list of stations that carried *Forum*) indicated that Weyher and the Pioneer Fund had an interest in providing financial support to the program. It is not clear that the $18,000 in donations that Simmons cited was in any way a product of an actual donation from the Fund, but Weyher's interest in Mississippi's civil rights struggle would become clearer as the civil rights movement gained traction.[45]

With a few exceptions, most *Forum* broadcasts in 1958 and 1959 featured southern guests. Though it maintained a distinct southern accent, over the course of nine years (1957–1966) *Forum* guests included Republicans and Democrats, politicians and religious leaders, military officers, and international figures, each of them with their own platforms in need of free publicity. *Forum* provided its guests with air time to articulate their agendas in a noncombative environment. Individual programs followed a scripted question-and-answer format, usually provided to the guest prior to the filming. It was also a way for elected officials to communicate with their constituents on issues that impacted them at home. At its foundation, however, *Forum* broadcasts sought to do what the Council movement had always done: to secure white unity in opposition to integration. Through *Forum*, Council administrators hoped to inspire white southerners to see themselves as part of a network of like-minded people across the country so that they would resolve to remain firm in their hometowns.

But tensions in its home state kept the Council on the defensive, especially toward the Coleman administration. In April 1959, a crowd surrounded the city jail at Poplarville, in the southern part of the state, abducted Mack Charles Parker, and lynched him. Charged with raping a white woman, Parker was awaiting trial at the time of his murder. The case against Parker was never conclusive, but given the evidence at the time and considering the history of Mississippi justice, his conviction was almost assured. The lynching sent shockwaves through the state within both the black and white communities and put Mississippi under the same national press scrutiny that followed the murder of Emmett Till. Governor Coleman immediately instructed Sheriff Osborne Moody to turn over all evidence to the Federal Bureau of Investigation (FBI) as a way to bring some stability to the environment and prevent further violence. His decision to do this outraged the Citizens' Council, whose entire defense of segregation rested upon the tenets of state sovereignty. To call in federal agents to investigate Mississippians' involvement with the murder of an accused black rapist was the ultimate betrayal.[46]

A month after Parker's lynching, the ACCM crafted its own response to the intense criticism directed at Mississippi. It circulated a letter to US senators detailing FBI rape statistics. Estimating fifty-seven rapes per day nationwide, the letter pointed out that Mississippi and other southern states were holding their rape numbers to "3 or 4 rape cases per year. . . . In other words," the letter asserted, "a woman is 76 times safer in Mississippi than she is in the average state in this nation, with regard to the crime of rape." To make the point more obvious, the letter also reminded its readers that 40 percent of the men arrested were black. "Since the protection of its womankind has always been a Caucasian tradition," the letter concluded, "these facts would certainly be of interest to every white American."[47] It is not clear exactly what this letter's intent was, but its timing suggests that the state association was aware of the impact that such bad press in the nation's capital could have on its infant broadcast. A lynching in 1959 could only confirm what most people in the country already believed about Mississippi and discourage potential congressional guests from accepting a *Forum* invitation.

Coleman's immediate call for an FBI investigation also worried Council leaders who carried a persistent fear of white moderation. The EFCC's campaigns in public high schools and among women, coupled with its reliance on the myth of the black rapist in 1959, suggested that Council leaders still considered sustained white support at home their top priority. Within the black community and among many whites, the Council's leadership seemed unchallenged even if the organization was not beloved. But ACCM correspondence indicated something different. Robert Patterson sent a letter to Council chapters in March 1959 that only barely concealed his frustrations with Council activity in the state. Citing monthly NAACP meetings as the standard the Council should emulate, Patterson posed the question, "Is it asking too much that each local Citizens' Council hold a meeting of it's [sic] Board of Directors at least once a month to discuss the many problems we face?"[48] Several months later, another letter went out, decrying the "complacency and apathy" that prevailed among whites in Mississippi. "Your State Association needs money and it needs it now," the letter concluded.[49]

Council influence in the state entered a critical year in 1959. Even as the ACCM oversaw more national efforts to market the defense of segregation, the battle at home was fierce. Coleman's administration was coming to an end and the state was in the midst of a gubernatorial election, signifying a new opportunity for the Council to embed its initiatives in the state's funding agenda. Unified white support of its mission was critical, and the "wait and see" attitude the organization perceived as the guiding principle of the Coleman administration was not considered adequate to the task.

Mississippi law prohibited an incumbent from being reelected to a consecutive term, so Coleman could not run again. The race pitted incumbent lieutenant governor Carroll Gartin against Ross Barnett, a Jackson-area attorney who specialized in civil suits against corporations. Gartin's reputation as an avowed segregationist was uncontested. He was a member of the Jackson Council, and he had appeared on an early broadcast of *Forum* before it moved to Washington. His advocacy for legislation to outlaw the NAACP in Mississippi had endeared him to Council leaders in previous years, but Gartin carried some liability. His involvement as lieutenant governor with the creation and oversight of the Sovereignty Commission worried Council leaders who had come to see the state agency as more of an obstacle than a handmaiden.[50]

Ross Barnett made his third attempt at the state's highest office in 1959, having lost elections in 1951 and 1955. Like Gartin, Barnett had been an early supporter of the Jackson Citizens' Council and participated as a surveyor in the 1959 "Freedom of Choice" survey. Many of his campaign stops included Citizens' Council meetings, and his 1957 involvement in the integration controversy in Clinton, Tennessee, underscored his loyalty to obstruction. His commitment to segregation in public schools mirrored Gartin's platform, but when the AFL-CIO endorsed Gartin's candidacy, rumors of CIO demands in exchange for its endorsement spread throughout the state, weakening Gartin's support enough to tip the election in Barnett's favor by less than 40,000 votes. His first official appearance as governor-elect was at a Citizens' Council fund-raising event for *Forum,* and in the weeks following his inauguration, Barnett devoted a significant portion of his schedule to meetings and fund-raisers for the Citizens' Council movement, including a visit to South Carolina to drum up support for Councils in that state.[51]

Barnett's election signified the Council's official entry into state government. Though the organization experienced a certain amount of deference in the halls of the state legislature prior to Barnett's administration, Governor Coleman's public disapproval of Council tactics prevented the organization's leadership from fully crossing the threshold into administrative influence. Shortly after Barnett's inauguration, the 1960 legislative session commenced, and the agenda filled with new anti-integration bills, a testament to the renewed hope that Barnett's administration brought to the segregationist cause in Mississippi. At session's end, twenty-one of those bills were new laws, many of which created a structure that would severely handicap the ability of civil rights activists to organize public demonstrations in the state. In addition to the guards against protesters, the legislature approved a measure that endowed the state's Institutions of Higher Learning (IHL) with the power to deny admission to any applicant to a state-funded college or university. The legislature also passed a bill that made it a felony to engage in a sexual relationship with a person from another race. The greatest legislative boon for the Citizens' Council, however, was the doubling of the Sovereignty Commission's budget, $100,000 of which had no specific allocation.[52]

Within a month of the legislative budget increase, members of the board approved an immediate dispersal of $20,000 to alleviate costs already accrued in the production of *Forum*. Additionally, $5,000 per month would go to the Council in support of the broadcast.[53] Oliver Emmerich, editor of the *State Times* in Jackson, described the allocation as "a grievous error." The Council's desperate need for financial assistance, he explained, proved that the organization suffered from waning public support, a fact that underscored the absurdity of diverting tax money to keep it afloat. Additionally, the Council's acceptance of state funding put a burden on the organization to justify its activities, a requirement that could place it under severe scrutiny.[54]

In addition to funneling Sovereignty Commission money to the Citizens' Council, Barnett expanded the agency's functions in a number of ways. He added three full-time investigators to the Commission's payroll and hired Erle Johnston, his former campaign spokesman, as the new public relations director. The Speakers' Bureau, under Johnston's guidance, created press packets, wrote speeches, and scheduled speaking tours outside of the South to win sympathy for the segregationist cause.[55]

It is not entirely clear whether the reinvigoration of the Sovereignty Commission's publicity efforts enhanced or undermined Council activities, but the campaigns remained separate from each other. Early efforts to mend the historical enmity between the state agency and the Council were mutually beneficial to both parties, but no sustained cooperation existed between the two. In later years, Erle Johnston, who served as director of the agency from 1963 to 1968, made this point clear, stating, "They were jealous of us and we were jealous of them."[56] At the very least, Barnett's commitment to increased surveillance freed the Council to focus more on its national campaign.

Securing state funding and an upcoming presidential election seemed to make a difference in *Forum*'s programming. Throughout 1960, Dick Morphew hosted an unprecedented variety of guests on the show. Out of thirty-three guests (some appeared more than once), all but three were members of Congress. Nineteen were from southern states, twenty were Democrats, ten were Republicans, and twelve represented states outside of the South. Out of forty-five episodes, fewer than half dealt with the civil rights movement (including pending legislation) or race. Topics ranged from FCC regulatory policies to loyalty oaths on college campuses and included discussions of military funding and foreign policy concerns.[57]

The cross-section of guests and topics on *Forum* was the foundation of the Council's national media blitz. Through weekly broadcasts with public figures in the nation's capital, the program became a legitimate public affairs program. Through the widening of its lens, the Council gradually attached the civil rights issue to almost every other pressing concern on the public agenda. A discussion about FCC regulations, for example, could easily turn into a conversation about the oppressive power of the federal government. Foreign policy discussions often led to statements about distractions at home and their impact on global security. When Congressman Edward J. Derwinski, a Republican from Illinois who would later serve as secretary for the Department of Veterans Affairs, appeared on the show in February, he identified the American tax burden as the top concern for his constituents. "I think that, basically speaking," he explained, "we need a decentralization of government and especially in those matters where local interests . . . could much more effectively administer a program than the far-off bureaucracy." Host Dick Morphew replied, "This sounds like a concept that we in the South have known for many years as 'states' rights.'"[58]

All *Forum* guests, regardless of region or party affiliation, represented a conservative perspective, so it was not difficult for Morphew to make obvious connections between the South's defense of segregation and the philosophical underpinnings of conservative ideology. Segregation did not have to be mentioned for listeners and viewers to recognize the language of state sovereignty and local control that accompanied the Council movement. Even on programs where guests dealt directly with civil rights activism or legislation, discussions remained safely confined within the boundaries of political ideology, with race as an incidental factor. Programs that featured discussions of pending civil rights legislation often examined the impact it would have on the party system or on private business. Robert T. Ashmore, a congressman from South Carolina, insisted that no southern congressmen he knew opposed equal access to the vote, but he saw a voting rights bill as an entry into the extension of federal power.[59]

Ashmore's colleague in the House of Representatives, F. Edward Hébert, Democrat from Louisiana, made similar predictions about the potential reach of civil rights legislation. He saw similarities between the media's focus on the South as the only obstacle to voting equality and the way in which journalists derisively labeled States' Rights party supporters "Dixiecrats," suggesting that the movement was regional. "I think the presentation being made in the few papers I've seen outside the Solid South . . . have missed the point entirely," Ashmore agreed, lamenting, "They talk about civil rights and voting privileges which are really not the issue."[60]

Forum broadcasts in 1960 were not completely void of more traditional race-baiting discussions, however, even if they were the exception. That year, two guests suggested the kind of connections the Council's work attracted within the larger network of white supremacy. Over the course of four programs, Morphew interviewed a religious leader from the Dutch Reformed Church of South Africa, Rev. D. F. B. DeBeer. DeBeer's description of South Africa's struggle to maintain its system of apartheid amidst global disapproval was a more direct discussion of race than normally appeared on the program. Asked to explain the system of segregation as it applied to South Africa, DeBeer defended his country's apartheid regime, describing it as "the differential development of each indigenous race . . . to its fullest extent and for the service of its own people and according to the innate characteristics of each race."[61] DeBeer's visit to *Forum* happened a few months after the Sharpeville Massacre, an event in which sixty-nine black protesters died at the hands of South African police. He described the situation as one in which police feared for their lives and acted in self-defense. Negative reaction to the murders in the global community, DeBeer argued, was a betrayal of the good relationship South Africa thought it had with the United Nations and with Western governments, including the United States.[62]

The Council's interest in South Africa was not a new development. Shortly after the organization began its work, Bill Simmons and S. E. D. Brown, the editor of the *South African Observer,* began exchanging correspondence. Specifically, they shared information with each other about the respective racial climate in each of their nations. A lot of that information ended up in both *The Citizen* and the *South African Observer,* in a trade intended to draw the two nation's experiences closer together. Brown reassured Simmons that an upcoming issue of the South African paper would contain "quite a lot" about the southern school situation, or what Brown called "integration . . . at bayonet point." But the two organizations also exchanged information about organizations and individuals they perceived as threats to white supremacy. This was the case in a letter Brown wrote in 1956 in which he provided Simmons with a list of "all the extreme liberals" under watch in South Africa for their suspected communism. He hoped Simmons could provide more information about the Americans on the list. In fact, shortly after the letter was received, Simmons wrote Mississippi congressman John Bell Williams, asking him to put the list through the House Un-American Activities Committee. When the chairman of that committee, Francis E. Walter, responded to the request, he claimed a "backlog of requests" and asked that an immediate response not be expected. Simmons replied: "If it could be expedited in any way, I would certainly appreciate your doing so. This information can be put to very effective use in South Africa, and we can use it here to show the international nature of the attack on segregation." The South African partnership would resurface in later years, but the *Forum* appearance from DeBeer, and the exchanges between Simmons and Brown, add another dimension to the Council's hopes for national sympathies. In truth, the Council's intent extended well beyond that to a minority white regime halfway around the world under global scrutiny for its own violent offenses against blacks.[63]

The second guest to appear on *Forum* in 1960 who dealt specifically with the issue of race was Carleton Putnam, author of *Race and Reason,* a defense of segregation that loosely relied upon history and anthropology as evidence of a natural racial hierarchy. Putnam first gained attention in a letter he wrote to President Eisenhower protesting the integration of Central High School in Little Rock, Arkansas, in 1957. The letter circulated among segregationist leaders soon after, and Putnam became a close ally of the Council movement. During *Forum's* tenure, Putnam appeared on ten different programs. His first appearance predated the publication of *Race and Reason,* providing free publicity for its upcoming release. The book would later appear on the Council's recommended reading list that appeared in *The Citizen* and in letter campaigns from the ACCM. During his visit, Putnam's remarks ran counter to the strategy other guests created through their discussion of issues that were not directly tied to race or the civil rights movement. Putnam disagreed with the use of constitutional arguments to defend segregation. The South, he insisted, must be vigilant about articulating the fundamental differences between the races or face a destruction of civilized society.[64]

Putnam's remarks were not at all contradictory to the Council's ideology, but they seemed to run counter to the tone that *Forum's* move to Washington sought to strike, underscoring the conflicts of interest that the program presented for the organization's campaign at home. *Forum's* location in the nation's capital held potential for connecting the defense of segregation with national issues, but at its heart, the organization believed fiercely in white supremacy and found a natural affinity for radical right groups and individuals who also found themselves marginalized from mainstream political circles. M. G. Lowman of the anticommunist group Circuit Riders, and Edward Hunter, a psychological warfare expert and author of a book on brainwashing, used *Forum* as a platform for their causes and played on the paranoia that some white southerners felt about communist conspiracies at work in the civil rights movement. And while political figures were the most frequent guests on the show, figures like DeBeer, Putnam, Lowman, and Hunter were not infrequent. Their appearances suggest that the Council's commitment to race-blind tactics was never deep enough to withstand the wave of civil rights challenges yet to come. White supremacy remained its central tenet, and the organization easily connected with causes that embraced similar principles.

One of those causes was *The Citizens' Voice,* a Michigan publication that represented the views of the National Civic Association, a body committed to opposing equal housing regulation in Detroit. In August 1960, Joseph Fisher, a resident of Pascagoula, Mississippi, sent a letter to the director of the Sovereignty Commission, Albert Jones, requesting money from both the state agency and the Citizens' Council to support the organization. Despite his request, however, Fisher cautioned against making support from Mississippi too public, warning that the time was not right to add a "southern flavor" to the campaign in Detroit. Covert financial support was, for Fisher, a much more practical approach.[65] Jones denied Fisher's request but recommended the Citizens' Council as a more likely benefactor. No evidence indicates that the Council complied, but Fisher's request is representative of the Council's identity as an organization that was sympathetic to a variety of conservative and radical causes, and it assists in understanding how *Forum* attracted some of its guests.

What most *Forum* broadcasts held in common, regardless of guest or topic, was the total avoidance of discussions about the civil rights campaign and its participants. Guests remained utterly silent about emerging leaders in the movement and never mentioned its objectives. Instead, guests often concealed the civil rights movement behind discussions of pending legislation, constitutional principles, competing political ideologies, or global conspiracies. Whatever else may have separated guests in their commitment to white supremacy, their shared whiteness and refusal to recognize black activism reiterated the Council's founding principle of white unity. The civil rights movement, under this reasoning, was little more than a front for other issues that promised deeper consequences.

At home, the Citizens' Council, despite the pockets of criticism it experienced, had achieved a façade of white unity by 1959. But that unity was always tenuous and dependent upon administrative favor and white moderates whose presence in the state was bigger than their relative silence portended. This was a phenomenon that Hodding Carter lamented in *The South Strikes Back,* a book that reflected on the Citizens' Council movement and the prospects of change in the state's race relations. De-

scribing the Council as the "cement" that held varying levels of white reaction together, Carter pointed out that despite signs of biracial cooperation prior to the *Brown* decision, the Council's ascendancy marked "the
decline of the Southern liberal (or moderate, as the term evolved). . . .
The moderate," he explained, "became first an isolated figure, then more
and more the subject of comprehensive efforts to silence him." The
forced silence reflected, in Carter's mind, an absence of "respect or tolerance for neighbors who did not believe wholeheartedly in its efforts."
Pretentions of conservatism would soon give way to the inevitable violence that a core constituency of Council membership craved. "The fact
still remains that the majority of the Council's members belong to it not
because of its 'respectability,' or its conservative credo" he insisted, "but
because it serves as an organized channel for their desire and intention
to maintain segregation and to freeze the Negro in his present status in
Mississippi."[66]

The Council's visible influence under Governor Ross Barnett's administration strained the coalitions that had made the organization's early
years so successful. Somewhat ironically, the achievement of state influence enabled the organization to begin cultivating higher ambitions
that would connect the segregationist defense to national networks.
Like many of the Council's other relationships, however, that transition
was somewhat uneasy. While *Forum* succeeded in attracting national political figures as its guests, the occasional iterations of white supremacy
and radical politics that some of its guests espoused prevented the organization from fully transitioning out of the ideology it had embraced
since 1954. With one foot in state politics and another in national political circles, the Council's focus seemed divided when the civil rights
movement in Mississippi caught its second wind in 1960.

The ascendance of the Barnett administration, its expansion of the
investigative functions of the Sovereignty Commission, and the financial support extended to the Council created a stifling atmosphere for
blacks in the state, but it also strengthened the resolve of leaders like
Medgar Evers to destroy it. Evers had borne witness to the tensions between the Council and the Sovereignty Commission under Coleman's
administration. An attempt to arrest Evers and NAACP executive director Roy Wilkins in 1959 ended when members of the Sovereignty Com-

mission intervened to stop it. The Jackson Citizens' Council initiated the arrest, and members of the organization were furious when Coleman's fear of negative press coverage prevented its completion. The incident exposed chinks in the armor of white resistance in Jackson and emboldened Evers to take advantage of that fact. As sit-in protests spread across other parts of the segregated South in 1960, Evers saw an opportunity to activate a similar movement in Jackson.[67]

Besides some early activity in the months following *Brown,* the state conference of NAACP chapters in Mississippi had not operated under a unified strategy for a number of years. Factions were split between older, more experienced leaders who favored legal challenges and younger, more militant members who saw the wave of demonstrations in other states as a clarion call for action in Mississippi. Medgar Evers was part of the latter faction, but as a representative of the organization in Mississippi he was obligated to wait for approval from national leaders. Despite his attempts at organized action, NAACP headquarters saw to it that his work remained mostly investigative, intended to provide substance for lawsuits. A change in leadership in 1960, however, represented a shift in that strategy. C. R. Darden stepped down as state president. His replacement, Aaron Henry, supported Evers's plea for direct action.[68]

On March 28, 1960, Evers attended a meeting at Campbell College in Jackson to discuss the potential for a boycott of Capitol Street, Jackson's main shopping district. With support from black leaders and a collection of black college students from Tougaloo, Jackson State College, and Campbell, the boycott was set to begin on April 10. Students distributed flyers encouraging blacks not to shop on Capitol Street until business owners changed their policies on segregation. Evers held a press conference announcing the campaign, during which he made assurances that the boycott would not result in demonstrations, especially considering new legislation passed to prevent such actions. Overall, the campaign was a success and served as the first organized civil rights protest in Jackson. It was so successful, in fact, that the Sovereignty Commission had its hands full gathering names of activists in the area who participated in the boycott's organization and the distribution of flyers. In his report to Ruby Hurley on the results of the boycott, Evers noted the reaction of local media, stating, "The radio, television and newspapers have been told to play down the movement and consequently we have not been getting the accurate and unbiased coverage normally given." Despite this "silent treatment," he wrote, reporters for United Press International (UPI) conducted a store-to-store survey to gauge the boycott's impact, finding that in some cases, businesses reported more than a 75 percent drop in their sales.[69]

Jackson was not the only city in Mississippi where activism began to appear. In April, under the leadership of Dr. Gilbert Mason, activists participated in a wade-in of a whites-only beach in Biloxi on the Mississippi Gulf Coast. Shortly after their arrival, black swimmers found themselves trapped in the water, facing an angry group of whites armed with bats, chains, sticks, and bricks. The standoff lasted well into the evening and resulted in multiple injuries for the black participants.[70]

The Council's failure to prevent organic black protest and white violence countermanded its entire raison d'être and threatened to undermine its legitimacy among white moderates. But the challenges in Jackson and Biloxi also underscored the need to maintain strict surveillance over black organizations and white equivocation. If anything, evidence of civil rights activity in Mississippi only further emboldened Council leaders to demonstrate zero tolerance for dissent.

In August 1960, the Council began an investigation into the activities of the managing editor of the campus newspaper at the University of Mississippi, Billy Barton. Barton had recently returned from a summer internship with the *Atlanta Journal* under the supervision of Ralph McGill, a well-known moderate within southern journalistic circles. While in Atlanta, Barton had come to the attention of one of the Council's sister organizations, the States' Rights Council in Georgia, for covering a sit-in demonstration in Atlanta in a way that reflected McGill's mentorship. Once informed, Bill Simmons alerted the Sovereignty Commission, explaining his alarm at the lengths to which "pro-integration groups" would go to infiltrate college campuses in Mississippi.[71] Letters to Barton's peers at *The Mississippian*, the campus newspaper, quickly followed, inquiring about Barton's associations and political leanings. Barton's editor balked at the inquiry, requesting more information from the Sovereignty Commission regarding its interest.[72] As the fall semester proceeded, rumors of Barton's association with the NAACP began to travel from Governor Barnett's office in Jackson to the chancellor at Ole Miss. Student informants became involved, and Barton's bid to become editor of the campus newspaper failed in the spring of 1961.[73]

Barton later claimed that the Council's attention to his candidacy resulted in a loss of the position and he sued for libel and slander. Included in his suit were the names of every individual and organization involved in his investigation—Governor Barnett and his secretary, Bill Simmons, Sara McCorkle, Albert Jones (director of the Sovereignty Commission), W. A. Luburrow (the informant from the States' Rights Council of Georgia), the Citizens' Council, and the Association of Citizens' Councils of Mississippi. The case was dismissed for failure to meet the standard expectation of evidence, but Barton's complaint was pointed in its criticism of the unethical combinations of power that conspired against him. It detailed the purpose behind the Council's organization and its extensive influence in a state where "open defiance and resistance [to federal law] is encouraged." In that atmosphere, the complaint continued, the rumors surrounding Barton about his involvement with the NAACP and civil rights activities were enough to make the accused "a leper and pariah in the eyes of his friends, neighbors and fellow Mississippians." Given its influence and its knowledge of the impact of the smear campaign against Barton, the Council should have been, in Barton's estimation, liable for damages.[74]

Barton's challenge was unusual in its directness, but it measured the widening network of Council surveillance and influence. Using informants in Georgia to activate a Sovereignty Commission investigation against a college student, the results of which were of interest to the governor, was an accurate example of the kind of police state the organization managed to create within six years of its founding. The Council was relentless in its pursuit of white unity, no matter how superficial. Its success in extracting a pro-segregation statement from Millsaps College in 1958, despite the institution's attempts to deflect compliance with Council demands, was only the first of a series of public pressure tactics against noncompliant whites. Barnett's election in 1959 seemed like tacit approval of its methods, and within months the Council was drawing money from state funds in furtherance of its national publicity campaign.

By 1960, evidence of Council success was in abundance. The organization served as a guiding hand for the governor, and it had secured a line of funding to expand its activities beyond Mississippi. Civil rights activity in the state was becoming more visible, but that fact only seemed to confirm the continued necessity of Council leadership. In general, while the details of local chapter activities may never fully surface, the state organization directed nearly all of its energies to maintaining white unity by silencing white moderates in the state. As Council leaders strategized about the future of their movement, they hoped for allies outside of Mississippi who would join them in speaking honestly about white supremacy as a natural fact, using their successes at home as a model for grassroots white activism. The first years of Council organization, however, were not predictive of the years to come, and the organization's early tactics could not survive the wave of black activism that was sweeping through the South. The Council's commitment to maintaining an atmosphere of fear as a way to cultivate white compliance created a tinderbox of white anxiety and underestimated the likelihood that the civil rights movement would make its way into Mississippi.

Meanwhile, Council movements in other southern states were reaching their peak, undermining the regional unity that earlier Council objectives had embraced. While the movements in Alabama and South Carolina would not officially see dramatic drop-offs until 1963 when the second desegregation of the University of Alabama and the desegregation of Clemson College commenced, the Louisiana movement saw shrinking membership as early as 1957. The Georgia and Florida movements never had a vibrant grassroots following, and, in Virginia, resistance more often emanated from the state's capital under the direction of public officials.[75] The Mississippi movement's investment in national coalition-building, then, over that of white unity within its own state or regional cooperation with sister organizations, made practical sense. It speaks directly to how the Mississippi Council managed to maintain relevance in the midst of the tumult still to come.

CHAPTER 4

THE CENTER WEAKENS, 1961–1962

The key point in evaluating Southern attitudes during Reconstruction is that the South did not overthrow the radicals until it was forced to do so by the sheer necessity for self-preservation. Southern opinion was by no means united until the later years of Reconstruction. There were moderates and compromisers. There were those who said it was, "bad for business" to resist Reconstruction. Some were apathetic or too busy to be bothered. Others were afraid of reprisals—in the form of federal bayonets. There are those who fear reprisals today—in the withholding of federal handouts.

—WILLIAM J. SIMMONS

One of the Citizens' Council's most reliable and widely read critics, Hodding Carter of the *Delta-Democrat Times,* remained nonplussed by the breadth of the organization's influence and how public it was, given its tactics of intimidation. In a November 1961 piece for the *New York Times Magazine,* Carter referred to Council administrator Bill Simmons as Governor Barnett's "constant companion," and he described Council literature as so widely distributed that patrons of restaurants could find it next to the toothpicks at the cashier counter. Increasingly, the targets of Council backlash were moderate whites like Carter, but as widely known as that fact was, the Council and its leaders maintained a nearly unanimous following among whites in the state who feared integration more than Council tyranny. Carter's certainty that fears of integration outweighed questions about Council leadership suggested that if civil rights activities increased in the state, support for the organization would strengthen.[1]

Carter was not wrong about the relationship between Council support and civil rights activity. The Council thrived when it was embattled, and its opponents were diverse. By 1960, with black challenges in the state nearly nonexistent, the Council's most pressing concern was maintaining a monopoly on white leadership in the state and successfully expanding its public relations campaigns into a national arena through *Forum* and related activities. But the growing strength of the southern civil rights campaign and its impact on Mississippi activists would soon interrupt those ambitions enough to put the Council under a microscope for its rapidly increasing budget and its instigation of federal defiance and violence at one of its most beloved institutions. The visibility achieved from the Council's successes and its constant demands for more money and more influence collided with some of the state's most troubling moments in the civil rights years. The intersection of Council tyranny and organic black protest from 1960 to 1963 gradually alienated the organization from suspicious white moderates who had only acceded to Council leadership as long as the stakes were comparatively low. As Mississippi became more of an outlier, even among its Deep South sister states, the Council's power in Mississippi changed from a security measure to a liability.

Council confidence was high in 1961, so high, in fact, that the Jackson Citizens' Council decided to commemorate May 17, the anniversary of *Brown*, as a date worth celebrating. In its "Seven Successful Years of Segregation" event, the Jackson Council featured Lieutenant Governor Paul Johnson Jr. as its keynote speaker. Newly elected ACCM president John Wright (son of former president Ellis Wright) credited the unity and determination of white Mississippians and the leadership of the Council with "peaceful race relations in a segregated society."[2] And indeed, the Council had much to celebrate. There were breaks in the dam of white resistance in the state, but overall the civil rights movement remained in its infant stages in Mississippi, even as it flourished in other southern states. In his address to event goers, Lieutenant Governor Johnson expressed the traditional assurances that black Mississippians were "thoroughly happy in the condition that they find themselves." Bill Simmons also spoke to the group, boasting of "the legend of invincibility" Mississippi had built up among civil rights activists and the presidential administration. "If and when the showdown comes in our city and state," he promised, "then the integrationists will learn what trouble really is."[3]

Simmons's remarks were not casual in their prediction about "if and when." The national NAACP had been reluctant to divert money and staff to Mississippi when campaigns in other states seemed much more promising. But its assessment of Mississippi as impregnable was changing. The Capitol Street boycotts and the wade-in in 1960 brought enough attention to Mississippi to force NAACP headquarters to reconsider the state as a target for an organized campaign. A fund-raising campaign began in February, and on April 7, 1961, "Operation Mississippi" was born in a meeting among local NAACP leaders in the state and the national office. The campaign included four initiatives: voter registration, desegregation of public facilities, equal employment, and attention to police brutality. In preparation, Mississippi NAACP field secretary Medgar Evers secured bail bondsmen and local attorneys who were committed to dealing with the aftermath of arrests.[4]

Before the official announcement for the campaign appeared, Jackson youth had already begun to challenge segregation in public facilities. Students at Jackson State College and Tougaloo College had long anticipated a direct action campaign in the capital city, but NAACP leadership never conceded because of the obvious obstacles to success that the city presented. A new state president (Aaron Henry) and the announcement of funding support were promising signs that the time had come to initiate Jackson's campaign. The first demonstration involved nine Tougaloo College students who, on March 28, 1961, staged a "read in" at the Jackson Municipal Library, a whites-only facility. Within minutes, Jackson police arrived and arrested all nine. Attempts to bail them out failed when the Hinds County sheriff could not be reached. Jackson State students staged a mass demonstration on campus in solidarity with their peers, turning out nearly eight hundred students in support. When Jackson State's president threatened participants with expulsion, students responded by refusing to attend classes the next day, and a group began a march to the city jail that ended with police dogs and tear gas.[5]

The court hearing the next day, however, suggested how tense the city had become. When the nine students arrived, a group of black supporters lining the sidewalk across the street erupted into applause, triggering a violent reaction from police officers armed with clubs and attack dogs. As news spread of the sit-in and the subsequent acts of support from the black community in Jackson, activism in the state exploded. Students staged similar demonstrations at the Jackson zoo, parks, and pools. In other areas of the state, boycotts and the desegregation of transportation facilities were the targets.[6]

The library sit-in and the events that followed, however, were not the only challenges to white authority in the capital city. The Freedom Rides, a campaign meant to test a recent Supreme Court decision declaring segregation in public transportation facilities unconstitutional, were gaining more press attention as they made their way from Washington, DC, to New Orleans. As Riders disembarked at various terminals in the Upper South, white backlash was almost nonexistent. But as the buses made their way through Alabama, the situation changed. During a stop in Anniston, a group of whites bombed one of the buses and beat riders as they tried to leave. A similar situation occurred in Birmingham. The Congress of Racial Equality (CORE), the civil rights group that organized the Freedom Rides, felt compelled to halt the bus campaign in light of these incidents, but the Student Non-Violent Coordinating Committee (SNCC) intervened, agreeing to contribute new Riders in order to complete the trip.[7]

The escalating violence as Riders moved further into the Deep South is a testament to the variations of resistance that existed in different parts of the South. Historian George Lewis cautions historians to project their understanding of these differences toward reaction, not sentiment. At each stop, the Freedom Riders challenged dominant white ideology against desegregation. But the violent reaction in Alabama forces a recognition that different constituencies triggered different responses. In Alabama, Birmingham's public safety commissioner drew robust support from Council and Klan members. His constituents championed his violent response.[8]

Events in Alabama did not bode well for the Riders' safety as they neared Mississippi, a state that civil rights leaders considered the most dangerous place for activism because of the solid resistance strategies the Council led. A series of frantic phone calls between the Kennedy administration and a slew of Mississippi officials took place in hopes of avoiding more violence. The compromise reached between Barnett (backed by the Citizens' Council) and Attorney General Robert Kennedy allowed Jackson police to arrest the Riders as soon as they got off the bus in exchange for Barnett's commitment to ensure the Riders' safety. Barnett kept his word, and when two buses arrived on May 24, Jackson police officers promptly arrested the passengers and escorted them to the city jail, where they awaited trial. Once found guilty and fined for breach of peace, the Riders refused to pay the bond and waited for the arrival of more Riders. Through the second week of June, waves of Freedom Riders continued to arrive in Jackson almost daily. With city and county jails beyond capacity, the Hinds County Board of Supervisors authorized the sheriff's office to transfer as many jailed Riders as was necessary to Parchman, the state penitentiary, a place infamous for its brutality.[9]

The Freedom Riders' arrival demanded a Council response. New arrivals of activists over the course of several weeks and the strains that arrests put on local facilities threatened to undermine the belief that the Council's presence was critical to keep civil rights campaigns out of the state. And while the public reactions of Jackson's black community were relatively muted, white officials were shaken.[10] On July 12, 1961, *Forum* released a statement announcing a series of programs dedicated to discussions about the Freedom Rides. Guests included state attorney general Joe Patterson and Mississippi Highway Patrol public relations director Grady Gilmore. The statement estimated that over four hundred stations from forty-two states would broadcast the programs. As soon as the programs became available, host Dick Morphew stated in the press release, Council offices had been "flooded with requests."[11]

In total, *Forum* dedicated four programs to the Freedom Rides. In addition to Gilmore and Patterson, Congressman John Bell Williams and Fred Jones, an early leader in the Council and the superintendent of Parchman, the state penitentiary, visited the program. Each guest expressed his certainty that the demonstration was not what it appeared. They warned that some of the Riders had received extensive training from communists in Cuba in preparation for the invasion. Attorney General Joe Patterson explained that among black Mississippians, the Riders had received a very poor reception. Referring to them as "agitatin' Riders," he took pride in the fact that "not a one of them has been a Mississippi nigra. They have all been outsiders and these wild-eyed radical whites that have come along with them."[12]

Grady Gilmore praised the foundational work already done to prepare Mississippians for the invasion. White reaction, he argued, was
admirable, thanks to local media and the Citizens' Council. During his
visit, Gilmore revealed the name of one of the participants, Katherine
Pleune, taking the extra step to spell her name for *Forum*'s listeners and
inform them that Ms. Pleune was white. Gilmore described her family
background, work history, and atheism. Asked why investigations into
CORE's communist affiliations had not been under way before the Freedom Rides, Gilmore lamented that "you just might as well talk to a brick
wall" as convince Mississippians that communists were in their state.
Recent events, he agreed, would go a long way to ensure greater vigilance, but he warned Morphew, "It's going to take a lot of hard work on
the part of people everywhere. Good, patriotic American citizens supporting all sound organizations that are fighting communism. If we are
going to turn the tide," he concluded, "all good people are going to have
to join in on the fight."[13]

Gilmore's and Patterson's reflections read like a Council membership
drive. Without total commitment from faithful white citizens, they implied, the Freedom Riders' entry into Mississippi could have developed
much differently. Neither made mention of the multiple phone calls between Washington and Jackson that preceded the arrests, an omission
that gave full credit to the Barnett administration for its wise leadership and the Citizens' Council for preparing Mississippians for these
invasions. Such an approach appealed to moderates in Mississippi by
emphasizing the avoidance of violence, a goal that white Mississippians
skeptical of the Council's value feared was not sustainable. Through the
Freedom Rides, the Council had the ear of those moderates and it took
full advantage.

The Council also answered criticisms of the decision to move forty-
five Riders to Parchman when they had only been convicted of breach of
the peace. Fred Jones, Parchman's superintendent and a Council member, visited *Forum* to counter accusations that the prisoners' treatment
had been less than humane. While they occupied maximum security
facilities in the prison complex, Jones explained, such measures were
taken for their own safety. The Freedom Riders, he pointed out, were
the first people to stay in the facility where prison officials placed them,

a new building that could hold up to six hundred prisoners "in case of an influx of these people to the state." As county convicts, Jones continued, the Riders were not sentenced to hard labor like other prisoners at the penitentiary. Investigators from Minnesota had concurred, according to Jones, that all were being treated perfectly well. Their treatment of prison officials, however, left something to be desired. He complained of singing and hunger strikes and demands for shared housing with fellow Riders as the greatest irritants to prison officials. In addition to their food provisions and fair treatment, Jones revealed that each prisoner was also given reading material: a Bible and Carleton Putnam's *Race and Reason,* a book that Jones described (not coincidentally given the Council's recent endorsement of the book) as "one of the best accounts of race relations" he had ever read.[14]

Jones's reflections were not entirely untrue, but they were far from accurate. Prison officials, under Barnett's orders, shielded the Riders from the typical brutalities that Parchman's regular occupants experienced. They did not perform prison labor, but officials confined them in nearly total isolation from each other. Only allowed out of their cells to shower twice a week, Riders rarely interacted with each other or anyone else. Sparse allotments of food and sleep deprivations, along with this isolation, constituted the extent to which guards could torture them under Barnett's orders. Barnett and his advisors were aware of the national scrutiny that the move to Parchman created for the state.[15]

The Freedom Rides initiated the first collision between a sustained civil rights campaign and white solidarity in Mississippi. With every confrontation, grassroots support grew, both in the white resistance movement and within the black community. By September, McComb, a city southwest of Jackson, began a campaign of its own, mirroring the Freedom Rides but extending into voter registration and lunch counter sit-ins. The campaigns drew press attention, and with more confrontations expected, frustrations reached a fever pitch, exploding when a group of white men in McComb physically attacked reporters covering the story. Erle Johnston, public relations director for the Sovereignty Commission and the head of its Speakers' Bureau, later recalled the resignation he felt after hearing about the violence in McComb, especially given the fact that he had just given a speech to a civic club in Pennsylvania about how peaceful race relations in Mississippi were.[16]

The Freedom Rides served as a measurable victory for both sides. The Council and its support of the Barnett administration, and vice versa, proved to be a beneficial collaboration in managing crisis, but the presence of black defiance, among both black Mississippians and activists from outside the state, could not be undone. Concessions in other states, the Council warned, could negatively affect Mississippi's resolve. Its leaders recommended that Barnett reach out to other southern states and lead them back to effective defiance. During the summer of 1961, Barnett hosted the Southern Governors Conference in Jackson, an event that Bill Simmons insisted *Forum* cover, requiring costs beyond its Washington allocation. In his monthly report to the Sovereignty Commission, Simmons claimed that requests for these special broadcasts more than doubled requests from the previous month, justifying the extra expense. *Forum* provided similar coverage to the Southwide Association of Municipal Officials annual meeting in Memphis in August, a group Simmons predicted would become "a powerful conservative force in the South."[17]

In total, *Forum* dedicated nine broadcasts to the Southern Governors Conference and the Southwide Association of Municipal Officials. The coverage of these events and their presentation on *Forum* aimed to place the Council at the center of a regional network of similarly minded leaders, each committed to uncompromising resistance to civil rights challenges. Given its questionable reputation at home, these broadcasts served as proof that the Council was not a maverick, power-hungry organization, but part of a legitimate political movement. Guest after guest emphasized the importance of southern unity against federal encroachments. One of the common themes they shared was their identification of the white South as the largest minority group in the country, the last region in the country to hold out against federal power. Mississippi's attorney general, Joe Patterson, appeared with his colleague, Alabama attorney general Macdonald Gallion, describing their respective jobs as virtually interchangeable since their problems were identical. "The only way in the world we can defend ourselves," Patterson explained, "is as a group and not just sit idly by and be clipped off one at the time."[18]

Patterson's remarks reflected a larger problem that the Council movement in Mississippi faced, and that was recognition from other southern states. Alabama, Georgia, and Louisiana had Council movements of their own, and cooperation was not unusual among the groups. But in other southern states, groups like the Citizens' Council were often singular and unlinked to statewide associations and thus not considered serious challenges to the political power structure. In states like Tennessee, Virginia, and North Carolina there was some reluctance to associate too directly with the Council given its reputation for terror and its demonstrated abhorrence for moderation on matters of race. The Southern Governors Conference was an attempt to address these differences, but given the limited number of guests to appear on *Forum* for the conference (four guests from three states, including Mississippi), it seemed unsuccessful in closing the gap between Council tactics in Mississippi and resistance movements in other states, a fact that underscores the weakening of resistance elsewhere (at least through Council organizations) and reinforces the fact that the Mississippi movement was unique in its ambitions.[19]

But the Mississippi Council's ambitions did not divorce it from a reputation, earned in its earliest days of activism and secured with the ascension of the Barnett administration, of violence and intimidation. As much as the Council wished to present itself as a nationally significant organization, elected officials in other southern states, confronting their own civil rights challenges and federal mandates, eschewed association with an organization openly committed to defiance. The intimate relationship between the Council in Mississippi and the state government enabled its growth. In other states, like Virginia, Council organizations garnered much less respect.

The Southwide Conference of Municipal Officials represented an opportunity to remedy these differences. With over three hundred attendees from ten southern states, the meeting gave *Forum* greater exposure and access to a wider range of attendees. Held in Memphis, the August 1961 conference was the first of its kind and represented an attempt to create a southern version of the American Municipal Association, committed to the unique issues facing southern cities. In its unanimously approved constitution, the association explained its commitment to community-centered policies, supporting federal action "only where the constitution clearly provides and then only in matters which are clearly beyond the resources of local or state government or in matters pertaining to national security."[20]

The link between the Southwide Conference of Municipal Officials and the Council movement is not entirely clear, but Jackson's mayor Allen C. Thompson, a member of the Jackson Citizens' Council, was in attendance, as were other Mississippi officials. The newly- formed organization was not unique in its objectives (the maintenance of segregation), but its presentation represented a softening of racist rhetoric and a magnification of principle. The municipal perspective identified the fiscal dependencies of cities on federal money as one of the gateways to federal intrusion. A city councilman from Danville, Virginia, John W. Carter, explained the need for "straight thinking and intellectual honesty" among citizens, who must come to terms with their role in selling their rights away by accepting federal money.[21] The mayor of Hartwell, Georgia, Lee Carter, also appeared as a *Forum* guest during the conference and urged regional support of an educational program to spread the message of the conference to the rest of the nation.[22]

The Council's interest in these attempts at collaboration likely rested in the hope that cooperative action would help underwrite their publicity expenses. As the uncontested leader in the field of resistance propaganda, the Citizens' Council stood to benefit greatly from regional unity. Its leaders had experience and proven success in selling their message to interested parties. Simmons's insistence on *Forum*'s coverage of the meeting, despite the additional expenses of doing so, suggests that he expected the investment to yield handsome rewards. In the meantime, he kept his *Forum* reports to the Sovereignty Commission relatively vague. While he often included some numerical indication of the program's success, the reports consisted of nothing more than a letter with assurances that increasing costs for the program were wholly justified. Meanwhile, the program provided free publicity to southern governors, city officials, conservative crusaders, and national figures with their own agendas. With those connections in tow, Simmons initiated the Council's entry into conservative grassroots activism.

But the demands for increasing financial support did not go unnoticed.

Discomfort with the Council's allocation of taxpayer money for *Forum* continued to surface in a number of corners, but most significantly from Erle Johnston, public relations director for the Sovereignty Commission. Johnston never believed the Council's claims that hundreds of radio and television stations regularly ran *Forum* broadcasts. In short, the cost of the program to the Sovereignty Commission was a major outlay if only a handful of (mostly southern) stations carried it. Using his connections with *Jackson Daily News* reporter Bob Pittman, Johnston began his own investigation into *Forum*'s audience. Johnston and Pittman sent out hundreds of postcards to stations the Council listed in its monthly newsletter as carriers of the program, and Pittman included the results of the survey in an article in August 1961, completely bypassing his editor to do so.[23] The survey provided no confirmation of *Forum*'s national audience. Pittman's article detailed station responses to inquiries about their inclusion of the program in their schedule. After collecting all of the replies, the survey showed that out of 308 stations, only seven responded that they used the program regularly and three of them were Mississippi stations. The remaining four stations were all in southern states: Georgia, Louisiana, Florida, and Virginia.[24]

Hal DeCell, longtime editor of the *Deer Creek Pilot*, had his doubts about *Forum*'s national reach as well. DeCell had served as the Sovereignty Commission's first director of public relations after successfully managing J. P. Coleman's gubernatorial campaign in 1955. In anticipation of the looming 1962 legislative session, DeCell predicted a debate in the state legislature over the fiscal wisdom of continuing to support *Forum* given the state's strained resources. Calling the allocation "unconstitutional," DeCell considered the $5,000 monthly allocation an easy cut for legislators looking to save some money. He considered the Council's monthly list of radio and television stations (included in each issue of the *The Citizens' Council*) an outright lie:

> Such claims emanating from the tweedle-de-dee and tweedle-de-dum of professional extremists are so blatantly naught but twaddle that I'm surprised even they can consider Mississippians so gullible. A fellow doesn't have to be a genius to realize that the Citizens Councils probably couldn't even buy time in the north to show their programs, much less get it free

as they claim. . . . How Governor Barnett and the members of the Sovereignty Commission can swallow such a farce is beyond comprehension.[25]

It is unclear what, if anything, Bill Simmons knew about Johnston's role in initiating the survey about *Forum* stations, but by the spring of 1962, the enmity between the two was obvious.[26] The diversion of state funds to support the Citizens' Council was never wholly accepted, even among Council supporters. The survey results came on the heels of a lawsuit initiated by Jackson attorney William Higgs and local activist Robert L. T. Smith protesting the use of taxpayer money to support a private organization committed to the preservation of segregation, a cause that many citizens did not support. The lawsuit included Ross Barnett, the Sovereignty Commission, and the Citizens' Council as equal contributors to the misuse of state money.[27] Although the plaintiffs failed to pursue the suit, its focus suggested a cause of much frustration for the Sovereignty Commission. For many Mississippians, the Citizens' Council and the Sovereignty Commission were indistinguishable from each other. Their publicity agendas overlapped, and it was often unclear which campaigns belonged to each organization, creating an atmosphere that left the Sovereignty Commission a beneficiary or victim of the Council's current popularity.

Erle Johnston, director of public relations for the Sovereignty Commission in 1962, attempted to remedy this confusion in an address he made to his alma mater, Grenada High School, in May. Johnston's speech stood out for its tone of practicality and moderation, reminiscent of his time with the Coleman administration. Johnston insisted that the activities of the Sovereignty Commission's Speakers' Bureau had counteracted some of the bad publicity aimed at Mississippi since he assumed its directorship in 1960. But while northern audiences had found some sympathy with the segregationist position, it was in no way a wholesale victory. Within minutes of opening his speech, Johnston declared that it was "wishful thinking" to believe that *Brown* would be overturned or that desegregation would never come to Mississippi, surfacing in full view the moderate position. In a statement directed at the Council's investments in *Forum,* Johnston did not equivocate: "We can expect no national movement of any strength which would support the southern tradition of segregated societies." No option existed, according to Johnston, to stave off the inevitable. Recent agreements between city officials and civil rights activists in Little Rock, Atlanta, Dallas, New Orleans, and Memphis, he imagined, were predictive of what was ahead for Jackson, and no amount of organization could prevent it.[28]

The only solution to maintaining segregated public schools in the state with growing pressures on all sides was, in Johnston's opinion, cooperation with the black community, who had much to gain economically from maintaining separate systems. But, he warned, black Mississippians had the backing of the federal government to advance their demands. They were educated and ready to exercise equal citizenship. He proceeded to encourage his audience to offer more recognition to black citizens in media coverage and in sporting events, a gross misreading of the deeper objectives behind the civil rights movement.[29]

Despite the paternalistic tone that Johnston's remarks struck, his insinuation that power rested in the hands of the black community to use at its will was remarkable. It signified a sentiment that the Council organization had successfully stifled since 1954. After the school closure amendment's passage that year, practical options that promised any measure of fairness to black Mississippians, as meager as those options may have been, were effectively removed from public conversations. Total resistance to both federal mandates and local black challenges was the only strategy that signified a true commitment to segregation. The Council had proven that in moments of confrontation it would err on the side of violence to defend the segregation principle rather than move toward compromise.

Johnston's true defection from the lockstep of segregationist rhetoric, however, came in his conflation of the Citizens' Council movement with the NAACP, neither of which he named outright, but whose identity was clear. He considered both groups "extremists." Toward the Council his tone was condescending: "They mean well. They are dedicated to their cause. But they have agitated the friction and bitterness and there is some question as to whether this attitude is a help, a hindrance, or merely creates hysteria." As an alternative, Johnston recommended that both black and white Mississippians adopt "practical segregation" as their objective, a system he saw as mutually beneficial for its maintenance of separate spaces, but with significant improvements to black facilities. It was, in short, a return to the last-hour improvements Mississippi attempted in the months immediately prior to and after the *Brown* decision.[30]

If there were any questions about the relationship between the Council and its benefactor, Johnston's speech answered them. His advocacy for practical segregation simulated the chords of moderation that had so vexed the Council under J. P. Coleman's administration. Additionally, Johnston's skepticism about the Council's campaign to convert other Americans into defenders of segregation (the entire purpose of *Forum*) was quite a blow. Simmons's reaction was immediate. He accused Johnston of surrendering, questioning his future with the Sovereignty Commission and casting a shadow over his reputation as a committed segregationist. Johnston responded, in part to correct false reporting of the speech and its reception, but his remarks escalated the public debate further, polarizing Council-friendly papers and their editors from newspapers more skeptical of the Council's tactics. The debate over Johnston's stance also brought form to the looming 1963 gubernatorial election, an election for which J. P. Coleman would be eligible.[31]

The most immediate concern, however, was Johnston's future with the Sovereignty Commission. Governor Barnett's connections with both Simmons and Johnston made for a difficult prediction. Firing Johnston was likely to meet with serious criticism from his allies in the political community and confirm the Council's tyranny over the Barnett administration. Retaining him threatened to weaken an already tenuous façade of white unity in the state by undermining the legitimacy of the Citizens' Council. After some maneuvering on Johnston's part, Barnett agreed to adopt a statement, with the support of the Sovereignty Commission's board of directors, confirming that both Simmons and Johnston were equally committed to preserving segregation and that both men had valuable contributions to make to that fight. In exchange for his immediate retention, however, Johnston agreed to resign his position by November if the situation worsened.[32]

As Johnston fielded criticisms about his advocacy of practical segregation and its suitability for a man in his position, the Council seemed to be getting further away from its founding mission at a time when its fiscal needs were increasing. As 1961 came to a close and 1962 began, *Forum* broadcasts increasingly featured foreign policy discussions to the exclusion of any other topic. Guests who participated in these discussions were almost always southern, however, including *Forum*'s most frequent guest, South Carolina senator Strom Thurmond. During the nine years of *Forum*'s programming, Thurmond appeared on thirty-six broadcasts, far more than any other guest on the show. His appearances often showcased his position on the Senate's Special Preparedness Investigating Subcommittee, charged with investigating allegations of the "muzzling" of military officials, a practice that sought to censor American military leaders from speaking directly about the communist threat and its practices.[33] In reality, the subcommittee formed after the Department of Defense issued a statement prohibiting military personnel from attending right-wing seminars. Senator Thurmond was especially alarmed at the Kennedy administration's silencing of anticommunist rhetoric among US military leaders, a strategy meant to ease American diplomacy with the Soviet Union.[34]

Thurmond's concerns paralleled the fears of conservative groups throughout the country who saw the administration's diplomatic stance as appeasement, evidence of decreasing American influence in the Cold War world. Thurmond's appearances on *Forum* articulated these anxieties, but the cause found a spokesman in retired Major General Edwin Walker, whose compulsory resignation from the army in 1961 made him a hero in radical conservative circles. Walker's career ended after the Department of Defense formally reprimanded him for his Pro-Blue Program, a self-designed training strategy that indoctrinated troops under his command with radical anticommunist propaganda, including literature from the John Birch Society.[35] In addition to his involvement with the muzzling controversy, Walker's career included supervision of the Little Rock desegregation crisis, a fact that turned Walker into a self-described expert on the relationship between communism and the civil rights movement.

Walker's advocacy of radical anticommunism, his claims about federal corruption in foreign policy, and his certainty that the civil rights movement was a product of both, made him a darling of the Citizens' Council and, on a broader plane, a popular spokesman for the burgeoning conservative cause.[36] As part of a speaking tour, he visited Jackson's City

Auditorium in December 1961, flanked by the governor, lieutenant governor, Jackson mayor Allen C. Thompson, and Congressman John Bell Williams. The Citizens' Council, through *Forum,* filmed the entire address as part of its "Project: Understanding" program, an initiative that focused on educational films for distribution among civic groups and schools. An article in the *Jackson Daily News,* a newspaper notorious for its support of all Council activities, estimated 4,000 people attended the event and claimed that Walker was "constantly interrupted by applause" as he described his audience as a fearsome display of white unity, "a symbol . . . of the cause of freedom everywhere."[37]

In addition to the Jackson speech, Dick Morphew hosted Walker on the first *Forum* broadcast of 1962. Walker's remarks during his visit reawakened the communist conspiracy rhetoric that had dominated white resistance in the 1950s. Walker urged viewers to "know [the] enemy" and to exercise skepticism about policies of "co-existence" on the battlefield.[38] His warnings drew from his experiences in the field but fit seamlessly with the Council's often militant language about preserving segregation. The Council embraced Walker's role as whistleblower and critic of federal military strategy. His willingness to risk his own career to protect his principles connected easily with the Council's defense of segregation in the midst of increasing isolation from public opinion.

But Walker's case also connected the Council and its supporters to conservatives throughout the country who saw some value in the general's case and what it represented. The January 1962 issue of *The Citizen* reprinted two national columns describing the impact of Walker's case upon the political spectrum. One of these columns was a piece by Holmes Alexander, a syndicated columnist whose opposition to desegregation was a cornerstone of his conservatism. In "Let's Choose Up Sides," Alexander argued that the political environment in which Walker resigned had polarized into two extreme factions: the Radical Right and the Lunatic Left. The former, defined through the platform of the John Birch Society, was "very strong for God and country, for free enterprise, local sovereignty and individualism." The latter, unfortunately, "put social welfare ahead of religion, 'the world' ahead of the USA, federal-aid-for-everything ahead of personal initiative, collectivism in everything from world government to fluoridation of water ahead of individualism." Given the clear difference between the two, Alexander warned readers to stop "pining" for moderation and choose a side.[39]

The focus on Edwin Walker and the muzzling hearings was one of the most significant convergences of white resistance to civil rights in the South with national conservative constituencies. For Strom Thurmond, one of the earliest Walker advocates, the hearings provided entry to an alliance with Sunbelt conservatives like Barry Goldwater, whose 1964 campaign for president, while unsuccessful, awakened conservative sympathies across the country. The support Thurmond sought from oil magnate and conservative media tycoon Dan Smoot and Tulsa's anticommunist evangelist Billy James Hargis signified a shift in both segregationist organizing and in Sunbelt conservatism. As historian Joseph Crespino aptly describes, the muzzling hearings and the support Walker enjoyed provided a wider, race-neutral base of support for the former and shed the racial innocence that Sunbelt conservatives had for so long claimed.[40]

It was within the emergence of the Sunbelt coalition that the South would find its most loyal allies. The Sunbelt migration that occurred from 1910 to 1970 brought more than 11 million southerners, more than half of them white, to Texas, Oklahoma, Arizona, and Southern California. Liberated from the racial politics that Black Belt areas of the Deep South demanded and increasingly protective of their newly achieved status as middle-class Americans, these migrants brought with them strands of plain folk religion and a belief that economic advancement resulted from hard work, not special treatment. Their politics, much less allegiant to the Democratic Party than the politics of the Deep South, provided a wide window for ideological experimentation and party affiliation, but both coalesced in a deep commitment to individualism. As the civil rights movement proceeded and violence moved out of the South into California, the tone that individualism struck converged with evolving desires for national sympathy among Deep South segregationists who feared their cause was lost.[41]

Forum did its part in helping cultivate that connection. In 1962, an unprecedented number of guests emphasized the same conservative talking points. In the midst of a midterm election year, the Kennedy administration's policies were clear targets for criticism. The slate of programs that defined the first half of 1962 represented an intersection of conservative threads that could speak to a variety of audiences: foreign policy, ideology, and religion. The Walker case awakened Americans to changes within the military regarding its training programs. Concerns about American influence abroad, its membership within the United Nations, and foreign policy expenditures already existed when the subcommittee hearings began in January 1962, and these fears were only magnified as more information became available. *Forum* guests who discussed the subcommittee hearings used the opportunity to further explain the Kennedy administration's mishandling of foreign policy and military strategy.[42]

Interspersed with the foreign policy programs were discussions about conservative ideology. Guests like Congressman James B. Utt, a Republican from California, and Senator John Tower of Texas, articulated the principles of conservatism for *Forum*'s audience, describing it as an ideology of "preservation" and natural change that valued stability and the rights of the individual.[43] But the issue that crystallized these principles was the Supreme Court's decision in *Engel v. Vitale,* the court case that declared school-sponsored prayer unconstitutional. Announced in June 1962, the decision brought form to the argument that the centralization of government in the United States and its increasing compromises with communism abroad would chip away at individual liberties and American sovereignty. Appearing with his colleague, Senator John Stennis from Mississippi, Virginia senator A. Willis Robertson feared the consequences of a decision that took away one of the fundamental differences between the United States and the Soviet Union: "We believe in God and they don't and . . . nothing would please [the Soviet Union] better than to see us abandon God and see God abandon us."[44] Congressman John Dowdy of Texas considered the decision another example of the protracted disintegration of the nation's moral fiber. While he defended the separation of church and state, Dowdy considered the decision too intrusive, stating, "God has to be a part of our government . . . I cannot see a nation long existing that tries to divorce itself from God."[45]

Forum benefited from the intersection of military anxieties, midterm elections, and controversial court decisions in 1962. The program attracted public figures eager to articulate their positions to their constituents. But at home, the Council faced the most direct challenge to white supremacy yet. In January 1961, an air force veteran and student at Jackson State College began what would turn into a nearly two-year process to desegregate the University of Mississippi. With the legal assistance of the NAACP, and the guidance of Mississippi field secretary Medgar Evers, James Meredith successfully moved his case through the court system until, on September 10, 1962, the Fifth Circuit Court of Appeals set aside all delaying tactics and ordered Meredith's immediate enrollment. Ten days later, Meredith arrived on campus in Oxford only to be turned away by the governor himself, who proudly announced his defiance to a cheering crowd waiting outside. On September 24, the Court of Appeals issued another order instructing the state's Institutions of Higher Learning to oversee his registration in Jackson instead. But tensions escalated when Barnett issued a directive to arrest federal officials who tried to enforce the order. Meredith left, only to be rejected a third time when he attempted to complete his registration in Oxford the next day. This time Lieutenant Governor Paul Johnson issued the denial. By the end of the day on September 26, both the governor and lieutenant governor had contempt orders against them.[46]

The Council's role in advising Barnett during the controversy is not entirely clear in the historical record but, given Barnett's previous relationship with Bill Simmons and his deference to Council advice in the past, it is likely that the Council had some influence in directing Barnett's response to the enrollment order.[47] The Council had every reason to believe that the successful resolution of this new crisis would bring another wave of membership increases and financial support similar to those in the months following the Freedom Rides. Nearly fifteen months had lapsed between the Freedom Rides and the Meredith case, however, bringing a slew of compromises in other states where the system of segregation was slowly falling apart with little fanfare. Mississippi was not alone in its defiance, but it was quickly becoming exceptionally stubborn in its refusal to yield anything that would weaken its position. Meredith's admission to Ole Miss, then, was especially shocking to white Mississippians who believed nothing like it could ever happen in their home state.

In the days immediately leading up to Meredith's official arrival on October 1, 1962, events developed quickly. Ross Barnett's defiant "I Love Mississippi" speech at an Ole Miss football game in Jackson assured white

Mississippians that, despite federal threats to enforce the order with or without Barnett's compliance, their governor would not back down from his position. With every successful denial of registration, the hysteria surrounding the standoff grew. Alabama's outgoing governor, John Patterson, expressed his support for Barnett in a telegram to President Kennedy. His successor, Governor-Elect George Wallace, also publicly declared his support for Barnett, along with Governor Orval Faubus of Arkansas and Virginia governor Albertis Harrison. Major General Edwin Walker encouraged Americans everywhere to "do whatever is necessary" should the federal government apply military force to ensure Meredith's admission.[48] In the days before Meredith's scheduled arrival, *Forum* rebroadcast a public address Barnett had made early in September in which he urged Mississippians to refuse to cooperate with the Kennedy administration's agenda, stating, "We will not drink from the cup of genocide."[49] The Sovereignty Commission printed over 1 million postcards addressed to the White House for citizens to express their opposition to Meredith's admission. And local newspapers inflamed fears through inaccurate, late-breaking coverage that painted Barnett as a hero.[50]

When Meredith arrived on the evening of September 30, the campus was a tinderbox. Federal officials comprised of federal marshals, Deputy Attorney General Nicholas Katzenbach, and representatives from the Department of Justice began arriving on campus late in the afternoon. Members of the Mississippi Highway Patrol, sent to maintain order between the gathering crowd and the federal marshals, dispersed shortly after the crowd began throwing bricks and setting vehicles on fire. They did so upon Barnett's orders, a reversal of his previous agreement with President Kennedy. At night's end, 3,000 people were on the Ole Miss campus. Some were students, but as the night continued and hostilities escalated, many of them retreated to dorms as more militant outsiders arrived. General Walker, who had encouraged such a standoff in previous remarks, was also on campus inciting the crowd to keep fighting.[51] At daybreak, more than 23,000 federal troops occupied the campus. Two people died, 160 marshals were injured, many of them from gunfire, and the campus looked like a war zone.[52]

Media coverage of the event was widespread. Many reporters had seen firsthand the development of the evening's events and phoned in their reports for October 1 editions. More in-depth stories from varying perspectives appeared over the next several days, including a piece from James Meredith in *The Saturday Evening Post,* where he described the events in his own words. Some reporters took more personal approaches, reflecting on the personal impact that witnessing such destruction on American soil had on them. NBC produced a special report on Monday, October 2, that included an interview with Attorney General Robert Kennedy during which he described the riots as a horrific experience for him, as it was upon his orders that the federal marshals held their fire even as they were being fired upon.[53]

The Council had its own reaction and used the riots as *Forum* topics through the month of October. Most national reports on the events of September 30 and October 1 detailed the actions of the on-campus mob and its harassment of federal troops. For white Mississippians, however, local newspapers emphasized the brute force of federal power over civilian protest, including a headline from the *Clarion-Ledger* that read, "Marshals Set Off Ole Miss Rioting."[54] *Forum*'s guests reiterated this account of the riots. Senator John Stennis blamed the premature use of tear gas as the spark that incited the riots, but spent much of his visit lamenting the fact that the Supreme Court's refusal to hear an appeal after the Fifth Circuit's ruling violated due process. But even as he wished for further judicial consideration, he argued that judicial decree could not supplant "the evolution of legislative enactments."[55] Council member and Hinds County judge Russell Moore, who was present during the riots, unequivocally blamed the federal government for the campus violence, describing Oxford as "a territory occupied by foreigners." Marshals issued the tear gas, he argued, "for some unknown reason." Moore insisted that Barnett refused to dismiss highway patrolmen, contradicting the widely reported fact that it was upon the governor's orders that they dispersed. He also reported frequent civilian harassments on the part of occupying troops in the days following the riots.[56]

William K. Shearer, a conservative newspaper editor from California and former legislative assistant to James Utt, also weighed in on the riots, stating that the situation arose from an attempt to enforce an unwanted social doctrine. "That same force," he warned, "can be used to close any newspaper in this country, to shut down any church, to close down free elections, to outlaw and wipe out any legitimate political party." The shock of this series of events, Shearer hoped, would convince conservative southerners to join with Sunbelt Republicans in the North and West, who understood that the civil rights movement was not about race at all but an economic battleground to promote welfare, public housing, and myriad forms of federal aid to black Americans.[57]

The battle that Shearer described was ideological, not moral, and it was a better reflection of an outsider's assessment of the Oxford tragedy than an accurate read of white Mississippians' reaction to the events. Meredith's enrollment countered the Citizens' Council's argument that outside groups were influencing local blacks to challenge the white power structure. Other than the critical assistance of the NAACP legal team, Meredith had no affiliation with civil rights organizations, local or otherwise. He declared no agenda other than his right as a Mississippian to attend a public university.[58] The events of September 30 and October 1 played out as a battle between Mississippi and the US government, not Mississippi versus James Meredith. Meredith undoubtedly experienced persistent harassment and intimidation during his time at Ole Miss, but in the immediate aftermath of the riots, white Mississippians concerned themselves more with the military occupation of Oxford. Ultimately, that polarization worked better for the Citizens' Council than a campaign against one black student, because it would outlast the controversy.

On October 24, 1962, the state association sent out a "Dear Friend" letter, calling for more organization, both political and economic, "against individuals and organizations which would destroy us." The "dark cloud" of federal occupation in Oxford had served to awaken white Mississippians to the threat of "racial perverts and ruthless politicians" bent on destroying the South. The letter was a call to arms, stating that the white South had only itself to depend on in the struggle against "Negro political domination and racial amalgamation." Within a couple of weeks another letter encouraged Council supporters to join the Minutemen, a national movement begun in 1961 to arm citizens against a communist takeover. The Council's endorsement of the movement was rare in its directness. The call for citizen soldiers to be part of a paramilitary organization was an indicator of the Council's ties to the radical right and its willingness to openly promote violence despite its earlier claims to sophisticated, nonviolent leadership.[59]

The Council's call to arms coincided with a reduction in funding from the Sovereignty Commission. Within a month of Meredith's entrance to the University of Mississippi, the Sovereignty Commission shrank its monthly support for *Forum* from $4,500 to $2,000.[60] The reduction in funds coincided with an increase in the Sovereignty Commission's Speakers' Bureau budget, which may have accounted for the change. Whatever the motivation behind the reduction, money was tight for both the state agency and the Citizens' Council, as they both escalated their public relations campaigns after Oxford.[61] What distinguished the state agency from the Citizens' Council, however, was its focused defense of the state of Mississippi. The Council's publicity campaign emphasized the national crisis of federal power and white victimhood over local conditions. By its own description, the Council saw *Forum* as "a basic course in American government, combined with a review of current events and issues."[62] By 1963, *Forum* reflected the Council's increasing interest in national and global events at a time when the civil rights movement at home was escalating, a transition that alienated its priorities from the Sovereignty Commission's function as a state agency. The reduction in funding ensured that, in pursuit of funding, the Council would have to find relevance outside of Mississippi.

As 1963 began, the limits of Council influence in Mississippi were palpable. The successful desegregation of the University of Mississippi provided some traction for the Council in terms of membership, but the growing distance from the Sovereignty Commission signified a loss of faith in the organization's efficacy as racial tensions escalated in the state. With a gubernatorial election looming, those signals mattered. The Council's success depended on the atmosphere of fear and isolation that hung over the state.

Increasing attention to civil rights challenges in Mississippi put the state under a microscope in other areas. As black activists attempted to organize rural areas of the state, particularly in the Delta, the true impact of discrimination came into focus. The economic disparities between blacks and whites in the state were dramatic, and poverty prevailed in rural, black-dominated areas of the state where the Citizens' Council had its earliest successes. The development of industry and farm mechanization in the 1930s turned scores of black plantation workers into the unemployed. Local distribution of commodity surpluses from the federal government somewhat alleviated this poverty, but it made recipients of assistance dependent upon white city officials for distribution and thus reluctant to join civil rights campaigns. Civil rights activist and Tougaloo professor John Salter did an eighteen-month study of poverty in Coahoma and Tunica counties, both in the Delta, during 1961 and 1962. During the course of his project he interviewed 259 individuals from 41 families. Nearly all of them lived in deplorable conditions and received no form of welfare assistance, a fact he attributed to "the negative attitude held by the dominant white power elite in Mississippi, with respect to Negro efforts to achieve basic American rights and human equality."[63]

John Salter's was not the only report that moved beyond the indignities of race-based segregation and disfranchisement and confronted the daily deprivations that those systems ensured. The Commission on Civil Rights conducted its own investigations in 1962 and issued a report in January 1963 that described an atmosphere of terror for black Mississippians and a state government committed to obstruction regarding racial progress. Jane Schutt, the chair for the Mississippi advisory committee, recommended a formal hearing to gather as much information as possible about the state of affairs in Mississippi, a state she deemed in more dire need than any other state in the South.[64]

Schutt and other native Mississippians represented a still vibrant, though cautious, group of white liberals who were full-fledged supporters of desegregation. Her work as chairwoman of the State Advisory Committee to the United States Commission on Civil Rights served as a pipeline for reporting conditions in the state. In her testimony to the Commission on Civil Rights in May 1963, Schutt described the state committee's work as the only lifeline "for those Mississippians who do not support the tenets of the Citizens Councils." White Mississippians, she explained to the commission, needed more awareness about the living conditions of their black neighbors and segregation's role in creating those conditions.[65]

The State Advisory Committee worked closely with the Mississippi Human Relations Council (MHRC) on collecting affidavits on police brutality and white-led violence against black citizens. Those efforts yielded scores of affidavits from black citizens about police harassment and violence, most of it unrelated to civil rights activity. The MHRC's correspondence includes references to the Council's intolerance and its manipulation of an ignorant public as the reason for the formation of the Human Relations Council. In a letter to MHRC chair Reverend Murray Cox, a concerned citizen described the Citizens' Council as an exploiter of the "lunatic fringe" in the state. To this writer, the Council and its leaders "love a diet of harassment, intolerant preaching, name calling, hate spreading, and . . . are happiest when sowing seeds of discord and turmoil where discord and turmoil will flourish best—among the ignorant."[66] These descriptions suggest an important point about the Council's work in Mississippi. The organization's tactics deliberately exacerbated existing conditions, conditions deeply rooted in the state's history of violence and white supremacy long before the Council's formation. When information about the daily conditions of poverty and terror that evidenced this history began to reach officials outside of the state, the reality of the Mississippi problem began to become clear.

Even as reports began to circulate about the severity of the situation in Mississippi, conditions worsened. In Greenwood, a Citizens' Council stronghold where SNCC-sponsored voter registration drives had been under way throughout 1962, local whites retaliated by eliminating federal assistance subsidies from the city's 1963 budget, a move that prompted an investigation by the Commission on Civil Rights, which recommended immediate federal intervention. Despite this recommendation, as winter set in, families starved from food shortages. But if white officials meant to weaken local black interest in voting, they misjudged the resources available to SNCC workers. The civil rights organization drew upon its national supporters to fill the gap, bringing regular deliveries of food to the area and drawing local blacks even closer to SNCC and its volunteers. As frustration grew among white leaders, retaliation seemed certain. In February, the black business district caught fire, allegedly in an attempt to destroy the SNCC office. Less than two weeks later, three SNCC workers left Greenwood on their way to Greenville and were fired on while driving, leaving Jimmy Travis, the driver, severely injured.[67]

The collection of events benefited the civil rights movement more than the white power structure. Attendance at meetings soared and applications for voter registration continued to increase at a phenomenal rate. The increase in support was so dramatic that both SNCC and the Council of Federated Organizations (COFO) sent more workers into the Delta to aid with food distribution and canvassing. National media coverage followed, shifting attention from the Ole Miss crisis to increasing local black activism. A standoff between white law enforcement and black demonstrators in Greenwood ended with a police dog attacking a popular black minister, an event for which the media was present. The Justice Department filed suit against the city of Greenwood, issuing an immediate restraining order prohibiting white city officials from interfering with local protests. After the events at Oxford, however, federal force was not a popular option. When Greenwood's city prosecutor issued a thinly veiled threat that federal interference would remove any guarantee of safety for local residents, the Kennedy administration backed down.[68]

The Delta was not alone in its activism. In Jackson, the Council's seat of power, the Jackson Youth Council began another economic boycott of downtown Jackson stores and participated in the first demonstrations on Capitol Street in December 1962. The most promising news for leaders like John Salter, who worked closely with his Tougaloo students in the boycott campaigns, was the media attention the demonstrations drew from the local press, a deviation from the typical silent treatment usually given such activities.[69]

To counter the impact of the boycotts, Citizens' Council member and Jackson's mayor, Allen Thompson, declared January 14 Willie Richardson Day in downtown Jackson. Richardson was a decorated black athlete and alumnus of Jackson State College, well known in the black community. The day included official honors at City Hall from the mayor and a parade through downtown Jackson. It was a countermove to the boycotts, meant to draw blacks into the downtown area and subject them to an elaborate display of how peaceful and respectful relations between whites and blacks truly were in Jackson. The *Clarion-Ledger,* in its coverage of the event, claimed that nearly 1,000 attended the events. According to John Salter, however, only 350 of Jackson's 70,000 black citizens were present, a disappointment that, if true, must have alarmed the white power structure, but attested to the inroads that local activists had made in drawing support from their communities.[70]

The Council's power in Mississippi thrived in an atmosphere of anticipation. When the Freedom Riders arrived in the summer of 1961 and were shuttled away to jail without violence, the organization was able to claim credit for the very thing it had promised white Mississippians since it became public in 1954. Despite the cooperation with the Kennedy administration that enabled Ross Barnett to secure the arrests, the Council's perceived success sustained its influence. After Meredith's admission to the University of Mississippi, the violence that accompanied it, and the persistent federal presence for months afterward, the Council's guidance seemed to ensure the very thing it purported to avoid— federal compulsion. The organization banked on local terror and white unity in the state to preserve white supremacy. Those factors, however, were codependent, and the failed attempt to preserve segregation at the state's oldest university became a tipping point for black activism in the state. When the anticipation of black challenge turned into a reality, the Council's ability to use it as a way to garner blind allegiance from whites in the state weakened. As national organizations like SNCC and CORE penetrated rural areas of Mississippi, the net of fear that isolated those communities and strengthened Council influence began to disintegrate, driving the Council to further cultivate partnerships already under way with conservative allies in California and elsewhere at a time when civil rights activities in the state began to gain momentum.

CHAPTER 5

ABANDONING THE HARVEST, PLOWING NEW FIELDS, 1963–1964

We found the general nature of [Greenwood] to be CLANNISH, from the bankers to the drunks about anything pertaining to [Byron De La Beckwith]. Everyone that we talked to seemed to know that we were in town and what we were after. Many of them on showing our credentials showed us their Citizens Councils cards. —POLICE REPORT ON BYRON DE LA BECKWITH'S WHEREABOUTS ON THE NIGHT OF MEDGAR EVERS'S MURDER

The successful desegregation of the University of Mississippi in the fall of 1962 was a signal defeat for the Citizens' Council in Mississippi. The Sovereignty Commission's funding reduction to *Forum* was only the first in a series of developments that suggested that the Council had reached the limits of its power. New voices of white protest as well as calls for moderation began to surface in 1963, shattering the façade of unity that the Council had claimed for years. These fractures grew in response to a burgeoning civil rights movement in Mississippi, one that was rooted in local activism and aided by national organizations that had gained experience in other parts of the South. White fears of local black protest had driven the Council's popularity in 1954 and 1955, but by 1963, the wave of civil rights campaigns across the South and the growing demands for congressional legislation created an environment that pulled the Council's focus further away from Mississippi and toward national issues.

The Council's attention to national concerns was not sudden. When the organization moved *Forum* to Washington, DC, in 1958 it did so in hopes of finding a diverse collection of allies, especially outside of the

South, who would find common cause with the segregationist defense. That objective was the brainchild of the Council's most influential administrator, William J. Simmons. As the Council's influence in Mississippi waned, it was Simmons who kept it afloat. He did so by pulling the Council's focus even further away from Mississippi and into national networks of white supremacy and conservatism, further jeopardizing Sovereignty Commission funding and increasing the need to find funding from other sources.

Simmons's public battle with Erle Johnston, over Johnston's public support for practical segregation in lieu of Council allegiance, drew attention to his looming influence over the state legislature and the Sovereignty Commission. While Simmons frequently denied that he held such authority over Mississippi's elected officials, the perception of his power was something quite different. Erle Johnston's oft-quoted branding of Bill Simmons as "the Rajah of Race" and "Mr. Citizens' Council" underscored the infamy of the Council leader, a fact that by 1963 had begun to overshadow the organization itself.[1]

In January 1963, the Memphis daily newspaper *The Commercial Appeal* ran a two-page story on Simmons, profiling his reputation in the state capital as well as his response to rumors about his influence. In the article, reporter William B. Street described Simmons as "one of Mississippi's most talked about people," though few Mississippians would recognize him if they passed him on the street. Articulate and well presented with a smile that "comes readily to his lips, seldom to his eyes," Simmons's disarming demeanor was a significant part of his success. His role in the Council movement, according to the article, was "little known" outside of political circles and other Council leaders, but within those groups his power remained unchecked. Street quoted an unidentified Jackson businessman who admitted that the Council had grown too powerful but knew that speaking against the Council would leave him branded as "a moderate, an integrationist, even a communist." Rumors of Simmons's influence over Governor Barnett, his attempt to get Erle Johnston fired from the Sovereignty Commission, and phone calls to a local Jackson business regarding the firing of black employees all appeared in Street's profile, as did Simmons's denial that he had any influence over administrative or economic matters.[2]

Similar descriptions peppered other profiles of resistance in Mississippi. In his presidential address to the Southern Historical Association in 1964, historian James Silver, author of *Mississippi: The Closed Society*, described a legislator's reaction to Bill Simmons's nearly constant presence in the state capitol during legislative sessions, declaring it all but impossible to objectively consider any bill without fear of the Council leader's "hot eyes" watching, ready to apply an "integrationist tag" to anyone who deviated from the Council's position.[3] Journalist Bill Minor, reflecting on his coverage of the civil rights years in Mississippi, conceded the impact of Simmons's presence but recognized his motives as far more calculating. He described Simmons as the "theoretician" of the Council, a "semi-intellectual" who provided "the spark of doctrinal genius" the organization needed to grow beyond its birth issue.[4]

Simmons's investment in the Mississippi Council movement is critical to understanding why the Mississippi Council structure remained intact while organizations in other states withered. No other resistance leader had the foresight and ambition that Simmons held. He was, at his core, a salesman, but unlike traditional southern race-baiters, he was not a politician peddling to the masses. His audience consisted of political leaders, local media outlets, and members of the business community in Jackson, individuals who knew enough to be skeptical of his tactics but had too much to lose to discount him altogether. Simmons believed it was among elite whites that the campaign would be won or lost. In recalling the first months of organizing the Jackson chapter, Simmons reflected that he sought to organize from "the top down" and to connect segregation to a network of similar issues to counteract the tendency of white southerners to isolate themselves into "places for lonely hearts."[5] His flair for intellectual engagement appealed to educated whites who craved an ideological home at a time when white supremacy was becoming less acceptable.

By 1963, Bill Simmons *was* the Citizens' Council. His editorship of *The Citizen* cultivated the language of resistance and connected readers with a community of like-minded organizations and individuals. *Forum,* a program almost wholly attributed to Simmons's leadership and maintenance, provided a platform for public figures eager to market their message to a broader audience, further embedding the Council movement within conservative politics. Publicity surrounding the Council, its principles, and its objectives came as a result of Bill Simmons's careful attention to marketing. The power that yielded, by 1963, was more closely identified with Simmons than it was with the Citizens' Council as an organization. And as the organization lost power, Simmons's leadership became especially critical to keeping the movement alive.[6]

William J. Simmons was born in Utica, a farming community a few miles south of Jackson, but a fire in 1925 forced the family to relocate to Jackson, where Simmons's father continued his career as a banker. Simmons graduated from Central High School in 1933, one year early, and spent some time as a student at Millsaps College before transferring and graduating from Mississippi College, a private Baptist college in Clinton, Mississippi, south of Jackson. Shortly after his graduation, he spent two years in Tours, France, studying French literature at the Institute of Touraine, where he was when World War II began. After a brief return to the United States in 1940, he departed for the West Indies. While in Trinidad, Simmons connected with the Royal Engineers, serving as chief draftsman for the British West Indian Command before he joined the Trinidad Volunteers and designed observation posts for ports on the island. After Pearl Harbor, he enlisted in the US Navy, where he signed up for deck officer's training before being discharged. As Simmons gained notoriety for his leadership role in the Council, rumors circulated that he had been a Nazi sympathizer, a fact that served as the motivation behind his discharge. Simmons consistently denied the accusation, attributing his discharge to a history of heat strokes during his time in Trinidad.[7]

In lieu of combat duty, Simmons traveled around during World War II, accepting a clerical position with the State Department in 1945, an experience that he described as "an overdose of the liberal point of view . . . devoid of any reality." He left his position to work with a high school friend who owned an airline, South Central Air Transport (later Gulf Airways), which specialized in transporting livestock. The venture never found stability, however, and Simmons soon moved into the natural gas industry in Lake Charles, Louisiana, where he remained for four years before starting his own produce brokerage business, a move that brought him back to Jackson shortly before the Dixiecrat revolt began to take shape in 1948.[8]

After several career starts in various fields, Simmons found his life's work in the fight to maintain segregation. Initially attracted to the states' rights movement, his investment in Council work lasted until the Council's demise in 1989. He described himself as an "unreconstructed" southerner with a great deal of admiration for Confederate leaders like Robert E. Lee, whose portrait hung alongside that of Stonewall Jackson in the Citizens' Council offices in downtown Jackson. Simmons's nostalgia, however, was not rooted in the Old South myths of cotton fields and hoop skirts. He considered the golden era in southern history to be the years from 1876 to a "few years prior to the Supreme Court decision in 1954." This period, of course, represented the years that followed Reconstruction, during which time the white South reasserted its dominance over black southerners through disfranchisement and legal segregation. Simmons's admiration for that period is instructive in understanding his strategy toward the Council. He considered the Council's work to be a modern version of the Mississippi Plan, a comparison that referenced the Democratic takeover in 1875 which initiated the end of the Republican Party and black voting in the state. The unity among whites across the South during that period, he believed, was misunderstood as aggression against black southerners instead of a defense of the white race. But his respect for the White League in Louisiana, an organization responsible for multiple acts of violence against Republican voters, black and white, suggests the superficiality of his claims (and thus, the Council's) that the Council was not a driver of violence in the state. For Simmons, the objective always took priority over the tactic. At his very center lay a commitment to white supremacy that overshadowed any misgivings he may have had about consequences.[9]

Simmons's exposure to the multiracial populations in the Caribbean convinced him that integration created chaos and left behind "in-betweens" who could claim neither white nor black identity and thus were isolated from both communities. Throughout his career, he maintained that racial characteristics defined the talents of every ethnic group, a point he reiterated in the multiple speeches and interviews he gave on behalf of the Council. In truth, he claimed sympathy for the Nation of Islam's position on racial coexistence. The only real solution, he explained in an interview in 1962, was the establishment of "a Negro state." Nothing short of a South African system that required physical separation of the races would work.[10]

Simmons's influence in the Council was felt more than it was seen. Just as Street's profile of him indicated, Simmons denied that he held sway over anyone in state government or in the business community. His accusers could rarely connect him directly to the character attacks that seemed to follow anything less than complete compliance with his recommendations. His dispute with Erle Johnston was an exception in that regard. In his monthly reports to the Sovereignty Commission, his tone remained grateful and cooperative, never openly combative, even when the two organizations were at their most estranged, evidence of his dependency on the agency for funding support.

Simmons's leadership was critical to maintaining financial solvency for *Forum* and the various travel expenses that accrued from the speeches he gave, but it did little for the rest of the Council organization. The Association of Citizens' Councils of Mississippi struggled to maintain the resources necessary to circulate literature and host speakers for its events. The state association hoped to exploit "the sentiment of resentment" in the wake of the Meredith crisis, targeting "those of wealth and position" in their fund-raising mailings.[11] Instead, the failed attempt to avoid a federal court order weakened the Council's position and, in the months that followed, a series of challenges arose that suggested the organization's inability to maintain stability in Mississippi.[12]

The first of these challenges came from twenty-eight young Methodist ministers, all of them native Mississippians serving in their home state. The "Born of Conviction" statement appeared in the January 1963 issue of the *Mississippi Methodist Advocate*. In the wake of the Meredith controversy, the North Mississippi Methodist Conference (the district to which Oxford belonged) endorsed the position that the churches were responsible for the failures in moral leadership that created an environment in which the Ole Miss riots would occur. Similar statements came from pastors of various denominations throughout the state, all of them regretful for the church's silence and its role in sanctioning racially motivated violence. But the continued silence of Bishop Marvin Franklin, the supervising bishop for the state, was noticeable. For young ministers in the state who wished to shore up unified support within Mississippi for the pro-integration position of the national Methodist Church, Franklin's silence was a problem.[13]

Citing the "grave crises precipitated by racial discord," "Born of Conviction" set forth a statement of the ministers' moral convictions that reflected the principles found in the 1960 Methodist Book of Discipline. Included in those principles was a confirmation of the brotherhood of man and discouragement of discrimination based on race, color, or creed. The statement unequivocally asserted the ministers' support of public schools, their opposition to tax-supported private schools, and their commitment to freedom in the pulpit. In their final point the ministers affirmed their continued opposition to communism, undoubtedly an answer to persistent accusations about the Methodist Church's suspicious connections.[14]

"Born of Conviction" was a tame assertion of moderation from a group of ministers vexed by the schism in their church, but in Mississippi it was tantamount to defection. Suspicions about Mississippi Methodists and their ties to a national church association that had declared its support of equality were borne out after the statement circulated through various media channels in the state. Three ministers who signed the statement found themselves promptly voted out of their congregations. Other congregants urged their ministers to recant. Some of the young ministers faced pressure to resign. All of them experienced ostracism in their communities.[15]

In a sharp departure from its history, the Council did not officially respond to "Born of Conviction." The organization's commitment to maintaining a collection of civic leaders from the ranks of the elite made ministers especially coveted as members. The Jackson Citizens' Council included among its most prominent members ministers from all of the major Protestant denominations in the city—Baptist, Methodist, and Presbyterian. The organization had a history of indicting religious institutions for their ambivalence about integration, and the Methodist church was a favorite Council target. The Millsaps College controversy in 1958, for example, grew out of a lecture questioning the relationship between segregation and Christianity. The publicity it received from the Citizens' Council spread quickly, forcing congregations to be skeptical of guest pastors from outside of the state who might be advocates of liberal theology and supporters of integration. In *Forum*'s first year of production, when it was still recorded in Jackson, local laymen and Council members visited the show to discuss church literature and the threatening trends of integration in children's devotionals.[16]

But when "Born of Conviction" appeared in January 1963, it was not the Council that guided the backlash. Another organization, the Mississippi Association of Methodist Ministers and Laymen (MAMML), stepped in and articulated a response that mirrored Council rhetoric in its accusations. Just as the Jackson Citizens' Council was a reinvigorated version of the Dixiecrat revolt, MAMML was a reorganization of the Voluntary Committee of Christian Laymen, a group formed in 1950 to protect the integrity of southern Methodists after the unification with northern churches in 1939. The organization went as far as submitting legislation that would enable local churches to split from their national denominations while maintaining control over their local church property, a bill that successfully passed both the House and State Senate in 1960. MAMML's list of members could easily be mistaken for a list of Jackson Citizens' Council leaders. Especially notable were Medford Evans, Council advisor and one of its most touted intellectuals; Ellis Wright, who led the charges against Millsaps in 1958; and attorney John Satterfield, who would later lead a fight with Senator Eastland to defeat the Civil Rights Act of 1964.[17]

The Citizens' Council shared MAMML's concerns about northern influence over Methodist churches in the South and the vulnerabilities it created within the segregationist bulwark. *Forum* regularly featured Meyers Lowman on its program, director of Circuit Riders, Inc., an extreme right anticommunist organization committed to exposing communist infiltration into religious denominations. Lowman was especially fixated on the Methodist Church.[18] He visited *Forum* twenty times, from 1961 to 1966, placing him among the most frequent guests. One of Lowman's more famous accusations was his statement that over 2,000 Methodist ministers had proven connections to communist or communist-supported activities, more than in any other Protestant denomination.[19]

MAMML issued its official response to "Born of Conviction" with a statement of its own in its monthly publication, *Information Bulletin,* entitled, "A Methodist Declaration of Conscience on Racial Segregation." Its author, Dr. Medford Evans, was a member of MAMML and a rising star in the Citizens' Council. With a PhD from Yale University, Evans brought a certain amount of sophistication to the white resistance movement in Mississippi. His résumé included a position as the chief of security training for the Atomic Energy Commission during World War II, and he later wrote a book about the development of the atomic bomb. His declared area of expertise involved communist infiltration, especially in the South. He was also a contributor to *Human Events,* a position that placed him firmly within the anticommunist strand of the conservative movement.[20]

In a statement three times the length of "Born of Conviction," Evans decried the hierarchy of the Methodist church and championed individualism as a guide for church governance, an argument that mirrored both states' rights ideology and Sunbelt conservativism. Claiming John Wesley's rejection of ecclesiastical authority as the definitive model for religious individualism, he saw in the "Born of Conviction" statement evidence that too many clergy had become "servile toward the episcopacy and supercilious toward the laity." The church, in Evans's perspective, was becoming an instrument of social revolution, and though freedom of the pulpit was not a principle with which he disagreed, he urged his readers to understand that consequences emanated from that freedom, especially regarding continued congregant support. Evans understood that the Meredith crisis lay behind the young ministers' statement of conscience, but he cautioned them against narrowly interpreting the events surrounding the actions of "an eccentric individual" as a moral call to action. Instead, he urged them to consider the desegregation of Ole Miss as only one event in a sinister plot to "warp the judgment of our governmental, academic, and ecclesiastical leadership." One need only look to events in the Congo, he argued, to understand how such seemingly minor occurrences wore down the consciences of white intellectuals until they believed, quite erroneously, that "all races are the same."[21]

Evans's statement emphasized the specter of worldwide communism and black domination as a tool to draw attention away from the shock of violence and rebellion that the Ole Miss riots conjured. The ministers' statement signified the kind of alarmed reaction that could threaten white solidarity. Evans countered that impulse by locating James Meredith within a series of global revolutions. In short, he urged white Mississippians to consider the wider consequences of consulting their consciences about local violence in lieu of considering Ole Miss as only one field of battle that, if lost, would bring white Mississippians closer to black rule. In doing so, he asked his readers to defy local ministers who evidenced a crisis of conscience about racial discrimination in the state or white violence that developed as a result of challenges to that discrimination. To better express the will of the people, Evans suggested that each Methodist congregation take a referendum, through secret ballot, on the issue of segregation in order to leverage popular sentiment against the authority of moderate ministers.[22] Whether upon Evans's advice or from internal pressures from their congregations, seventeen of the twenty-eight signors of "Born of Conviction" were in different churches within six months. A year later, eighteen had left the state altogether.[23]

MAMML's response to "Born of Conviction" and the subsequent resignations and reassignments were evidence that the Council was not the only organization acting to suppress dissent. It is possible that the Council deliberately delegated official response to "Born of Conviction" to MAMML as a way to distance itself from another controversial slander campaign at a time when the organization was becoming less popular and losing state funding. There is no evidence of that connection except shared ideology and membership. It is not entirely clear, either, that MAMML's response was wholly or even mostly responsible for the backlash to the "Born of Conviction" ministers. The Council had, from its earliest days, aligned religious-based racial reform with liberalism. No denomination was safe from the organization's criticism. In equal measure, Baptist, Lutheran, Presbyterian, and Catholic ministers who suggested support for integration as a Christian mandate found themselves accused of misrepresenting biblical scripture and divine intent for racial separation. Worse, they were labeled "liberals," "socialists," "one-worlders," and "do-gooders," epithets that aligned their ideology with the forces of communism. At its heart, the Council's embrace of religion as a defense for segregation was rooted in the evangelical strand of Christianity that was thriving in the Sunbelt. That particular thread of religious fervor, deeply conservative and committed to conversion, stood in opposition to more progressive religious movements committed to racial reform.[24]

In short, the Council's rhetoric about threats to segregation, whether secular or sectarian, had matured over the course of several years. It had become so deeply embedded that white reaction to dissent was nearly automatic and followed a particular pattern. White resistance activism, whether within the Council organization or not, was broad and deep and, regardless of the Council's popularity at any given moment, did not wholly depend on the organization's presence to thrive. The Citizens' Council's visibility in Mississippi mattered less than the paradigm of resistance it had created.

In MAMML's reaction to "Born of Conviction," Medford Evans urged white Mississippians to see James Meredith within the context of global events, all of which pointed to racial upheavals. That perspective was a common one for the Council in 1963. In its monthly publication, *The Citizen,* and on *Forum,* global events took priority over local civil rights challenges, even as civil rights activity in Mississippi continued to escalate and white dissent grew.

The temporal proximity of federal occupation of the University of Mississippi and the Cuban missile crisis provided an ideal connection between the local crisis and the Council's claims about communist involvement in racial agitations. Within three weeks of the events in Oxford the Kennedy administration faced another immediate threat, this one to national security. The discovery of missile sites in Cuba, ninety miles from the coast of Florida, brought the United States to a state of brinkmanship with the Soviet Union. The eventual disarmament and restoration of stability between the two countries was a victory for Americans terrified by the prospect of nuclear war, but for conservatives and anticommunist hardliners, Kennedy's management of the situation was a missed opportunity to prove American superiority.

Forum featured seventeen consecutive programs on the Cuban situation in early 1963, months after the standoff ended but coinciding with MAMML's reaction to the "Born of Conviction" statement. Guests repeatedly expressed their disappointment in Kennedy's handling of the situation, reading it as another example of the protracted weakening of

American foreign policy toward communism, an appeasement approach that ensured future standoffs.[25] In addition to foreign affairs, *Forum* returned to its earlier emphasis on communism, a topic it had begun to supplant with conservative themes in 1962.[26] Bill Simmons, in his monthly report to the Sovereignty Commission, described this series of programs as an attempt to be responsive to the issue "uppermost on the minds of Americans . . . as posing the most acute threat to our national survival." The sharp contrast between the weakness of Kennedy's position toward Cuba and his "aggressive action in Mississippi" was, to Simmons, further justification of the emphasis on foreign policy in *Forum*'s most recent broadcasts.[27]

With half of its programming dedicated to foreign affairs and communism in 1963, a year that saw more civil rights activity in Mississippi than any other thus far, *Forum*'s focus was revelatory of its connections with political figures committed to their own agendas. Mississippi's senior senator, John Stennis, chaired the Senate Preparedness Subcommittee, the investigative committee charged with gathering intelligence on the missile crisis and assessing the decision-making process. His position on the committee may have held some influence over Bill Simmons and host Dick Morphew as they scheduled guests. Other guests like William Cramer (Florida), James Utt (California), and Senator John Tower (Texas) were all Republicans and returning guests to the show. Their *Forum* appearances helped connect white resistance to southern Republicanism, a nascent movement in 1963 but one that would take a more visible form in the figure of Arizona senator Barry Goldwater, the 1964 Republican presidential nominee. Three years earlier, Goldwater's *Conscience of a Conservative* evidenced the convergence of aggressive foreign policy, individualism, and moral responsibility into a conservative ideology that had special resonance on the West Coast. Southern Californians embraced Goldwater's unapologetic support for displays of American superiority on foreign fields, a position that won him criticism from other groups who considered him too "trigger happy" to be president. His prioritization of states' rights over civil rights and his opposition to government intervention in education would appeal to white southerners, earning him 78 percent of Mississippi's popular vote in 1964.[28]

The diversity of *Forum*'s guests also helped make the case for its continued funding. Simmons saw *Forum* guests as important salesmen for the program. In his April 1963 report, he took pains to describe the way in which particular guests connected with *Forum*'s mission, their reputations among constituents and colleagues, and their success in advertising the program to their state's television and radio stations. All of this, according to Simmons, was to great effect, as the program had received requests for its Cuba programs from over 200 stations, making a total of 550 stations carrying *Forum* in the month of March. In addition to monthly numbers, Simmons also indicated growing international interest in *Forum*, claiming that stations in the British Isles and in South Africa had requested copies of programs.[29]

But as Simmons touted the successes of the Council's Washington program, civil rights activism in Mississippi finally found a foothold. Meredith's successful integration emboldened young activists throughout the state to gather more support and organize more direct challenges to segregation, a reaction that Erle Johnston described as "openly . . . exuberant."

In Jackson, however, the movement depended almost entirely upon college students and their mentors. Members of the black business community were reluctant to risk their livelihood to stand against white supremacy in a city where the Council wielded the most influence. The presence of Tougaloo and Jackson State College, as well as the state's NAACP headquarters, provided the structure and support to help grow a local movement, but a sustained direct action campaign in Jackson remained elusive. The NAACP was reluctant to throw its full financial support behind a campaign that was sure to yield thousands of arrests, possibly to no beneficial end. As other areas of the state began to break open, however, Medgar Evers, Mississippi's field secretary, and other activists in Jackson grew impatient as they watched other civil rights organizations like SNCC and CORE win the trust and commitment of black Mississippians while the NAACP clung to its integration petitions and lawsuits.

The organization's perspective began to change in April, however, when the confrontation between marchers and white law enforcement in Birmingham drew an unprecedented amount of national media coverage for its brutality and for the dynamism of Martin Luther King Jr., who represented the Southern Christian Leadership Conference (SCLC). The NAACP had good reason to believe that Jackson was next in the SCLC's direct action campaign. The organization had a number of allies in Mississippi, including the state's NAACP president Aaron Henry, and a number of SCLC members, Reverend Fred Shuttlesworth among them, had already invested money in the Mississippi movement. By May, the Birmingham campaign showed signs of victory, and the NAACP national office pledged its financial resources to support a sustained direct-action campaign in Jackson.[30]

The support of the national office was a major turning point for the Jackson Movement. A collection of demands and a publicity campaign was already well under way when the NAACP officially gave its blessing. On May 13, 1963, John Salter and Medgar Evers, with the cooperation of the Jackson Youth Council and North Jackson Youth Council, drafted and sent a letter to Mayor Allen Thompson, the Mississippi Bank Association, the Junior Chamber of Commerce, the Jackson Chamber of Commerce, the Mississippi Economic Council, and the Downtown Jackson Association, detailing their determination to "put an end to all forms of racial discrimination in Jackson" through a "selective buying" campaign. The boycott, mostly focused on the downtown shopping district on Capitol Street, would last until complete desegregation of public facilities occurred.[31]

Mayor Thompson responded as expected, addressing Jacksonians over television and radio, assuring them that there was no better city for blacks than Jackson, where they were appreciated and protected. Racial agitators, he declared, would not create chaos in an otherwise peaceful city. A few days later, Medgar Evers stood before the television cameras at WLBT, the location of the first *Forum* broadcast, and directly rebutted the mayor's remarks, describing the unbearable conditions black Jacksonians endured at the hands of white law enforcement, white politicians, and poorly funded schools. He concluded his address with an appeal to the "silent, responsible citizens of the white community who know that a victory for democracy in Jackson will be a victory for democracy everywhere."[32] With that statement, Evers showed his deep understanding of the city's greatest weakness in the fight against segregation.

The Jackson Movement's greatest impact came on the first day of demonstrations. On May 28, a group of Tougaloo students and faculty, including John Salter, took their seat at the Woolworth's lunch counter as a challenge to its whites-only policy. After white students poured in from a nearby high school, the demonstrators withstood two hours of threats and assaults. The images of stone-still activists perched on stools, covered in condiments and surrounded by angry white youth, would become one of the most recognized moments in the civil rights movement. It also transformed the protest into a full-fledged movement.[33]

Over the next several days as demonstrations continued, police arrested hundreds and the *Clarion-Ledger,* the state's leading newspaper, covered story after story, tracking the status of activity in the Jackson area. Next to reports on demonstrations and arrests stood editorials assuring unity and urging calm in the midst of chaos. The Jackson Citizens' Council issued its own statement, quoted in full text in the *Clarion-Ledger.* In it, the Council reminded readers that unity had been its purpose since its founding. "We have been trying," the statement read, "to inform our people of the need for unity of purpose and action in time of crisis. Having grown to be the largest organization in Jackson we are determined to resist integration by every lawful means." The Council urged full support for local law enforcement and the mayor, lest Jacksonians find their city under federal occupation.[34]

In addition to the Jackson Council's press release, the Council's monthly magazine, *The Citizen,* featured a panel interview among Simmons, *Forum* host Dick Morphew, and Dr. Medford Evans, now a "full-time consultant for the Council." During the course of the interview, the three men discussed the Jackson Movement, a surprising display of acknowledgement for Council leaders who largely ignored local challenges unless they could be nationally marketed. Evans's purported expertise on anticommunism naturally drove the discussion into the connections between civil rights challenges in Mississippi and the communist agenda, associating the Jackson Movement with a "world-wide racial revolution . . . an attack on the United States and on world civilizations as we have known it." But the discussion did not read like a typical sublimation of race to global politics. Simmons placed great emphasis on the need for continued white support of the mayor and other city officials, arguing that integration only came to cities when their leaders panicked and compromised. Simmons praised the "good sense" and restraint of law enforcement and white citizens, an accomplishment achieved under conditions of "extreme provocation." Jackson, he reassured his fellow panelists, was presenting a "completely solid front."[35]

The racial strife in Jackson was an open challenge to the Council's collective economic power. When Evers and Salter drafted the letter to Mayor Thompson and the leading civic organizations in Jackson, it could have been addressed to the Jackson Citizens' Council, considering its representation in organizations like the Chamber of Commerce and the Downtown Jackson Development Association. The Capitol Street boycott was a direct assault on white business interests in Jackson, a rich field for Council membership. It was that deep infiltration of the political and business elite, however, that enabled Council leaders to remain invisible even as their influence could be seen in the mayor's decision-making.

Mayor Thompson refused to meet with Medgar Evers or John Salter, selecting representatives of the black community not associated with the Jackson Movement and weakening the position of the NAACP in achieving its demands. As arrests increased, Jackson police removed detainees to the Mississippi state fairgrounds, where they stayed until bond was posted. In answer to criticisms of the inhumane facilities at the fairgrounds, Thompson vowed to support a bond bill to construct more jails, a taunt meant to convey his indefatigable commitment to stopping the demonstrations. Governor Barnett praised Thompson's handling of the continued demonstrations and demands for desegregation, and rumors circulated about a gubernatorial run for Thompson.[36]

As the mayor stonewalled, events outside of Jackson were accelerating at a rapid pace. On June 5, the University of Mississippi admitted its second black student, Cleveland McDowell. Despite efforts to obstruct his enrollment, Governor Barnett called it "unwise and futile . . . to enter into a physical or shooting combat with the United States army." In Alabama, Governor George Wallace's efforts to forestall integration at the University of Alabama reached a necessary end. These events stood adjacent to news of the Jackson protests and praise for Thompson, creating a rapidly shifting environment for Jacksonians. Locally, it seemed the status quo might survive, but only a few hours to the north and to the east, change was already visible. On June 11, 1963, President Kennedy addressed the nation to announce his full support for sweeping civil rights legislation.[37] A few hours later, Medgar Evers, the first full-time NAACP field secretary for the state of Mississippi and leader of the Jackson Movement, lay in his driveway within minutes of death, shot at the hands of a member of the Greenwood Citizens' Council, Byron de la Beckwith.[38]

Mayor Thompson, Governor Barnett, and other prominent members of the Citizens' Council who held public positions decried Evers's murder, vowing to apprehend the responsible party through all reasonable efforts. It is unclear how soon they realized that one of their own members was the chief suspect, but the Council organization never released any official statement about Beckwith's membership in the movement, though the *Clarion-Ledger*'s article announcing his arrest described him as "one of the first to join the Citizens' Council."[39] Bill Minor, a veteran Mississippi journalist who closely covered the civil rights movement in the state, later recalled that Beckwith was a major admirer of the Citizens' Council. In a letter to the *Commercial Appeal* in 1958, Beckwith wrote as much, stating, "If there is anything bestowed upon us since the birth of Christ any better for the white race and our nation than the Citizens Council, then God must have kept it up in heaven for Himself."[40]

Whatever the organization's knowledge of Beckwith, his politics and his involvement with Evers's murder, at the very least he stands as an example of the seeds that the Council movement sowed among its constituents. Despite its mission to cultivate elite leaders in lieu of Klan-like organizations, the rhetoric of the movement, its race-baiting literature, and its endorsement by the most powerful and visible leaders in Mississippi was a deadly combination in a state where working-class whites frequently heard their leaders describe civil rights gains as threats to their livelihood and status. Pulitzer Prize–winning writer and Jackson native Eudora Welty described in astonishing detail the profile of Evers's killer, hours after the murder and days before Beckwith was identified as a suspect. In "Where Is the Voice Coming From?," a short story published in the *New Yorker* less than a month after the murder, Welty drew a portrait of a poor, undereducated white man, emasculated as he watches a black man give an eloquent speech on the local news station. In her description of the killer's thought process, the intricacies of class and race in Mississippi become clear, an indication of the rural soil in which the Citizens' Council grew.[41]

Greenwood, a moderate-sized town in the Delta, sat in the heartland of the Council movement. Only a few miles away from the organization's birthplace in Indianola, it served as the headquarters for the state association and exemplified the local power of a white minority united in their commitment to put down black mobility. Greenwood had drawn attention in 1962 for the widespread presence of deep poverty within the black community. And it won the attention of the Kennedy administration when white leaders withheld government assistance as punishment for local organizing efforts in cooperation with COFO activists.

Beckwith would have seen those events unfold in his hometown, and the development of visible organizing in Jackson by the end of 1962, alongside James Meredith's admission to the University of Mississippi, undoubtedly rattled his faith in the Council's leadership. Beckwith, who later boasted that he was an "honorary life member" of the Citizens' Councils of America, had a keen sense of the organization's function as early as 1957. In a letter he wrote to the *Jackson Daily News* he seemed to be answering a question about the Council's purpose, evidence perhaps of continued ambiguity about the organization in its first few years of existence. Beckwith thought highly of the organization. He identified it as "the catalyst" of a larger movement that would ultimately save the nation from "mongrelization, totalitarianism and judicial dictatorship." He saw the Council as a connection between the typical white citizen and the men elected into power. "Politicians don't lead," he stated, "they follow. They find out which way the people are going and then they run get in front of them and lead them there. The Citizen's Council showed them which way the people were going. The Citizen's Council destroyed the integrationist doctrine of inevitability."[42]

In their interviews with Beckwith's acquaintances in Greenwood, Jackson police noted a general impression among people who knew him that he was nice enough, but not someone with whom you wanted to get involved in a conversation. Coworkers and neighbors alike noted that he easily became agitated on the topic of integration, and he was frequently described as "radical" on the race question. This description among Greenwood residents is notable, considering the area's commitment to the Council. Beckwith, somehow, stood out as too extreme, even in the midst of the state's most loyal segregationists.[43]

But police investigations also noted that despite the almost universal sentiment that Beckwith's position on race was comparatively extreme, even for the Delta, the very same people assured his innocence. In fact, a few months after the first round of interviews, police officers noted a distinct change in the way that the community had closed ranks around him. In the days and weeks following Evers's murder, interview subjects had been forthcoming about Beckwith's views on race. By January, however, a report described an environment where those same people seemed to feel like "it would be better not to say any thing [sic]." Investigators speculated that this might be due to the fact that most of them now believed him to be guilty. One report noted the closing remarks of Greenwood's mayor as he left an interview with the investigating officers: "Not much more was said in regards to Beckwith but when the Mayor started to leave he turned and said for us not to find too much on Beckwith while in Greenwood."[44]

The Council's involvement with Beckwith's defense was not difficult to detect. His attorney, Hardy Lott, was a former president of the local Citizens' Council. Two Greenwood police officers, Hollis Cresswell and James Holly, provided Beckwith with an alibi at his first two trials, a fact they never shared with Jackson police during their investigation in the months following the murder. Though the Council name was never attached to the effort, a number of Council members led a fund-raising effort to pay Beckwith's attorneys. The Sovereignty Commission provided extra insurance for Beckwith's freedom by investigating potential jurors to aid in jury selection. There was more visible support as well. Ross Barnett and General Edwin Walker, both recognized as Council supporters, attended Beckwith's trial in January 1964, shaking his hand and hugging him.[45]

Nothing better exemplifies the Council's complicated identity than its connection with the Evers murder. Beckwith could have been acting on his own, but the way in which Council leaders in Greenwood worked in his defense reflects Simmons's commitment to objectives over tactics. To allow justice to proceed uninterrupted against Beckwith would have signaled a weakening in white supremacy's defense. Even if the Council purportedly abhorred violence, its leaders understood that, in some ways, it was inevitable among a membership base that included "radicals" like Beckwith. In fact, that reality underscored the Council's insistence that no civil rights challenges could be allowed to develop without consequence. At the same time, the Council's protection toward Beckwith threatened to work against the Council in its national campaigns.

In its official capacity, the Council pursued business as usual. Council activities seemed to venture further and further away from the strife in Mississippi as the Evers murder investigation moved closer to Beckwith. In the summer and fall of 1963, the Council's message emphasized its growing popularity outside of the South through its "Operation Information" project. In October, the Citizens' Councils of America hosted a leadership conference in Jackson where Council administrators detailed the breadth of activities overseen by the Council in 1963. Reports included the multiple invitations given Bill Simmons and other Council representatives to give speeches to college campuses and appearances on various television programs to discuss the race question. In addition to its speaking engagements, the Council claimed *Forum* appeared on more than 1,500 stations in all fifty states, making it "the number one public-affairs series . . . used by more stations than any other public-affairs program." But membership in the organization and the dues that came with it remained a major concern. *Forum* host and Council administrator Dick Morphew, in his speech to the leadership conference in Jackson, explained that the funding structure allocated 20 percent of monthly dues for Operation Information (i.e., *Forum*), a model he compared to missionary work.[46]

Council activities, as evidenced through the new Operation Information series, drifted more and more toward ideology and away from issue-driven campaigning at a critical moment in the civil rights movement. The violence in Birmingham and Medgar Evers's murder gave urgency to President Kennedy's demand for civil rights legislation. In Mississippi, the prospect of congressional legislation threatened to unravel the entire fabric of resistance, which had largely rested upon the constitutionality of the Supreme Court's desegregation decision. Federal legislation, under that interpretation, would be much more legitimate. But with the

Council's priorities elsewhere, the organized challenge to pending civil rights legislation came from an entirely new organization, the Coordinating Committee for Fundamental American Freedoms (CCFAF).

In a meeting in Washington, DC, in June 1963, Senator James Eastland, Sovereignty Commission director Erle Johnston, attorney John Satterfield, and Hugh White Jr., a leader in Virginia's resistance movement and son of Hugh White (governor of Mississippi from 1951 to 1955), met to discuss a national campaign to defeat the civil rights bill pending in Congress.[47] The coordinator for the committee, John Satterfield, was a longtime supporter of the Citizens' Council. He had been a critical advocate for the Council's position towards Millsaps in 1958 and had drafted the bill enabling tax money to support the organization's educational activities.[48] Despite his previous connections with the organization, Satterfield did not include any Citizens' Council administrators in the planning of the campaign. The Council had already shown some acumen for fleshing out connections with conservative groups throughout the country, especially in its Cuba broadcasts, but its tendency to attract right-wing radicals and its reputation as a heavy-handed defender of segregation in Mississippi might have proven a liability in a campaign meant to lobby a national following. Recent civil rights activity in Mississippi may have also weakened the Council's reputation as an influential stakeholder. Erle Johnston's ascendance to director of the Sovereignty Commission, in spite of previous efforts to remove him, and his involvement in the CCFAF probably also played into the Council's exclusion. With his approval and Governor Barnett's, the state agency committed $10,000 to the CCFAF, money that could have gone to *Forum* instead. Taken together, all of these factors suggest that the Council's exclusion was deliberate.

The CCFAF followed the same script as the Council in its massive mailing campaigns and in Satterfield's numerous appearances on conservative talk shows like the *Wayne Poucher Show* and *Manion Forum*. It drew donations from a number of conservative organizations as well as business interests who feared the impact of civil rights legislation on employment practices and wage requirements. With offices in Washington and full-time staff members committed to its success, the CCFAF brought to life the threats that had been circulating for years, namely, that civil rights legislation would reach far beyond racial equality into pocketbooks, real estate markets, human resources departments, and education.[49]

The CCFAF had an ally in the Virginia Commission on Constitutional Government (CCG), a state agency created in 1958 to preserve segregation and draw in northern allies. Committed to conservative issues like fiscal accountability and law and order, the CCG, from its inception, wished to avoid reactive approaches to *Brown* that were sure to incite rebellion by baiting the deepest fears of certain groups of white southerners. The CCG's successful alliance with Pennsylvania Republicans in 1962 signified that southern Republican tremors existed prior to 1968 and that, in some cases, it was resistance groups that initiated them.[50] The CCFAF, however, in contrast to its counterpart in Virginia, is unique in its appearance in a Deep South state. As noted earlier, the Council movement existed in Virginia but took a distinctly different form there than it did in Mississippi, where race-baiting literature and an atmosphere of fear penetrated political spheres even as the Council pursued other tactics with venues like *Forum*. The CCFAF abandoned race-baiting altogether, a tacit rejection of the hybrid approach the Citizens' Council embraced as a way to keep grassroots support and elite leadership in balance. Instead, the CCFAF replaced those well-worn tactics with colorblind warnings of economic intrusions and violations of property. In that capacity, the proposed civil rights bill, according to CCFAF literature, sought to do much more than desegregate public accommodations. This approach marked a closer alliance with Sunbelt conservatism than it did with the form of organized resistance that the Council represented.

Despite the fact that the Council was not involved in the CCFAF, it provided a platform to publicize the campaign. It helped distribute the CCFAF's pamphlet, "The Blueprint for Total Federal Regimentation," and during the last few weeks of 1963 and well into 1964, *Forum* featured guest after guest who stood in stark opposition to the pending legislation. John Satterfield and the CCFAF's full-time director, John J. Synon, a protégé of conservative journalist James Kilpatrick, also appeared on the program.[51]

The *Forum* programs that dealt with what would become the Civil Rights Act of 1964 showcased the embrace of colorblind conservatism within the white resistance movement. In pursuit of national allies, leaders of the CCFAF set aside race-baiting language and used economic arguments to draw support from business leaders. In his appearance on *Forum* in 1963, for example, John Synon argued, "this bill . . . is about 10 percent civil rights and the rest is a blueprint for total regimentation . . . the manifestation of a longtime plan to control the economy and actually the lives of the people in this country." Citing threats to union solidarity, individual employment practices, and religious freedom, Synon urged viewers and listeners to contact their senators and ask them not to support "the most frightening bit of legislation that has ever been drafted."[52] John Satterfield reiterated these threats a few weeks later, adding that every homeowner, employer, employee, union member, civil service worker, bank depositor, loan recipient, farmer, parent, voter, Social Security payee, and veteran would find themselves impacted if pending legislation passed. Nothing short of a "federal police state," he predicted, would result from its success.[53]

Throughout all of the broadcasts about pending legislation, guests emphasized that the civil rights bill was not intended to address issues of equality, but rather assured increasing federal oversight. These claims were not a dramatic shift from the way the Council generally spoke about civil rights issues, but they insinuated that for Americans in favor of securing racial equality this bill was not the right fit. Council leaders regularly relied on the cultivation of defiance as a way to maintain support. The incorporation of the CCFAF's campaign objectives within the *Forum* programming schedule, however, marked a subtle difference between issue-driven activism in the CCFAF and the Council's reliance on white supremacy as self-explanatory. For the former, the personal economic impact of civil rights reform provided a tangible understanding of what equality meant for people already empowered: land ownership, autonomy, individualism. All of those values were race-neutral, relieving reluctant whites of any notion they may have had that their opposition to civil rights legislation reflected their racial prejudice. The Council's tactics, in contrast, generally remained unapologetic about the embrace of white supremacy as a natural defense against federal legislation, compliance with judicial decisions, or local civil rights challenges at home. Through *Forum* it entertained a variety of approaches to resisting racial reforms, but it never abandoned its deep belief in white supremacy as its most foundational and consistent principle. But in these programs, George Lewis's identification of the "slow evolution" from defending segregation as natural order to defending it as a critical expression of individual rights, becomes clear.[54]

The CCFAF's efforts failed and President Lyndon Johnson officially signed the Civil Rights Act of 1964 into law on July 2, 1964. But months before its passage, the CCFAF's administrators were already seeking to delve back into the ideology of white supremacy as a more effective strategy. John Satterfield wrote a letter to Mississippi governor Paul B. Johnson Jr. in March, arguing that the recent onslaught of civil rights demonstrations had proven that fundamental racial differences should be clearly articulated in the defense for segregation. Opposition to civil rights demands had consistently relied on arguments that avoided this fact and unwittingly played into the hands of equalitarianism. To Satterfield, the erroneous belief that "'skin is only skin-deep,' that a Negro is simply a white man with a black skin," was a deeply troubling misunderstanding of biological characteristics. To counter that misunderstanding, he proposed a public relations campaign that would emphasize the anthropological "story" of racial difference, using "emerging African nations, their obvious inability to govern themselves, [and] their inherent inadequacies" as an example of where civil rights successes would lead the United States.[55]

Satterfield's proposal to Johnson praised the Citizens' Council's ongoing efforts as "outstanding," describing the Council as "well organized" and "necessary." His proposal should not, he argued, be construed as a replacement for the organization.[56] But Satterfield's emphasis on national networks of conservatism, civic action, media venues, and educational outreach suggested that he saw the Council as a local body of resistance with limited potential for national impact.[57] The messages of the Council and Satterfield's new organization, however, were very similar in their recognition that intellectual unity among white Americans was the only hope for avoiding black gains. For that reason, the new organization must remain disaffiliated from political connections or campaigns as well as steer clear of the "lunatic fringe," something that would make Council cooperation difficult.[58]

What separated these organizations was the delivery method. While the Council had taken advantage of radio and television as media of delivery alongside print campaigns, Satterfield proposed guerilla tactics within existing venues. The following passage from his proposal is telling in this regard:

> No recommendation for the use of radio is submitted. At the outset we should not try to reach the broad spectrum of people, not retail our arguments to the people, directly. In the case of printed media, it is the editors and publishers who are, at the point of our development, the important people. So, we go *through* them—educate them—and accept, as a bonus, the residual benefits to be had from the publication of our arguments. Radio and TV have no such people. They are "show biz," with neither the background nor the desire to evaluate material submitted. They follow the popular trend. They are the eunuchs of thought.[59]

Satterfield's organization sought to revolutionize gatekeepers within the news business, bypassing the general public altogether. His suggestions mirrored early Council objectives, before the organization became public, when it seemed realistic that indirect control and suppression would be enough to prevent change. The embrace of a covert white supremacy campaign, even as Satterfield worked to defeat civil rights legislation through the CCFAF using race-neutral rhetoric, suggests a total abandonment of the grassroots investment that the Citizens' Council had found so critical to its existence. When the CCFAF dissolved in June 1964, John Synon, who directed the organization's office in Washington, DC, immediately shifted his efforts to the Putnam Letters Committee under the leadership of Carleton Putnam, which would "emphasize ethnic differences between the races."[60] Satterfield continued to pursue the establishment of a conservative organization in Washington that would work to infiltrate news outlets and worked closely with the Mississippi State Sovereignty Commission to match donations from "eastern interests" with a stake in making white supremacy a more commonly held ideology, especially in the wake of the Civil Rights Act.[61]

These developments marginalized Council input and moved efforts previously aligned against specific civil rights issues into a campaign for ideological transformation. As the Sovereignty Commission aligned itself with Satterfield's efforts for a Washington office, it requested an increase of funding for "special projects." Probably not coincidentally, *Forum's* monthly allowance was reduced to $2,000, a $2,500 decrease from its payment under Barnett's administration, but those payments ended altogether in December 1964. The appearance of a new organization committed to similar objectives and with committed funding from a state agency signified the prioritization of new initiatives in lieu of Council support.[62]

In addition to losing its power among the state's leaders, the Council's claims of suppressing violence collapsed among the unprecedented escalation of white violence throughout Mississippi in 1964. A report from the Civil Rights Division of the Department of Justice in July listed fifty-two Klan-related incidents across the state, including multiple cross burnings, church burnings, house bombings, beatings, and shootings. Among those events was the disappearance of Michael Schwerner, Andrew Goodman, and Meridian native James Chaney, the three civil rights workers later found shot to death and buried outside of Philadelphia.[63] The influx of civil rights activists that summer, of which Schwerner and Goodman were a part, represented a final breakdown of Mississippi's defense against change. Freedom Summer was proof that the Council's promises were hollow. Voter registration and education campaigns across rural areas of Mississippi made it clear that the organization's heyday had ended. The Council's success in pulling together diverse coalitions of whites in the wake of *Brown* was now being challenged by the very organization that it had contrasted itself with.

Rumors of another group dedicated to resisting the Civil Rights Act began to circulate in the summer of 1964, as well. Organized in May 1963, in Natchez, Americans for the Preservation of the White Race (APWR) pledged "to maintain the traditional heritage of the purposes upon which the United States of America was founded" and "to promote domestic tranquility and solve the problems of the intruder and the agitators that we have been encountered with recently and to provide a common defense against such."[64] Most of the APWR's efforts involved boycotts of businesses that showed signs of complying with the Civil Rights Act, whether by hiring black employees or by targeting black business owners who had some affiliation with the civil rights movement. By the summer of 1964, as civil rights activists migrated around the state, the APWR moved beyond Natchez and prepared to begin a letter-writing campaign to Governor Paul Johnson for the removal of Erle Johnston as director of the Sovereignty Commission. Their demands came in response to Johnston's opposition to the Carthage chapter's plan to begin a white boycott of any businesses in the area caught supplying or patronizing a black-owned business. Johnston's opposition to the boycott came from fears of white division at a time when violence was already escalating in the state and civil rights activity showed no signs of abating.[65]

The increase in Klan activity and the spread of the APWR throughout the state shattered any illusions left about unified white action. The big tent the Council had claimed in its earliest days devolved into its constituent parts, with elites and non-elites migrating into their own organizations. The success of the Civil Rights Act and the continued presence of black activists, both native to and from outside of the state, yielded a variety of responses from white Mississippians that ranged from total compliance to violent backlash. The presence of each seemed to reinforce the other. More moderate whites migrated away from stalwart resistance as Klan-initiated violence spread across the state. In a similar way, whites who comprised the extreme right of the Council's resistance moved into organizations like the APWR or the Klan. Transformations in political circles also became visible. This trend was especially notable in the figure of Governor Paul Johnson who, as Barnett's successor, began his term with a visible commitment to race-baiting campaign promises. In the wake of violence, however, his position dramatically weakened, and his refusal to cooperate with the Citizens' Council's agenda signified a shift in the state's support for organized resistance. In total, unified white resistance fractured beyond repair, and the threats to black safety varied according to local conditions, mirroring the environment in which the Council first exerted its power in 1954 and 1955.[66]

By 1964, the Council's visibility relied on the continued activity of the Jackson chapter, the Citizens' Councils of America's *Forum* broadcasts, and a newly formed Council School Foundation dedicated to creating all-white private schools as a solution to the beginnings of desegregation in Mississippi's public schools. The Jackson Citizens' Council acted in very similar ways to the original Council model, which relied on local white leadership to stave off civil rights activities and, purportedly, violence. In the wake of passage of the Civil Rights Act, the JCC announced the beginnings of a campaign to repeal it and discouraged white Mississippians from "hastening into blind compliance" until the statute made its way into the court system for review. In an ironic twist, the JCC's statement to the *Clarion-Ledger,* the state's leading newspaper, quoted the Thirteenth Amendment's prohibition against involuntary servitude as evidence that a business owner could not be forced to "serve another against his wishes."[67]

The Jackson Council still boasted an impressive collection of the state's most prominent business leaders, but its statement called for white boycotts of any businesses inclined to comply with serving black clients, an action that threatened to severely undermine the financial health of small business owners in the capital city. Pushback to the organization's suggestions was swift. A local restaurant owner and attorney, Howard E. Ross Jr., predicted that compliance with the Council's demands would most assuredly bring steep federal fines and bankruptcy. Aleck Primos, president of the JCC and a local restaurant owner himself, issued another formal statement in response to Ross's, reiterating the necessity of unity: "Our very best hope is for us to all stand together and fight and die if necessary, for most certainly if we do not we will be picked off one by one."[68]

Primos's description of the "one by one" weakening of white resistance was prescient. Beginning in August 1964, thirteen different schools in three districts in Mississippi admitted their first black students. Jackson was among them, with eight of its city schools admitting black students without significant white flight.[69] The reality of these changes drove the Citizens' Councils of America to begin the Council School Foundation, a fund-raising effort to begin a series of Council-backed private schools in the Jackson area, the first of which opened in October 1964 in a private home where classes met until separate facilities were completed in November.[70] It did so at the same time that the APWR chapter in Leake County (one of the school districts that integrated in 1964) opened its first all-white private academy.[71] Both benefited from a newly passed tuition grant law from the Mississippi state legislature that promised $185 to alleviate the costs of private school for white parents.[72]

Despite new investment in what would become a rapidly growing private school movement, the Council's power waned alongside the myriad organizations and white resistance efforts that existed in Mississippi by the fall of 1964, when the reality of change became clear. White unity, if it ever existed, splintered into radical organizations unwilling to accept federal mandates or moderate efforts that pursued limited accommodations through the token desegregation that marked the 1964–1965 public school year.

Forum also showed signs of weakening. The diminishing variety of national political figures who appeared on the show in 1964 was evidence of the Council's occupation of an obsolete position. Council administrators' appearances on *Forum* increased and resembled the program's first year of broadcasting when local Council members were the most frequent guests. But the program strived to maintain national relevance, despite struggles in its home state. Council administrators who visited *Forum* focused on urban unrest in cities outside of the South, and on the nascent private school movement at home.[73]

Despite its efforts to remain relevant, nothing could bring the organization back to life in its home state. While the Jackson chapter stayed relatively active, other chapters fell dormant, and by the end of 1964, the Council's work in Mississippi was limited to its private school program, still very much in the early stages with only one school in Jackson. The mark that the Council left on white resistance in the state, however, was visible in the organization of APWR chapters, the continuing work of the Sovereignty Commission, and increasing violence throughout the state. The Council's persistent influence withered against the wave of defeats that white resistance faced, most especially the success of the Civil Rights Act. But its cultivation of white leadership at the local level and its philosophy of defiance ensured that its tactics would survive without the Council moniker. The inability of the organization to adapt to changing circumstances in Mississippi isolated its leaders from elected officials from whom the Council had once received predictable support. In October, Jackson mayor and former Council member Allen Thompson denounced the Council, claiming, "Not once did they offer to help work out our problems through the courts. . . . They just wanted stand-in-the-door resistance, regardless of the consequences to the city and its citizens."[74] The culture of resistance that the Council reinvigorated in the first few years after *Brown* had clearly become a liability for leaders in the state who sought stability and compromise in light of escalating violence. The Council's unapologetic embrace of white supremacy was persistent, however. Yet, while its tactics at home were less popular and its competitors seemed to multiply, its national prospects improved as the political climate shifted into new configurations of party alliance that welcomed defiance as a permanent fixture within the American political landscape.

CHAPTER 6

FLIGHT AND WHITE REUNION: THE CITIZENS' COUNCIL AFTER 1964

It is no news that people feel alienated and powerless, and believe that
their institutions have abandoned them and even turned on them. But the
difference here is that the people who start and support the new schools
are taking action in a specific way. They are taxing themselves heavily to
open alternative schools, ones that stress their values, their attitudes,
their principles of morality and right. It is no accident that the schools
oppose the thrust of the society as a whole. That is their purpose.
—*The Schools that Fear Built*, 1976

O n May 17, 1965, at the Mississippi State Coliseum in downtown Jackson, George Wallace headlined "White Monday," an event marking
the eleventh anniversary of *Brown v. Board of Education*. The Citizens'
Council captured the events on film, and its coverage opened with the
procession of pallbearers surrounding a casket draped in the Confederate flag. Former Mississippi governors Hugh White (1951–1955) and
Ross Barnett (1959–1963) occupied the stage alongside Wallace and Jim
Clark, the sheriff of Dallas County, Alabama, home of the Selma voting
rights campaign where Clark's forces perpetrated one of the most violent
confrontations of the civil rights movement. The collection of speakers
represented the long trajectory of white southern resistance to the civil
rights campaign, from legislative stopgaps under White, to police brutality under Clark. And Wallace's keynote signified a reinvigoration of white
defiance that would carry resistance into the new post–civil rights era:

Even though we have suffered some loss of battles here, we haven't lost the war yet, because when the American people are sufficiently aroused in sufficient numbers, in my judgment . . . we're going to see some reaction differently on the part of those in public office and not only the states in our own region but those who hold office in other parts of these United States.

With a closing shot of the crowd cheering and "Dixie" playing in the background, a voiceover began: "This is why I'm happy to support the Citizens' Council movement: a united and determined white majority with a responsible and effective leadership can accomplish virtually any goal. Won't you join with me?"[1]

In contrast to the somber "Black Monday" moniker that circulated alongside Judge Tom Brady's book in the months following the Supreme Court's monumental desegregation decision, "White Monday" signified a triumph, an unapologetic seizure of white identity that resembled the post-Reconstruction, or Redemption, era in southern history. For the Council and sympathetic white allies across the country, the achievement of sweeping civil rights legislation signified the defeat of pre-1964 white resistance. But it also provided stabilization after years of ambiguity about the future of legalized discrimination. In many ways, the Civil Rights Act of 1964 and the Voting Rights Act of 1965 provided renewed clarity to Mississippi Council administrators who remained active for another twenty years. In the years leading up to 1964, the organization struggled to balance its local priorities in Mississippi against its efforts to achieve national significance. As support at home dissipated, however, the Council looked elsewhere, not only for allies but for mentors who would offer alternative paths of white activism. By the 1980s, this search fully converged with the political ideology of conservatism. But in the interim, the Council recommitted itself to white supremacist ideology through widening networks of white power that led its administrators to participate in a variety of movements and reactions which varied in their applications, but remained consistent in their embrace of white supremacy: white flight through the private school movement, white majority politics in California and George Wallace's presidential campaigns, and the defense of white minority regimes in southern Africa. In short, after 1964, the Council's white supremacy merged with a rising tide of white reaction across the country, breathing new life into a movement that its critics had already declared dead.

As the Council pursued outside support, local activities in Mississippi remained comparatively dormant. While the Jackson Citizens' Council remained active, it did so largely as a franchise of the Citizens' Councils of America, the umbrella organization that sponsored *Forum* and had the most connections to outside financing and initiatives. The Jackson Council continued to have annual meetings during which its members elected a board of directors and someone associated with the CCA or one of its initiatives provided a keynote address. The Jackson chapter also set up a phone line under its "Dial for Truth" program where callers could listen to a detailed recording about a particular topic, like school integration. It also published a monthly newsletter, *Aspect,* which detailed local concerns in the capital city, announced upcoming meetings, and provided information about making donations to the organization.[2]

Indications of growth across Mississippi and the South were sparse but appeared occasionally in local newspapers or were self-reported in Council publications. *The Citizen,* from 1975 to 1977, devoted a few pages in each issue to a section entitled, "What Is the Citizens' Council Doing?," which highlighted recent activities in various chapters and excerpted letters from Council supporters who praised the organization for its continued work. The December 1976 issue described events going on in the St. Louis, Memphis, Central-Illinois, Carroll County (Mississippi), and Grenada (Mississippi) chapters.[3] In January 1977, the column claimed 182 new members in the Jackson Citizens' Council, forty-three new members in Brookhaven, and thirty-one new members in Pike County.[4] Growth was up "1000%" in Attala County, according to the column, all thanks to general store owner and supporter of private schools, Donald Oakes.[5] In February 1977, "What Is the Council Doing?" announced syndication of a CCA column, "Citizens' Council Forum," and by the next issue it claimed space in forty-four newspapers.[6] Other news included an announcement from the Central-Illinois Citizens' Council regarding its organization of a "Reverse Discrimination" seminar in March 1977. Readers of *The Citizen* could also learn about a letter recently sent by the Memphis Council to the Tennessee General Assembly requesting the inclusion of a white studies program in the state's universities. The Memphis branch and "other patriotic groups" also claimed credit for winning a campaign to fly the Confederate flag year-round at three city parks in October 1978.[7] The most consistent news about other Councils, however, came from the St. Louis branch, where a collection of chapters in the area established a Fairness in Broadcasting Committee to monitor media coverage of news events. These chapters also supported their own radio program in 1976 called "Silent Majority Speaks." The radio program, according to the chapter's own description, would focus on presenting listeners with "in-depth views and conservative opinions" often ignored in mainstream media coverage but representative of the views "held by a majority of the citizens."[8]

If these reports are to be believed, the Council movement was not dead in the 1970s. At the very least, people active in Council structures managed to merge their consistent embrace of white supremacy with related concerns among other Americans. The frequency of Council events and campaigns, however, is impossible to determine, as are the membership lists for these groups. A more productive measure of Council activity was the CCA's efforts toward the private school movement. It was the most visible and long-standing legacy that the Council left on its home state. When desegregation began to take place in Mississippi schools in the fall of 1964, the Council immediately set up a small school with around twenty students, grades 1–6, in the home of one its members, Dr. Charles Neal, a local neurosurgeon who became president of the Council School Foundation in December. Council School No. 1, as it came to be called, offered all twelve grades the next school year and, in the spring of 1966, graduated its first four seniors. In September 1966, Council School No. 2 opened in southwest Jackson as an elementary school, and Council School No. 3 opened in north Jackson as a high school.

Both schools were renamed for their locations: McCluer Academy and Manhattan Academy, respectively, rather than for Confederate generals, a move that Bill Simmons later recalled was deliberate in order to make Council schools a product of their own era rather than a venue for the worship of "dead Confederate heroes." Council leaders worked closely with a local architect and designed the schools to reflect modern designs and educational priorities, including science labs and a library. More importantly, Simmons insisted that the schools not be "experimental" in their mission. The integration of public schools, in his perspective, was little more than a social experiment that would severely disrupt the learning environment.[9]

The Council Schools in Jackson saw a sharp increase after the Supreme Court announced its decision in *Alexander v. Holmes* in 1969. In it, the court declared an end to "all deliberate speed," demanding that the dual school system (still largely intact in Mississippi) be abolished without further delay. The decision came out in late October and required full integration in some districts by January 1970 and all districts in the state by the fall.[10] In areas of the state where the black population outnumbered the white, white students immediately fled into private academies, filling makeshift facilities beyond capacity. In Jackson, where the numbers of black and white students were nearly equal, the response was similar. Over 40 percent of the white students in Jackson Public Schools left in 1970. There were other private school options in the Jackson area, and some students moved to other districts where the white population made up the majority, but of the white students who attended private school in Jackson in 1970–1971, 60 percent of them went to a Council School.[11]

The Council had a six-year head start on most private school organizers, who hastily coordinated facilities, teachers, and curriculum in the fall of 1969, but even Simmons felt overwhelmed by the rapid flight of white students into Council Schools. Between the fall term in 1969 and January 1970, Council School enrollment increased from 300 to 1,500, forcing the schools to operate on two shifts until new construction was completed.[12]

The popularity of private school as an option for white students, by Simmons's estimation, drew in white moderates who had only tolerated the Council before.[13] More importantly, it provided a protected space where white supremacy could thrive. The Council School Handbook opened with the schools' history, explicitly noting the timeline of federal interference and its detrimental impact on the public schools. But the language was mild compared to that in other Council literature. The handbook did little more than imply a continuation of the system of segregation, but its descriptions of the basic curriculum and philosophy of the schools gave evidence of a softened version of the Council's standard message, with particular emphasis on authority, the absence of indoctrination, and high standards of performance.[14]

The private school phenomenon was not limited to Mississippi. Council School formation was only one example of a general flight out of public school systems across the South. In their study on the out-migration of white students into alternative schools, David Nevin and Robert E. Bills identified a "fundamental and dangerous dissatisfaction in American society." The formation of religiously affiliated schools was part of this response and reflected a widespread belief that the country was in the midst of a moral crisis. In the minds of anxious parents, increasing acceptance of divorce, premarital sex, drug use, crime, and abortion, demanded alternative educational environments that could isolate their children from these influences. The Council Schools, however, were more focused in their defiance. As late as 1975, the enrollment application for admission to a Council School included a statement by the Board of Directors that identified forced integration as "a moral wrong" and "disastrous."[15] The Council's alignment with wider trends of white flight, however, is important. It suggests the organization's place within larger conservative movements. For years the Council had cultivated its ideology to blend in with issues outside of segregation. As groups of Americans responded with alarm to urban unrest, inflation, and assaults on traditional structures of power, their refusal to accept changing circumstances was, in itself, a form of defiance. Ever and always, however, what set the Council apart from sister movements within conservatism was the centrality of white supremacy.

The apparent stagnation of the Council's growth in Mississippi outside of the private school movement was difficult to detect in light of the organization's financial investments. In the fall of 1967, the Jackson Council announced recent approval of the construction of a modern, state-of-the-art building in downtown Jackson that would serve as the new headquarters for the Citizens' Councils of America and provide space for the Jackson chapter. With over 6,000 square feet of offices, archival space, and covered parking, the new building reflected what the announcement described as "thirteen years of success in the nation" and promised to be a "major step" toward a new wave of "expanded activity." Completion of such a "magnificent structure" should also, the announcement noted, "prove to the doubters that the Citizens' Council movement is not dead—as has been erroneously reported in some quarters of late—but that the movement is just beginning to take on the outward character of its inward purpose—WE HAVE ONLY BEGUN!"[16]

As proof of the organization's continued vibrancy, an entire special section of the *Clarion-Ledger*'s Sunday paper was dedicated to the building's ribbon-cutting on August 11, 1968. Coverage included quarter-page color photographs of the building and detailed descriptions of the interior offices. An article on the property's history followed coverage of building details. Speakers at the event stood in front of three flags placed on the front corner of the building: American, Mississippi, and Confederate.[17]

In his opening remarks, Robert B. Patterson, founder of the first chapter in Indianola, reiterated the Council's purpose for a post–civil rights America: "to restore domestic tranquility to our streets . . . preserve the rights of our people to educate their children and to govern their local affairs." Judge Tom Brady, author of *Black Monday*, the book that created an outline for Council organization, provided his own remarks; his presence was a reminder of the Council's roots and its continued relevance. In total, eight pages of the *Clarion-Ledger* marked the Council's reintroduction to its home state. Most of that coverage, however, detailed Council activities, reminding readers that the Council's work was thriving. Write-ups about success in the Council Schools and in the organization's Leadership Conferences were placed among dozens of ads from local businesses, evidence that the Council still had support. At the very least, local business owners were not averse to being connected with the organization.[18]

The dedication of a new headquarters for the Citizens' Councils of America and its expanded activities was a product of Bill Simmons's indefatigable commitment to the Council. Robert Patterson said as much in his remarks at the ribbon cutting, when he referred to Simmons as "the chief architect in the construction of this National Headquarters." Citing his "vision and . . . ingenuity," Patterson placed Simmons "among the greatest assets of our organization."[19] Indeed, Simmons had long been the centerpiece of Council strategy. During Ross Barnett's administration it was Simmons's influence that was cited as the most definitive factor in the governor's decision-making process. The most active arm of the Council movement, the CCA, was Simmons's creation, and it was his efforts that cultivated relationships with outside groups, contributors, and donors. Simmons traveled extensively on behalf of the Citizens' Council as well, giving dozens of speeches across the country about Council ideology and organization.[20] He was the managing editor of *The Citizen* during most of its existence, and he was creator and manager of *Forum,* a program that ended in 1966 following the sudden death of its host, Dick Morphew.

In short, Bill Simmons *was* the Citizens' Council. His involvement across the various activities, investments, and partnerships that the organization sustained over the course of its existence provided consistency and enabled enough overlap to compensate for diminishing support. After 1964, Simmons's interests reflected the alliances he forged and informed a new phase of Council activism that considered the fact of racial difference and natural white superiority an underarticulated point.

The commitment to racial difference as a central strategy was not a dramatic shift from the Council's philosophy, but intervening years had led the Council down numerous roads, most of them political and aimed at obstructing the passage of civil rights legislation. Integration presented an opportunity to draw attention back to the Council's foundational commitment to white supremacy without the burden of legalistic arguments. It is unlikely, however, that the Council would have so fully embraced this strategy without the guidance and support of the Pioneer Fund, a New York–based research foundation committed to supporting scientists who devoted their careers to proving natural racial differences. The founder of the Pioneer Fund, Wycliffe Draper, and his successor, Harry F. Weyher, had shown interest in the southern white resistance movement for years, donating money and connecting Pioneer Fund grant recipients to organizations like the Citizens' Council. As early as 1959, Weyher was in communication with Simmons about *Forum* costs and budget projections.[21] It is also likely that the Pioneer Fund was a major donor to the Council School Foundation and possibly contributed funds to the Council's new building.[22]

The embrace of racial difference as a Council strategy was only the most recent attempt to offer the issue of natural racial hierarchy as a counternarrative to the argument for equality. These efforts gained visibility in 1958 with the founding of the National Putnam Letters Committee (NPLC). The NPLC's founding followed the circulation of a letter that Carleton Putnam, a former airline executive and author of *Race and Reason* (1961), sent to President Dwight Eisenhower in protest of the *Brown* decision. Through the NPLC, Putnam sought to bring more attention to the scientific argument against racial equality by using paid advertisements in northern newspapers, and he used Pioneer Fund money to do it.[23] The Pioneer Fund was also the driving force behind the CCFAF and came close to colluding with Mississippi governor Paul Johnson Jr. in 1964, when he accepted an initial deposit of $50,000 from the organization with a promise of $150,000 more upon the state's commitment to matching funds through a readjustment of the Sovereignty Commission's allocations. All of the money was pledged toward a Washington office, under the name "Fund of the Founding Fathers," which would support a variety of covert media infiltration strategies as a way of controlling the message about race. At the center of these strategies was a commitment to "honesty" about natural racial differences.[24]

The proposal to readjust Sovereignty Commission funds to support Fund for the Founding Fathers was considered possible, in part, because funding of *Forum* officially ended in December 1964. The state agency's director, Erle Johnston, had long doubted Bill Simmons's claims about the number of radio and television stations carrying the program. After an inquiry to dozens of stations yielded few confirmations that *Forum* was part of their schedule, Johnston recommended that funding of the Council's program should end.[25] The Council was not without options, however. Satterfield's vision for the campaign depended upon the governor's support. The escalating violence during the summer of 1964 led Governor Johnson to return the initial $50,000 deposit, and the original version of the plan never developed.[26] The Citizens' Council became the natural alternative. After Governor Johnson returned the $50,000 deposit, the Pioneer Fund, Carleton Putnam, and John Synon turned to Bill Simmons.

The Council's history with both Carleton Putnam and the Pioneer Fund made the switch an easy adjustment and provided the organization with a new campaign. The relationship extended as far back as 1960 when Putnam first visited *Forum.* In total, Putnam appeared on ten *Forum* broadcasts and served as a featured speaker at Council events. His book about natural racial difference, *Race and Reason,* received regular endorsements in the Council's monthly magazine, *The Citizen,* and was the focus of "Race and Reason Day," a Council event held in Jackson in 1961. The Council was also familiar with the work of the Pioneer Fund through *Forum,* which hosted a number of biologists who supported the tenets of scientific racism and had connections to the New York–based organization.

When John Synon and Bill Simmons began communicating in 1965 about a new Washington-based organization, all parties—Simmons, Putnam, Weyher, and Synon—were familiar to each other. In December, John Synon, who joined the National Putnam Letters Committee when the CCFAF was disbanded in 1964, provided Simmons with a detailed proposal that included an annual budget estimate of $35,692.80, none of which would come from the Council. Synon's proposal involved lobbying efforts and the publication of a monthly column, as well as a network of researchers and writers to contribute pieces on what he referred to as "our subject."[27]

Simmons agreed with the spirit of Synon's proposal but balked at the suggestion that the Citizens' Council serve only as a stakeholder for the work and not Synon's employer. He was especially opposed to the removal of the Citizens' Council name from the organization. In Simmons's reply to Synon, he explained that "potential contributors" would respond best to a Citizens' Council office in Washington, and suggested that all funds come from the Council given its connection with "outside sources" that were already familiar with the organization's experience "in the field of the Negro Revolution." His mention of Harry F. Weyher, president of the Pioneer Fund, is a good indication of who those outside sources were.[28]

It is not clear how Simmons and Synon resolved the discrepancy of funds and branding, but there is some evidence that an agreement existed. In 1965 and 1966, *Forum* devoted some of its broadcasts to discussions about racial differences with Carleton Putnam and Robert Gayre, editor of *Mankind Quarterly,* a pseudoscientific journal focused on genetic differences among the races. Both Gayre and Putnam were, at various times, on the payroll of the Pioneer Fund.[29] Dr. Henry Garrett, another recipient of Pioneer Fund money, appeared on two programs in 1964 and served as a regular contributor to the Council's monthly magazine, *The Citizen.* Garrett was a psychologist who taught at Columbia University for thirty years before he left to devote his time to the segregationist cause. His résumé showed that in addition to the honor of serving as president of the American Psychological Association, Garrett had briefly served as president of the Pioneer Fund from 1971 to 1973.[30]

More damning evidence exists in the Council's attention to developing events in southern Africa. In John Synon's proposal to Simmons, he included what he referred to as a "press junket" for South Africa, a letter with enclosures from Synon to Dr. E. M. Rhoodie, secretary of information for South Africa. In it, Synon recommended that Rhoodie consider "an educational-advertising campaign, whose overt appeal would be potential emigrants, people the Union of South Africa would welcome as newcomers. Its covert significance would lie in the opportunity the ads would afford South Africa to tell its story." Synon's suggestions included ads that would capture South Africans working, state their average pay and access to educational opportunities, and profile stories that would bring South African culture to life. The circulation of positive images of South Africa, he argued, would have a significant impact on Americans' opinion of South Africa.[31]

Clearly, the South Africans to whom Synon referred were of European descent, and his opening remarks to Rhoodie underscored this point: "There is no nation, anywhere, nor has there ever been a nation so like America as is South Africa: Its genesis, its development, its culture, its economics, the whole of its history is remarkably similar to that of the United States." Those commonalities, he argued, should serve as the centerpiece for the public relations campaign with deliberate examples of common elements in both countries, "South African housewife-to-American-housewife, South African mechanic-to-American-mechanic," each aiming to "convince the American people, segment by segment, their South African opposites are counterparts."[32]

Synon enclosed his letter to Rhoodie in his December letter to Bill Simmons because of Simmons's impending trip to Pretoria, South Africa, a trip that Synon understood to be in pursuit of "snagging South Africa as an 'account' of one sort or another."[33] There is no evidence that such an account ever crystallized for South Africa, but Simmons spent three months traveling around southern Africa (South Africa, the protectorate of South-West Africa, and Rhodesia) early in 1966 and, while there, recorded eleven *Forum* broadcasts with various guests who discussed at length the history, culture, economy, and racial system of the region.[34]

When Bill Simmons reported back on his impressions of the region at a Jackson Citizens' Council event in the spring of 1966, Synon's suggestions were evident. He described a utopia where "whites are so united on the race question that even 'moderates' believe in and advocate social separation of the races." School integration was considered "so outlandish as not to merit even a passing thought." A strong economy, high white birth rate, and white leadership that had a "will to rule, a will to assume responsibility" combined to bring a general "absence of race tension." He also noted the success with which the region had encouraged white immigration.[35]

Simmons's trip and the sympathies for Rhodesia and South Africa that were clear in the Council's publications were not unique. As Zoe Hyman's work reveals, the John Birch Society also contributed space in its publication, *American Opinion,* to support white minority rule. Black newspapers, like the *Chicago Defender,* listed the Citizens' Council among organizations bent on popularizing the South African model of oppression, including the Ku Klux Klan.[36]

Simmons's visit and the nature of his remarks upon his return may well have been directed toward improving the region's reputation as a way to interest white Americans in the possibility of migration. But the trip was only one piece of a broader push for empowering the white majority at home. If a white minority in southern Africa could maintain stability in the midst of global revolution and international disapproval, a unified white majority in the United States could initiate its own racial revolution.

The Council's interest in southern Africa and its connection with the Pioneer Fund, especially after 1964, reveals a clear connection with a rising tide of Radical Right movements that, by the 1970s, had become well funded and influential. While the Council's enthusiasm for Ronald Reagan's election as president in 1980 speaks to the formal marriage of white southern resistance with the Republican Party and its conservative base, the late 1960s and 1970s were critical to securing the Council's relationship to radical organizations, a relationship that preceded and perhaps even grounded southern entry into the conservative ascendancy that the 1980s oversaw.

Political scientist Kirkpatrick Sale, author of *Power Shift*, cautioned his readers in 1975 against undervaluing the radical strands of conservatism that included such movements as Friends of Rhodesian Independence, the John Birch Society, the American Nazi Party, Sons of Liberty, the Minutemen, and the Liberty Lobby. Among all of those organizations and movements, Sale included the Citizens' Council.[37] And while historians have marked the Council's influence to have been in steep decline after 1964, taken as a national movement within the Radical Right, its contribution cannot be dismissed. The fact that it would soon find a comfortable home within the Republican Party suggests that Radical Right contributions were critical components for the party realignments that defined southern politics post-1964.

The factor enabling Council relevance when its fight to maintain segregation at home ended was its merger with Sunbelt conservatism. Sale's warning about Radical Right influence in 1975 identified the Southern Rim as the most active area of organization for these groups. From "the reactionaries of Orange County to the rednecks of South Carolina," the Southern Rim of the United States contained the deep pockets of manufacturing, agribusiness, defense plants, and oil interests, all of them joint stakeholders and deeply suspicious of federal power. Sale made a sharp distinction between this ideological alliance and that of conservative intellectuals like William F. Buckley Jr., who saw the Republican Party as the most practical pipeline for conservative ascendancy. In contrast, the Far Right element in the Southern Rim was decidedly "non-scholarly, earthy . . . and given to speechifying, in the tents and on the airwaves." And while Sale recognized the disparate elements that contributed to this alliance, racism among them, he saw the common embrace of "*adversarianism*, a being-against*," as the core of their partnership.[38]

Each of these groups, standing alone, was radical enough to remain in isolation and irrelevant to national politics. But their convergence and common "adversarianism" stoked grassroots activism at a time when the sparks enflamed by the civil rights movement could easily have flickered out after sweeping congressional legislation became a reality. As the Citizens' Council movement did in the wake of *Brown* in 1954, when existing political leadership remained ambivalent as it waited to see whether and how the decision would take effect, Radical Right organizations stepped into a vacuum of leadership post-1964 when the aftermath of the new racial order was still unclear and full party realignment remained unrealized. The Council, again, benefited from an atmosphere of uncertainty, but this time its search for national alliances was less elusive.

The Council's plummeting memberships in Mississippi demanded expansion elsewhere, and by 1964 administrators began organizing the state of California in partnership with a conservative journalist, William K. Shearer, editor of the *California Statesman,* a newspaper published in San Diego.[39] In October, the San Francisco Citizens' Council had formed and planned its first invitation-only membership event with an agenda that included presentations by Bill Simmons and Louis Hollis from the Citizens' Councils of America, and Kent H. Steffgan, field director for the California Councils.[40] Another chapter formed in Sacramento shortly after and contributed support for California's Proposition 14, a proposed amendment to the state constitution that would allow property owners the freedom to discriminate against prospective buyers.[41] Voters approved the initiative in the 1964 election, a significant victory for advocates of white majority politics and a positive sign for future Council chapters in the state. To celebrate, *Forum* featured three programs on location in San Diego to discuss the successful amendment and what it meant for the future of white politics. William Shearer appeared on two of the programs and described in some detail the process of getting an initiative on the ballot and tips on effective grassroots organizing.[42] While he insisted that only groups opposed to Proposition 14 made the initiative a "racial issue," he emphasized the election's outcome as proof that a "white protest vote" existed that must be mobilized in future elections if candidates wanted to ensure victory. "The majority community,'" he argued, "has legitimate interests to protect just as do other segments of society. . . . [T]here is no validity to the philosophy that every group except the white majority has a right to mobilize and be represented."[43]

Shearer's remarks in 1965 echoed the dominance of race-neutral rhetoric within Sunbelt conservatism. The emphasis on property, and thus individual, rights in the Proposition 14 campaign embraced strategies that marginalized racism as a problem deeply embedded within the individual, not institutions. Organizers who campaigned for approval of the amendment removed race from their rhetoric altogether, forcing their opponents to campaign in similar ways in order to capture critical white votes. In the process, anti–Proposition 14 supporters excluded the NAACP, the United Civil Rights Committee, and the Mexican American Political Association, a choice aimed at avoiding narratives of discrimination in favor of ideological argument. The consequences of that choice collapsed political positions into a battleground of white racial identity.[44]

Victory would not last, however. Shearer appeared on *Forum* again in 1966 to discuss the California State Supreme Court's decision to overturn the amendment based on the its determination that Proposition 14 violated the Fourteenth Amendment. His remarks in 1966 struck an angrier tone, one that described a "polarized" environment between whites and blacks in California, a product of the wave of violence that had plagued the Los Angeles area since the outbreak of the Watts riots in August 1965. He described current white sentiment as a "rejection" of the black community that affected innocent and guilty alike, but was likely to reap reactions from "the majority community . . . in some other way than through the civil process." Shearer warned that if extralegal tactics on either side took over, nothing short of a "holocaust" would develop. Interestingly, he suggested "separate development" as a solution, the term regularly applied to the system of apartheid in South Africa and Rhodesia.[45]

The intersection of California's conservative movement with white southern resistance is more revelatory of a shift in the former's priorities than in an expansion of Council ideology. For California conservatives in 1966, urban riots butted up against deeply held beliefs about their own racial innocence, especially in comparison to the violence committed against blacks in the Deep South during the height of the civil rights movement. Caught between the reality of racial violence at home and their wish to avoid a reaction akin to that of white southern segregationists after *Brown,* California conservatives began advocating for a "responsible Right," one that understood in equal measure that the issue of race, whether employed to justify the preservation of segregation and disfranchisement or to promote a more robust reform movement through federal welfare programs, skewed political priorities in dangerous and destructive ways. Their solution was what Darren Dochuk tags as a "liberation" from both. California conservatives, then, were more attracted to Ronald Reagan than they were to George Wallace by 1968.[46]

The distinction between Wallace and Reagan blurs, however, in light of the connections the Mississippi Council had with Californians like Shearer. Differences between evangelical conservatives and John Birch conservatives, for example, suggest complexities within the California movement and underscore the importance of that state in securing a unified conservatism that could shape up in a number of different ways. The fact that the Council could find allies in California is evidence that one of those options was the ascendance of the Radical Right over that of evangelicals and other strands of conservatism jockeying for dominance in the 1960s.

The wave of race riots that ripped through the nation's cities in the late 1960s provided a linking issue that helped crystallize the bond between white southerners and their counterparts in California. Nine *Forum* broadcasts in 1965 and 1966 dealt with erupting violence in various cities across the country. Each of the guests who spoke about the riots denied the role of poverty and police brutality in motivating the riots, at times appearing smug about the "arrival" of racial conflict in cities outside of the South. In their estimation, the atmosphere of lawlessness cultivated in the midst of the civil rights movement created a sense of entitlement in black communities. After viewing some of the damage in the Watts neighborhood during a trip to Los Angeles, Bill Simmons returned to *Forum* proclaiming, "The constant barrage of propaganda directed at the Negroes, excusing them for their delinquencies and crime . . . directly encouraged the Los Angeles riots." South Carolina senator Strom Thurmond blamed the Johnson administration for creating "resentment" within black communities, making them "feel that they are oppressed and that they are not treated properly." Alabama congressman Joe D. Waggoner blamed "people in high places, people in government, people who fill the pulpits of this land" for "preaching and teaching disrespect for law which does not suit them."[47]

The ultimate example of blatant disregard for the law in black communities was the accusation that law enforcement officials were guilty of race-driven harassment and brutality. Not surprisingly, *Forum* guests and contributors to *The Citizen* declaimed the honesty, duty, and courage of white law enforcement in the face of "destruction, terrorism," and attacks from protesters. The earliest discussions of police-led violence against protesters came out of the Selma voting rights campaign after local police brutally beat scores of peaceful marchers as they attempted to cross the Edmund Pettus Bridge. Selma stands out as one of the last Council strongholds in Alabama and, within the context of the Alabama movement, one of its most radical chapters. George Lewis describes the Council's impact in the city and in Dallas County as so effective that it precluded any chance of moderate, progressive reform in response to mass demonstrations.[48]

Alabama governor George Wallace appeared on *Forum* shortly after "Bloody Sunday" to defend police actions in spite of his admission that "some excesses" could have happened "in the tumult and the confusion." Had marchers not openly defied orders to stay off of the highway, he argued, those "excesses" would have never occurred.[49] Wallace further lamented the wave of vitriol directed at American law enforcement officers in the wake of racial demonstrations throughout the country. Their burden, he explained, was a heavy one in light of the rapid escalation of "lawless elements" in the nation's cities.[50]

The defense of white police officers was an important component of the commentary that Council leaders, *Citizen* contributors, and *Forum* guests made regarding race riots and deserves a deeper examination. Because police authority was local in nature, it excluded, at least in the short term, other intervening systems of power. The goal of immediate stability enabled swift reactions from police officers who could, as George Wallace stated, act with the necessary amount of force "to preserve law and order." Without their rapid reactions, he concluded, anarchy was inevitable.[51] Bill Simmons argued a similar point on a program in 1966, when he discussed the history of race riots in the United States. Simmons detected a notable difference in the present wave of riots in northern cities. Previous incidents, like the riots that followed the end of World War I and World War II, he argued, were clearly the product of racial tensions between whites and blacks. In contrast, the riots in 1965 and 1966 involved "Negro mobs against the police."[52] In Simmons's estimation, law enforcement was neutral and acted only in the interest of ensuring stability through the restoration of law and order. Medford Evans, a Council administrator and former chief of security training for the Atomic Energy Commission, took the point even further, arguing that "the law on the books is one thing, but the law in action is whoever has the power to make arrests." Since most arrests were made at the local level, he continued, sheriffs and chiefs of police had a "more realistic understanding of the day-to-day problems in an age of revolution, which we know this [wave of riots] is." Their authority to arrest, and thus obstruct, civil uprisings, made them the next natural target of subversive forces in the United States.[53]

Evans's remarks drifted toward the anticommunist warnings that prevailed in the early days of the civil rights movement, but the general assumption that law enforcement was race-neutral and loyal only to the system of law it sought to enforce, cast black rioters and demonstrators as lawbreakers whose cries of police brutality were carefully orchestrated attempts to undermine sanctioned (white) authority. The law enforcement angle played a unique role in the Council's message after 1964 because it represented one of the last bastions of unchecked, local white authority, the very thing the Council hoped to preserve in the first few months of its existence, when it sought to stay out of the public eye.

The topic of riots and police procedure toward suspected criminals was not one the Council abandoned quickly. Its identification of the natural criminal tendencies of black Americans fit comfortably with the innate racial difference argument that the Pioneer Fund and their southern African allies championed. John Synon was specific in his connection between natural racial hierarchy and urban unrest in an article he wrote for *The Citizen* in January 1968, entitled, "Daddybird, Riots, and the Unemployed." In it he reflected on the soon-to-be-released Kerner Report, the final report on a seven-month study on the causes of urban rioting. Synon, anticipating explanations related to disproportionate unemployment among black Americans, described rampant joblessness as a symptom of unnatural pretenses about black equality. The liberal "fiat" that forced the concept of economic equality into mainstream political priorities, he claimed, set up unrealistic expectations for people of African descent who naturally possessed lower IQs than Caucasians. The intelligence difference, he concluded, meant that the ability of black men to work in jobs equivalent to white men's was severely circumscribed by biological predispositions. It also (and perhaps this was the true irritant to Synon) left a vacuum in more appropriate fields of employment where white people needed black workers: "Where once we had a man to cut the grass and do the garden, now Pappa rides the range on a power mower and—excuse it, please—the flowers 'go to pot.' In general, the grinning face that once gave the fillip to life has disappeared along with yesterday's good will."[54] The editorial essay in the April 1968 issue continued Synon's sentiment, stating, "When our national press finally decides to tell the American public the truth, that the races are different, the first step towards a solution to the race problem will be made."[55]

The integration of denials about racial differences with the breakdown of law and order in the nation's cities underscored the Council's assessment that the surrender of white leadership to minority interests had created chaos. White liberals were frequent targets of this perspective, but in a more general appeal, Council leaders and contributors urged a reinvigoration of white leadership that would trust the natural talents of the race to protect and control their black neighbors. The chaos of riots at home and revolutions abroad was a predictable outcome of the actions of a race of people biologically incapable of self-regulation and without effective white oversight. If white Americans wished to see stability restored and have practical governance prevail, they had to accept the fact of white dominance and the responsibility that accompanied it. To drive home the point, Bill Simmons seized upon the nostalgia of slavery and white paternalism as ideal examples of the proper role that whites should assume. Support for black power and integration, he argued, was little more than "attempts by participating whites to get rid of their own responsibility toward the blacks." That approach, Simmons explained, was "hostile to the whole American tradition of white responsibility."[56]

In the field of white leadership, the Council practiced what it preached. Since 1956, the Citizens' Councils of America hosted an annual leadership conference to bring together members of the Council movement across the South to explore a common theme pertinent to current challenges. All of the conferences focused on organization-building, but the years after 1964 are especially revelatory of the Council's commitment to white coalition-building as a way to overturn civil rights successes. Those conferences, rather than encouraging outright defiance, sought to preserve white authority through existing institutions like law enforcement and the private school movement, while leveraging white anger to activate sustained grassroots support. Some examples of conference themes were, "How Can We Educate Our Children?" (Chattanooga, 1966); "Stand Up for America!" (New Orleans, 1967); "The Road Ahead" (Jackson, 1968); "Law and Order" (Memphis, 1969); and "Citizen Power" (Atlanta, 1970).[57]

Leadership conferences also provided material for *The Citizen*, where speeches from the conferences appeared in print throughout the year. The common sentiment among all of the leadership conference themes was that the current two-party system left no room for the average white American and his concerns. In the process of catering to special interests, white political power was devalued and politicians became further removed from mainstream America. The Council had occasionally identified conservatism as a productive connection for these disillusioned Americans, but it consistently considered white supremacy a better fit. That left the organization alienated from both parties, neither of which directly used common whiteness as a strategy for support. In an editorial entitled "Heart of America," which appeared in *The Citizen* in April 1971, the point was made clear. "It seems unfortunate," the piece read, "that so few outside Citizens' Council circles will face squarely the crucial role of race in the world revolution. One hears futile arguments as to whether conservatives should be concerned with "the [communist] Conspiracy" or with "race."[58] The equivocation was untenable for Council leaders like Simmons who worked closely with organizations like the Pioneer Fund that were fully committed to proving that a natural racial hierarchy existed.

But there was much more to the argument than the assumption of black inferiority. Being white in the United States had become, according to Council literature, a liability in the aftermath of civil rights legislation and race riots. Skeptical whites who doubted the legitimacy of campus uprisings and urban riots, for example, found themselves victims of "abuse" from the very people who had experienced the greatest benefits from the American system. Black Americans and college students, according to Bill Simmons, denounced what most white Americans considered virtuous: "patriotism, hard work, cleanliness, self-reliance."[59] William Lowndes, president of the Southern States Industrial Council, a conservative group of southern business leaders, complained that the current climate had neutralized the white working man into a victim of increasing entitlement programs that devalued his identity as a "law-abiding, respectable, hardworking individual." Months before Richard Nixon would use this same descriptor in his acceptance speech at the Republican National Convention, Lowndes described the "Forgotten Man," a man who, year after year,

> watches his earnings siphoned away to support global aid programs. . . . [He is] allowed a $600 yearly tax deduction to raise and educate his child while the unwed mother on relief gets many times that amount in welfare checks to support her burgeoning brood. [H]e is a 'bigot,' a 'racist,' and a veritable beast if he has any personal preference as to the buyer of his dwelling.[60]

That forgotten man was only one among many, in the Council's estimation. If most white Americans felt the same way, it could create a political revolution that had the potential of rolling back the gains of the civil rights movement. The attention given to race in previous years, according to Bill Simmons, raised the consciousness of white people who, he predicted, were ready to "close ranks" in order to avoid integration. "White public opinion," he stated, "is a sleeping giant . . . and when opinion finally unites and moves toward its own self-preservation . . . the majority of whites in the United States will not tolerate the loss of their personal freedoms."[61]

Support for a white counterrevolution aligned the Council's priorities with a political insurgency that extended well beyond the South. The most visible evidence of that movement was in the presidential campaigns of Alabama governor George Wallace in 1964, 1968, and 1972. Wallace's platform represented the full flowering of white backlash to the social movements of the 1950s, 1960s, and 1970s. Up until his campaign in 1964, Wallace had been best remembered for his "segregation now . . . segregation tomorrow . . . segregation forever," declaration. Neil McMillen describes the Alabama Council movement as having the most impact through leaders like Wallace who internalized the power of the Council message and turned it into political currency.[62] His presidential aspirations represented a more ambitious agenda that went beyond opposition to the civil rights movement to leverage white anger about social movements that threatened American values. In his speeches, Wallace articulated the concerns of the "forgotten man" that William Lowndes referenced, defended the rights of property owners that California's Proposition 14 sought to enshrine, and confirmed the local authority of police officers to protect their communities.[63] His politics and the rhetoric of his campaigns enlivened conservative ideology by applying its principles to the plight of the (white) working man. He did so by creating two poles of threats: the lawless and the bureaucrats. Between those poles was a wide center that included those Americans committed to God and country, heritage, and hard work. In the process of championing them, he helped transform white resistance into the ultimate form of patriotism. In short, Wallace's campaigns converted conservative ideology from a philosophy into a movement.[64]

Wallace began appearing on *Forum* in 1962, shortly after his first election as governor.[65] During his first presidential campaign in 1964, however, his connection to the Council became much more visible. He appeared on the program four times in 1964 and spoke at length of a white protest vote that his campaign captured during the primary season in places like Wisconsin, where he won nearly 300,000 votes. Wallace acknowledged that his election to the presidency was a long shot, but he described those votes as a message to leaders of both parties that "good conservative people" would no longer remain silent. He described his supporters as defenders of "individual liberty and freedom . . . the incentive and initiative system . . . property ownership, [who] have been . . . afraid to speak because the liberal, left-wing news media has called [them] racist, bigot, prejudiced, ignorant."[66]

The Council was more than just an outlet for Wallace's publicity, however. The organization directed a significant amount of its publications, events planning, and personnel to his campaign. In 1967, Bill Simmons took a leave of absence from Council activities in order to work on Wallace's campaign for the 1968 presidential primary.[67] Advertisements for Wallace's campaign appeared in *The Citizen* regularly throughout 1967, even though paid advertisements were never part of the format of the monthly magazine. Subscribers could tear out an order form inside their monthly issue and acquire campaign paraphernalia like bumper stickers, lapel pins, and a souvenir coin. The magazine dedicated most of its June issue that year to an interview with Wallace. The June, July–August, and September issues featured a three-part travel log from Wallace's campaign stops by an anonymous writer (likely Simmons) who called himself "One Who Went Along." In addition to his keynote address at the "White Monday" rally in 1965, Wallace also headlined the "Stand Up for America!" CCA Leadership Conference in 1967, the title of which was a nod to a pamphlet about Wallace's career that the radical-right organization, the Liberty Lobby, published in 1965.[68] Council founder Robert Patterson made speeches on Wallace's behalf, presenting components of his platform as solutions to the crises of anarchy, treason, and federal ineptitude that plagued the nation.[69]

Wallace's relationship with the Citizens' Council provides some assistance in locating the Council's activity in a breach between their segregationist origins and what would become the "new conservatism"—a coalition of traditional Republicans committed to small government and fiscal balance, their moderate faithful, and a new cohort of radical activists committed to white supremacy.[70] The Council's connections to the Pioneer Fund and its renewed embrace of racial difference after 1964 made the organization more compatible with its radical peers than with conservative moderates, but by 1968 it had found, in some form, the white unity for which it had always fought. After Richard Nixon's victory in the 1968 presidential election, the Council crowed about its victory even though Wallace's hopes of winning enough votes to prevent an electoral victory for either party were not realized. In his keynote address to the 1969 CCA Leadership Conference, Bill Simmons predicted success for Wallace in 1972. But perhaps more significant was his declaration that the Wallace movement differed from the Dixiecrats who, he explained, quit too soon. Wallace and his supporters, in contrast, were part of a permanent political force of disaffected white Americans.[71] Robert Patterson, in his remarks at the conference, put an even finer point on the election's meaning. Wallace may not have won, he argued, but his campaign helped ensure that all of the "Negro and left wing votes" went to the loser, Democratic nominee Hubert Humphrey. For Patterson, that fact portended the reassertion of white political power after years of marginalization.[72]

Council leaders were not alone in their assessment of the 1968 election. Political scientist Kevin Phillips in *The Emerging Republican Majority*, published in 1969, flatly declared, "The South is turning into an important presidential base of the Republican Party." The simultaneous defection from the Democratic Party by both the Upper and Peripheral South (who voted for Nixon in 1968) and the Deep South (who voted for Wallace) would eventually result in a total migration into the Republican Party once the third party threat dissipated. The Nixon administration's approach to enforcing civil rights legislation and Great Society programs would, he argued, determine how rapidly that threat would disappear.[73]

The 1972 campaign season brought that threat to a close when Wallace suffered paralyzing bullet wounds at the hands of Arthur Bremer. But the 9.9 million votes he won in 1968, over 40 percent of which came from outside of the Southern Rim, had already shifted party priorities and fulfilled Kirkpatrick Sale's prediction that, "Even if Wallace himself should retire from the scene, it seems likely that 'his voters' will remain a constituency with which all future politicians will have to contend. Wallace-ism, in short, seems powerful enough to survive George Wallace."[74]

The Council was a major contributor to keeping Wallace's law-and-order message alive and applicable to rising fears over crime. Throughout the 1970s, the Council frequently described a general environment of lawlessness that threatened white security. Not surprisingly, they blamed the civil rights movement for beginning the chaos and in so doing secured the Council's resistance to it within the nostalgia of a pre-*Brown* America. It was not unusual, for example, for *The Citizen* to reprint articles from the civil rights years as a way to drive home the correctness and consistency of the Council's position. That point was underscored by nearly every monthly issue of *The Citizen*. The magazine contained pages of crime reports from various cities throughout the country. Black-on-white crime and stories about media bias were the most frequent topics. One particular issue included page after page of titles that pointed to a genuine crisis of white safety, black immorality, and government corruption: "Memphis Woman Raped in Home, Negro Nabbed," "Girl, 17, Beaten, Raped by Negro in Rear of Store," "Black Congressman Diggs Indicted in Fraud Counts," "Charles Evers Escapes Re-Trial on Tax Charge," "Rape Threats Terrorize Elderly Whites in Dallas," "Puerto Rican Poverty Unit Accused of Wasting Millions," "Woman, 91, Beaten, Robbed as Blacks Ransack Home."[75]

Other articles were more direct in their connection between the civil rights movement and increased crime. In a May 1974 article, Council founder Robert Patterson marked the twentieth anniversary of *Brown v. Board of Education* as "loosing" the black revolution that created all of the crises currently facing the United States. Integration caused the decline of the public school system, destruction of neighborhoods, and lowering of morale in the armed services, police and fire departments, and countless other institutions throughout the country. With the help of a biased media, he argued, whites had become "mesmerized" into feeling guilty about being white and accepted justifications for crime. But the benefit of increasing crime in northern cities, he predicted, could "at long last" draw whites across the country together. "The South," he argued, "does not have the political and economic power to solve the problem by itself. It needs help from the rest of our nation."[76]

White unity had always been the Council's clarion call, but in the 1970s, a time where the organized civil rights movement dissipated into local campaigns for fair housing and equal employment and sat beside panic over crime in the cities and forced busing, white unity seemed to hold more promise than it had in the 1960s. On the back end of integration, the Council's earlier predictions of disastrous consequences seemed prescient. Perceived white marginalization—in politics, education, employment, and countless other areas—emanated from Council commentaries on current affairs. Bill Simmons described a general sentiment among whites that they were strangers in their own land, walking down familiar streets but confronting "bushy Afros with pointed goatees and insolent eyes, Aunt Jemima in hot pants, long-haired hippies on the main corner peddling pornographic underground papers, weirdos and freaks of both sexes and of several degrees in between." His explanation was that integration had so blurred the lines between black and white that the first generation of white students to experience integration had "adopted the habits and customs of the so-called Black ghetto: the deliberate uncleanliness; the foul language; the sloppy dress; the loping, pendulum-like walk; the amorality; the dehumanizing of romantic love; the subculture of drugs; rock music; self hate, self death."[77]

Politically, such ideas had nowhere to go. The shooting in 1972 moderated Wallace's position too much for the Council to continue supporting him as its candidate. Richard Nixon's and Jimmy Carter's presidencies held little hope from the Council's perspective, and *The Citizen* continued to belabor the point that without white conservatives both Democrats and Republicans would struggle to find dominance. An editorial in the January 1977 issue noted that between the parties, not "a dime's worth of difference" existed.[78]

At home, conditions also seemed discouraging for a Council resurgence. The organization's dimming relevance was detectable as early as the 1967 gubernatorial campaign, during which the Council sponsored a debate for the candidates. The first question, "Why haven't our ideals of States Rights and racial integrity been featured in this campaign as in the past?," pointed directly to the Council's dramatic loss of influence in state politics. Another question, "How would you have handled the James Meredith affair?" reflected the organization's nostalgia for Ross Barnett, but it also indicated whom its members were likely to support, given that Barnett was a candidate in 1967. In contrast, candidate John Bell Williams, a congressman and previously a staunch Council supporter, urged Mississippians to elect a candidate who struck a balance between extremists on both sides. "We cannot reach our goals as a state," he explained in his campaign announcement, "by following prophets of doom and despair and by clinging blindly to the past. Nor can they be attained through a molly-coddling, fearful, vacillating approach to our problems in an attempt to placate all factions of our body politic." Willliams, who ultimately won the race, publicly distanced himself from the Council in those brief remarks. Two months later, he was even more pointed in locating his place among a field of candidates that not only included Barnett but, at the other end of the spectrum, William F. Winter, who would go on to become one of the state's most progressive governors, especially regarding race. It was clear where Williams felt electoral strength lay: moderates. He described his platform in contrast to that of Barnett, "whose reckless actions and questionable deals previously brought grief and tragedy to the state of Mississippi." A few months later, Charles Griffin, Williams's assistant, responded to an inquiry about the status of *Forum*, explaining that Williams had no dealings with the Council anymore since Council leaders were "bitterly opposing . . . Williams in the Governor's race."[79]

Occasionally the Council would surface in local newspapers in which the leadership would articulate its position on a contested issue, but increasingly, there was little to differentiate its positions from that of Byron De La Beckwith who, when he ran for lieutenant governor in 1967, claimed, "The white segregationists of Mississippi, and that is most of us, are sick and tired of the cowardly, do-nothing leadership that has been coming out of the state's capital in Jackson for the past several years."[80] Beckwith, whose two trials for Medgar Evers's murder both ended in a mistrial, had, by 1967, migrated into Klan circles. The distance he identified between "most" white Mississippians and their leadership certainly pertained to the Council after Williams's election.

The Mississippi Council worked tirelessly to create alliances that would make its position politically relevant after 1964. But its natural connection with Radical Right movements and George Wallace's third party challenge in 1968 kept Republicans like Richard Nixon wary of openly coveting its support. While his campaigns in 1968 and 1972 appealed to white suburbanites and Upper South elites in areas of the South where radical defiance never fully flourished, capturing the Council vote in Mississippi was beset with difficulty. The Republican Party organization in Mississippi remained undecided about whether it should pursue newly liberated black votes or those of former white segregationists. Their ambivalence reflected sentiments at the national level. The Nixon administration expressed sympathy for the South's position but refused to support defiance of federal mandates. Its refusal to openly denounce *Alexander v. Holmes*, the Supreme Court decision that demanded immediate compliance with desegregation orders, and *Green v. Connolly*, the decision that threatened to remove tax exemptions from private schools that discriminated against students based on race, evidenced the lack of sympathy for stalwart segregationist positions. Ultimately, by 1972, Nixon did enough in his recognition of white southern discontent to win 78 per cent of the popular vote in Mississippi. In the same election cycle, Mississippi elected two Republicans to Congress, Thad Cochran and Trent Lott.[81]

The Republican victories in Mississippi in 1972, however, did not match Council priorities as much as they signified a reentry of the state into national politics. Council ideology was not irrelevant to that transition. In fact, Council ideology and its commitment to white supremacy made the Republican Party structure in Mississippi unique in comparison to national and regional models of Republican ascendancy. In his study of Mississippi politics after 1965, historian Chris Danielson describes Republican growth in Mississippi as a product of growing dissatisfaction with black political empowerment, especially in black-dominated areas of the state where local Democratic Party structures came to reflect the color of their constituents. Local political realities and the absence of widespread suburbanization in Mississippi drove the Republican Party structure in the state away from early attempts to capture black votes and toward rural white constituencies that responded to racist appeals.[82]

But the persistence of white defiance within Mississippi's Republican Party left it further to the right of the national party than other constituencies migrating into GOP allegiance by 1980. In January 1980, Bill Simmons made public a letter he sent to the chairman of the Republican National Committee, Bill Brock, in which he urged Brock to remember that organizations like the Citizens' Council were "representative of a cross section of the kind of conservative patriotic Americans on whose support the Republican Party must depend if it hopes for success in this part of the country."[83] Simmons's letter was one of the few direct acknowledgements that the Republican Party was the organization's party of choice. In general, the Council repeatedly declared that not enough difference existed between Democrats and Republicans, and that fact made the organization much more likely to drift toward a third-party option.

Reagan's election in 1980 changed that pattern. After years of self-described marginalization in a political system dominated by liberals and moderates, Reagan's election warranted a celebration. While the Council never actively endorsed Reagan prior to the election, his victory made the cover of the December 1980 issue of *The Citizen,* complete with a photo of the first couple and a headline that read, "Ronnie and Nancy!" Inside, the editorial's title, "New Hope for America," encapsulated the triumph that his election symbolized for the organization.[84] An editorial in the January 1981 issue described Reagan's election as "almost too good to be true." His persona evoked a sense of "independence and rugged individualism" that proved that candidates no longer had to bow to pressure groups or depend on regional loyalty in order to win an election.[85]

Council leaders perceived in Ronald Reagan a true reflection of their politics of defiance. In him, their suspicions of federal intrusion and the value of their whiteness over liberal fantasies of equality, and worse, entitlement, became normalized. Reagan campaigned with white southern sensitivities in mind, vowing to scale back assistance programs to the poor, cut taxes for white working-class Americans, and reassert American superiority in foreign policy. His experience with Sunbelt conservatism in California at a time when it was developing common ground with white southerners was critical to political gains in the Deep South. White southern realignment into the Republican Party was well under way by 1980, but Council support of that switch remained elusive. It was in the figure of Ronald Reagan that the organization's goals seemed satisfied. Given the Council's loyalty to white supremacy, Reagan embodied the formula of conservative white leadership and defiance that the organization embraced.

Prior to 1980 the Council never expressed its support for a sitting president. From its founding under Dwight Eisenhower's administration through five more administrations, much of its message depended on the persistence of Washington's bureaucracy, liberalism, and obsession with bloc voting to stoke the anger of its white supporters into political defiance. The Council had gone as far as to describe itself as a minority group in 1960 when it supported independent presidential electors. The transition into white majority politics, begun in the wake of sweeping civil rights legislation, seemed to reach its logical end in 1980 with the ascendancy of conservatism. *The Citizen* reprinted articles by the likes of Newt Gingrich, Patrick Buchanan, and George Will, each emerging voices for the New Right coalition of evangelicals, fiscal conservatives, and foreign policy hardliners.[86]

But the trope of white victimization did not disappear so quickly. Even in the midst of a more sympathetic political environment than it had experienced in over thirty years of existence, the paranoia that characterized the Cold War–era defense of segregation persisted, making any deviation from hardline conservatism untenable. Less than two years after it declared victory in the White House, a Council editorial headline asked the question, "'Me-Tooism': Will Republican Liberals Drive Voters into New Third Party?" The question referred to the proposed twenty-five-year extension of the Voting Rights Act, and it predicted a southern defection akin to 1960 or Wallace's third-party movement in 1968 if it passed.[87]

The ease with which the Council dove back into the margins of mainstream politics is evidence of the "adversarianism" that Kirkpatrick Sale identified in 1975. As had been true from its earliest days, the Council relied on vacuums of power for growth. The conservative ascendancy and the alliance between Deep South and Sunbelt conservatism that the election of 1980 signified, made it difficult to remain in a contrarian position. Its position was especially difficult to maintain given the race-neutral slant that multiregional alliances required of conservatism.

The Citizens' Council's easy transition back into defiance, even after hailing Reagan's victory, is evidence of this fact. In an interview with Howard Raines in 1979, Council founder Robert Patterson looked back on twenty-five years of white resistance. Insisting that white Americans would never accept integration, he continued to deny the success of the civil rights movement, stating, "Civil rights organizations never mobilized blacks. They mobilized reporters and Freedom Riders and politicians." The machinations of white liberals, in other words, forced change on the South, and now the rest of the country had become their new target. In reaction, Raines pressed Patterson to account for the lack of white southern support for the Council, asking him if it reflected white Mississippians' acceptance of the new racial order. Patterson offered another explanation:

I don't believe that. If they do [accept the new racial order], why do they all live in the suburbs, and why do they move out of the neighborhood when Negroes move in? And why do they send their children to private school? And why do they manipulate and move to go out to an area that doesn't have many Negroes in it so they can send their child to a virtually all-white school? . . . They haven't accepted integration. They've run from it.[88]

Patterson's remarks are revelatory of the way in which white supremacy, even as it became enshrined within a national political party, defined Council identity more than anything else. It is easy to see in the Council movement a long journey to Republican identity. But a look at the organization in the post–civil rights years suggests that the Council was much more comfortable within Radical Right networks than it was in mainstream politics. The distance it kept from more respectable networks of power enabled a condescension toward white self-denial that Patterson's reflections on white flight evidenced. That approach also enabled the ideology of defiance to survive political shifts that accrued within party structures.

The Citizens' Council in Mississippi survived the civil rights movement because it maintained that stature of defiance while its sister organizations, some of them from their moment of birth, strived for political relevance. In the process, organizations in North Carolina, Virginia, and Tennessee abandoned race-baiting rhetoric and sold their objections as conservative ideology. The Council in Mississippi experimented with these approaches but only as long as it complemented white supremacy as its raison d'être. The reinvigoration of defiance through the success of George Wallace's third-party challenge in 1968 was critical to maintaining that commitment, but more significantly, it proved that disaffected whites were a constituency in their own right and one worth pursuing. In its unapologetic embrace of white supremacy, and its political endorsement of George Wallace in 1968, the Council secured a place for defiance within the existing two-party structure. This defiant strand of conservatism was not peculiar to the Deep South, and it would continue to resurface and demand deference at critical moments of American crisis.

CONCLUSION

On April 11, 1985, the Citizens' Councils of America moved out of its modern headquarters in downtown Jackson and into more modest facilities, and within four years, in June 1989, the organization closed its doors for good. Robert B. Patterson seemed resigned about it, attributing the end of thirty-five years of resistance to a simple fact: "We had no program left." The end of segregation laws, he argued, rendered the Council's influence obsolete.[1] The timing of his surrender is curious considering that school integration in Mississippi had been in place for nearly twenty years by 1989. The Council's defense of segregation could have ended with the passage of the Civil Rights Act of 1964. But the organization persisted. Its leaders endured more than two decades of legislative defeats and court orders, all aimed at dismantling state-sanctioned vestiges of white supremacy and black marginalization. At any one of those points, the organization could have—perhaps should have—folded. The fact that it survived could be attributable to any number of factors, both practical and intangible, but a significant component of that survival was the organization's patient commitment to white supremacy and the renewed relevance of that position once white Americans outside of the South confronted, and then embraced, their own racism.

This book has emphasized the contexts within which the Citizens' Council acted from 1954 to 1989. That time period saw years of manic defiance from white segregationists forswearing compliance with federal mandates. But it also included dramatic changes at the hands of tireless black activists and sympathetic members of the white power structure. In the midst of those changes the Council did not evolve from its original position. Its leaders and the breadth of their work are evidence of the incredible adaptability of white supremacy and the variety of institutions that have accommodated it.

Scholars have relied on the Citizens' Council to represent white opposition to the civil rights movement, its power, and its excesses. But that use has severely circumscribed our understanding of the complexities of white resistance and discouraged deeper investigations of the Council's post–civil rights migrations. For the Citizens' Council, its influence and model of defiance seeped into organizations like Americans for the Preservation of the White Race, initiated white flight to private schools, and connected white Mississippians to a conservative movement within a political party that for over a century had represented the northern antislavery conspiracy and Reconstruction. Perhaps when we track the relative successes and failures of an organization like the Citizens' Council, we should be more mindful of the ways in which social movements, regardless of the success or failure of their particular campaigns, impact attitudes and offer platforms that are often adapted and co-opted to other purposes and other movements.

Historians' assessment of the Council has been situated within its most powerful years, 1954–1964. For Council administrators, however, measures of success became less clear-cut as distance grew from those heady years of organization and terror. In a letter to former Sovereignty Commission director Erle Johnston in 1987, Bill Simmons looked back on those years with some wistfulness, ambivalent about whether the years of Council activism were triumphs or failures. If the circumstances of 1987 could serve as any kind of measure, he reflected, the latter was more fitting:

We are seeing the bitter fruit of the Voting Rights Act . . . so interpreted as to mandate gerrymandering for the advancement of black political power; school desegregation to mean busing to achieve racial balance . . . ; black takeover of the sports scene and much so-called entertainment; a total reversal of racial politics; the reduction of once-sovereign states to mere federal dependencies; affirmative action; minority set-aside programs; skyrocketing crime; . . . the transformation of major areas of Mississippi's capital city into a ghetto that reaches from North West Street to Clinton and from I-20 West to Madison County. In retrospect, as I looked through some of our archives in an effort to refresh my memory . . . MISSISSIPPI, THE AGONY YEARS began to look more and more like, "the good old days."[2]

Ultimately, Bill Simmons's final word on his life's work is instructive. His obituary upon his death in 2007 (a piece that reporters speculated to be self-written) never mentioned the Citizens' Council. Instead, the profile explained his return to Jackson in 1954 as the beginning of thirty-five years of "publishing, school administration and foundation administration work," during which time he traveled for speeches, made multiple television appearances, and published articles.[3] Perhaps the cumulative wearing away of the "good old days" that he identified in his letter to Johnston undermined his faith in the value of decades-long defiance. More likely, he wished for his legacy to rest within the more general realms of education and activism, an embrace of half-truths that concealed his role in assaulting those very categories.

Read differently, however, Simmons's work and the work of the Council lost its distinctiveness when the tenets of their ideology became absorbed into mainstream political threads, polarizing rhetoric, and white flight from integration. Council administrator Medford Evans made a similar point in 1985 in response to the Council's move out of its modern, custom-built facility into leased office space. The Council's founding purpose, he explained, was to protect schoolchildren. And it was in that purpose that, he argued, the organization had found the greatest success through the network of private academies that dominated Mississippi's educational landscape. Their success was, to Evans, a symbolic passing of the torch from the Council's earliest work to local communities. In that scenario, the Council's influence was less necessary, as "community after community has learned that political guidance and control by educationists, politicians, and agitators is generally more of a hindrance than a help."[4]

The Council's prioritization of white unity through various iterations of civil rights activism, success, and white backlash ensured that white resistance would remain relevant regardless of its victories and losses. Because the organization persisted after the civil rights movement dissipated, its alignment with national sentiments about race and difference, equality and entitlement, was more seamless than history has recognized. Just as Citizens' Council leaders pulled lessons from the defeat of the Dixiecrats in 1948, the experiences that accompanied organized white resistance to civil rights cultivated white activism and dissent as part and parcel of the American political system. The patient cultivation of white supremacy through organizations like the Citizens' Council and its network of allies ensured that the legacies of segregation, disfranchisement, and institutional discrimination would not be lost to history but find new ways to survive and divide.

NOTES

INTRODUCTION

1. Lola Lee Bruington to Neil R. McMillen, March 10, 1967, Folder 4, Box 1, M-99, Citizens' Council Collection, Special Collections, McCain Library and Archives, University of Southern Mississippi.

2. Andrew Ferguson, "The Boy from Yazoo City: Haley Barbour, Mississippi's Favorite Son," *Weekly Standard,* 27 December 2010, www.weeklystandard.com/articles/boy-yazoo-city_523551.html.

3. Neil McMillen, *The Citizens' Council: Organized Resistance to the Second Reconstruction, 1954–64,* 2nd edition (Urbana: University of Illinois Press, 1994), 299–304.

4. Stephanie Rolph, "The Citizens' Council in Africa: White Supremacy in Global Perspective," *Journal of Southern History* 82, No. 3 (August 2016): 617–50; Daniel Geary and Jennifer Sutton, "Resisting the Wind of Change: The Citizens' Councils and European Decolonization," in *The U.S. South and Europe: Transatlantic Relations in the Nineteenth and Twentieth Centuries,* ed. Cornelius A. van Minnen and Manfred Berg (Lexington: University Press of Kentucky, 2013), 269–79; Thomas Noer, "Segregationists and the World: The Foreign Policy of the White Resistance," in *Window on Freedom: Race, Civil Rights, and Foreign Affairs, 1945–1988,* ed. Brenda Gayle Plummer (Chapel Hill: University of North Carolina Press, 2003), 141–62; Zoe Hyman, "American Segregationist Ideology and White Southern Africa, 1948–1975" (PhD diss., University of Sussex, 2011), 108–88.

5. McMillen, *Citizens' Council,* 352–54; Dan T. Carter, *The Politics of Rage: George Wallace, the Origins of the New Conservatism, and the Transformation of American Politics* (New York: Simon and Schuster, 1995), 335, 343.

6. George W. Shannon, "Editor Scores Book for Bias," *The Citizen* 16, No. 5 (February 1972): 18–22; John J. Synon, "Underwritten Carpetbagger," *The Citizen* 16, No. 5 (February 1972): 23–26.

7. Shannon, "Editor Scores Book for Bias," 20 and 22.

8. McMillen, *Citizens' Council,* xiii.

9. The scholarship on the impact of white southern resistance continues to evolve, but some of the most significant contributions include Numan V. Bartley, *The Rise of Massive Resistance: Race and Politics in the South during the 1950's* (Baton Rouge: Louisiana State University Press, 1969); Carter, *The Politics of Rage;* Kari Frederickson, *The Dixiecrat Revolt*

and the End of the Solid South (Chapel Hill: University of North Carolina Press, 2001); Clive Webb, ed., *Massive Resistance: Southern Opposition to the Second Reconstruction* (New York: Oxford University Press, 2005); George Lewis, *Massive Resistance: The White Response to the Civil Rights Movement* (New York: Bloomsbury Academic, 2006); Kevin M. Kruse, *White Flight: Atlanta and the Making of Modern Conservatism* (Princeton, NJ: Princeton University Press, 2007); Matthew D. Lassiter, *The Silent Majority: Suburban Politics in the Sunbelt South* (Princeton, NJ: Princeton University Press, 2007); Joseph Crespino, *In Search of Another Country: Mississippi and the Conservative Counterrevolution* (Princeton, NJ: Princeton University Press, 2007); Joseph E. Lowndes, *From the New Deal to the New Right: Race and the Southern Origins of Modern Conservatism* (New Haven, CT: Yale University Press, 2008); Jason Morgan Ward, *Defending White Democracy: The Making of a Segregationist Movement and the Remaking of Racial Politics, 1936–1965* (Chapel Hill: University of North Carolina Press, 2011); and William P. Hustwit, *James J. Kilpatrick: Salesman for Segregation* (Chapel Hill: University of North Carolina Press, 2013). Scholarship on white resistance and conservatism outside of the South includes George H. Nash, *The Conservative Intellectual Movement in America Since 1945* (New York: Basic Books, 1976); Jonathan Schoenwald, *A Time for Choosing: The Rise of Modern American Conservatism* (New York: Oxford University Press, 2001); Lisa McGirr, *Suburban Warriors: The Origins of the New American Right* (Princeton, NJ: Princeton University Press, 2002); Donald T. Critchlow, *The Conservative Ascendancy: How the GOP Right Made Political History* (Cambridge, MA: Harvard University Press, 2007); Daniel K. Williams, *God's Own Party: The Making of the Christian Right* (New York: Oxford University Press, 2010); Clive Webb, *Rabble Rousers: The American Far Right in the Civil Rights Era* (Athens: University of Georgia Press, 2010); and Darren Dochuk, *From Bible Belt to Sunbelt: Plain-Folk Religion, Grassroots Politics, and the Rise of Evangelical Conservatism* (New York: W. W. Norton, 2012).

10. Penny M. Von Eschen, *Race Against Empire: Black Americans and Anticolonialism, 1937–1957* (Ithaca, NY: Cornell University Press, 1997); Peniel Joseph, *Waiting 'Til the Midnight Hour: A Narrative History of Black Power in America* (New York: Henry Holt, 2006); Clayborne Carson, *In Struggle: SNCC and the Black Awakening of the 1960s* (Cambridge, MA: Harvard University Press, 1995); Nico Slate, ed., *Black Power beyond Borders: The Global Dimensions of the Black Power Movement* (New York: Palgrave Macmillan, 2012); Gerald Horne, *Black and Red: W. E. B. DuBois and the Afro-American Response to the Cold War, 1944–1960* (New York: State University of New York Press, 1986); Brenda Gayle Plummer, *In Search of Power: African Americans in the Era of Decolonization, 1956–1974* (Cambridge: Cambridge University Press, 2013), 24–61; and Brenda Gayle Plummer, *Rising Wind: Black Americans and U.S. Foreign Affairs, 1935–1960* (Chapel Hill: University of North Carolina Press, 1996), 167–298.

11. George M. Frederickson, *White Supremacy: A Comparative Study in American and South African History* (New York: Oxford University Press, 1981), xix.

12. Grace Elizabeth Hale, *Making Whiteness: The Culture of Segregation in the South, 1890–1940* (New York: Vintage Books, 1998), xi.

13. Joel Williamson, *The Crucible of Race: Black-White Relations in the American South since Emancipation* (New York: Oxford University Press, 1984); Stephanie McCurry, *Mas-*

ters of *Small Worlds: Yeoman Households, Gender Relations, and the Political Culture of the Antebellum South Carolina Low Country* (New York: Oxford University Press, 1995); Paul V. Murphy, *The Rebuke of History: The Southern Agrarians and American Conservative Thought* (Chapel Hill: University of North Carolina Press, 2001); Stephen Cresswell, *Rednecks, Redeemers, and Race: Mississippi after Reconstruction, 1877–1917* (Jackson: University Press of Mississippi, 2006); Trent Watts, *One Homogeneous People: Narratives of White Southern Identity, 1890–1920* (Knoxville: University of Tennessee Press, 2010); Nell Irvin Painter, *The History of White People* (New York: W. W. Norton, 2010); and Kristine Taylor, "Untimely Subjects: White Trash and the Making of Racial Innocence in the Postwar South," *American Quarterly* 67, No. 1 (March 2015): 55–79.

14. The term *moderate* applies to elected officials, journalists, and other public figures who questioned the wisdom of open defiance as a response to federal directives. The term had varying meanings in each state, but in Mississippi moderates like Governor J. P. Coleman embraced "practical segregation," a defense of the existing system that, in Joseph Crespino's description, "advocated realistic approaches that tried to maintain good relations with local African Americans and minimize outside attention and federal interference." See Crespino, *In Search of Another Country*, 19. The Mississippi State Sovereignty Commission, the state agency created for the purposes of improving the state's image, was an example of the vision behind practical segregation. Moderates saw the Council as exacerbating the worst elements of racism in Mississippi through its frequent calls for stalwart defiance, its use of white supremacist dog whistles in its publications, and the local terror it advocated to eliminate dissent. During the Council's most popular years, moderate leadership was less outspoken than it would be after the Meredith crisis in 1962. In addition to *In Search of Another Country*, see Robert E. Luckett Jr., *Joe T. Patterson and the White South's Dilemma: Evolving Resistance to Black Advancement* (Jackson: University Press of Mississippi, 2015).

CHAPTER ONE

Note to chapter epigraph: James Graham Cook, *The Segregationists* (New York: Appleton-Century-Crofts, 1962), 80.

1. Association of Citizens' Councils of Mississippi, "The Citizens' Council," Pamphlet, November 1954, 5, Archival Reading Room, General Collection, Mississippi Department of Archives and History, Jackson, Mississippi.

2. George H. Nash, *The Conservative Intellectual Movement in America Since 1945* (New York: Basic Books, 1976), 3–5.

3. Ibid., 55–56.

4. Ibid., 81–82.

5. Ibid., 82; Albert Jay Nock, *Our Enemy the State* (New York: William Morrow, 1935), 4 and 7–8.

6. Nock, *Our Enemy the State*, 13.

7. Nash, *The Conservative Intellectual Movement*, 5–8.

8. Friedrich A. Hayek, *The Road to Serfdom* (Chicago: University of Chicago Press, 1944), 32 and 59.

9. Ibid., 76–77.

10. Peter Viereck, *Conservatism Revisited* (New York: Collier Books, 1949), 32–33.

11. Ibid., 143.

12. Bernard Iddings Bell, *Crowd Culture: An Examination of a Way of Life* (New York: Harper and Brothers, 1952), 53–56 and 69.

13. Jonathan Schoenwald, *A Time for Choosing: The Rise of Modern American Conservatism* (New York: Oxford University Press, 2001), 14–34.

14. Ibid., 15–16.

15. *Facts Forum*, Vol. 1, No. 4, 1952, Microfilm, Reel 46, Series F8, and Vol. 2, No. 1, January 1953, 3, The Right Wing Collection of the University of Iowa Libraries.

16. Ibid., Vol. 1, No. 10, October 1953.

17. Ibid., Vol. 3, No. 4, April 1953.

18. Ibid., Vol. 1, No. 11, November 1953; Schoenwald, *A Time for Choosing*, 96.

19. Ibid., Vol. 1, No. 2, September 1953.

20. Ibid., Vol. 4, No. 2, February 1955, 20.

21. Ibid., 22–23.

22. Richard H. King, "The Struggle Against Equality: Conservative Intellectuals in the Civil Rights Era, 1954–1975," in *The Role of Ideas in the Civil Rights South*, ed. Ted Ownby (Jackson: University Press of Mississippi, 2002), 116–18.

23. Glenn Feldman, *The Irony of the Solid South: Democrats, Republicans, and Race, 1865–1944* (Tuscaloosa: University of Alabama Press, 2013), 2.

24. Kari Frederickson, *The Dixiecrat Revolt and the End of the Solid South* (Chapel Hill: University of North Carolina Press, 2001), 118–23.

25. Ibid., 133; Jason Morgan Ward, *Defending White Democracy: The Making of a Segregationist Movement and the Remaking of Racial Politics, 1936–1965* (Chapel Hill: University of North Carolina Press, 2011), 104–5.

26. Frederickson, *Dixiecrat Revolt*, 5–7; Ward, *Defending White Democracy*, 99–104; Numan V. Bartley, *The Rise of Massive Resistance: Race and Politics in the South during the 1950's* (Baton Rouge: Louisiana State University Press, 1969), 28–35.

27. Joseph E. Lowndes, *From the New Deal to the New Right: Race and the Southern Origins of Modern Conservatism* (New Haven, CT: Yale University Press, 2008), 11–39.

28. Frederickson, *Dixiecrat Revolt*, 198.

29. American States' Rights Association, Pamphlet, 1953, Folder: 1953, Civil Rights, Box 34, Subseries 1, File Series 3, James O. Eastland Papers, Archives and Special Collections, J. D. Williams Library, University of Mississippi, Oxford, Mississippi.

30. Dixiecrats Democratic Association of Louisiana, *The Dixiecrat: Sentinel of the South*, 1951, Folder: 1951, Civil Rights, Box 34, Subseries 1, File Series 3, Eastland Papers.

31. Ward, *Defending White Democracy*, 103–4 and 120; Frederickson, *Dixiecrat Revolt*, 187–216.

32. Patricia Sullivan, "Southern Reformers, the New Deal, and the Movement's Foundation," in *The Civil Rights Movement*, ed. Jack E. Davis (Malden, MA: Blackwell, 2001), 12–29.

33. John Dittmer, *Local People: The Struggle for Civil Rights in Mississippi* (Urbana: University of Illinois Press, 1995), 25–26 and 28–29.

34. Ibid., 20.

35. Walter Sillers Jr. to Governor Hugh White, 14 September 1953, Folder 5, Box 3 (3:5), Walter Sillers Jr. Papers, University Archives, Delta State University, Cleveland, Mississippi.

36. Charles C. Bolton, *The Hardest Deal of All: The Battle over School Integration in Mississippi, 1870–1980* (Jackson: University Press of Mississippi, 2005), 33–49.

37. Ibid., 49–58.

38. Ibid., 43.

39. *Brown v. Board of Education of Topeka* 347 U.S. 483 (1954).

40. Thomas P. Brady, Interview by Orley B. Caudill, 7 March 1972, Jackson, Mississippi, Civil Rights in Mississippi Digital Archive, University of Southern Mississippi Digital Collections, digilib.usm.edu/cdm/ref/collection/coh/id/9309; George Lewis, *Massive Resistance: The White Response to the Civil Rights Movement* (London: Hodder Arnold, 2006), 43.

41. Lewis, *Massive Resistance,* 17–18.

42. Tom P. Brady, *Black Monday* (Winona: Association of Citizens' Councils of Mississippi, 1955).

43. Ibid., 67–77.

44. Ibid., 84–85.

CHAPTER TWO

Note to chapter epigraph: Sam H. Bowers Jr., Interview by Debra Spencer, January 30, 1984, Florence, MS, 17, www.mdah.ms.gov/arrec/digital_archives/bowers/transcript.php?page=17.

1. James Graham Cook, *The Segregationists* (New York: Appleton-Century-Crofts, 1962), 49 and 52.

2. Ibid., 53.

3. Paul Anthony, "Pro-Segregation Groups' History and Trends," *New South* 12, No. 1 (January 1957): 4–6, Allen Eugene Cox Papers, MSU; Neil McMillen, *The Citizens' Council: Organized Resistance to the Second Reconstruction, 1954–64,* 2nd edition (Urbana: University of Illinois Press, 1994), 18–19.

4. James C. Cobb, *The Most Southern Place on Earth: The Mississippi Delta and the Roots of Regional Identity* (New York: Oxford University Press, 1992), 91–97.

5. Ibid., 99.

6. Ibid., 200–1.

7. Anthony, "Pro-Segregation Groups' History," 5.

8. Ibid., 7.

9. John Dittmer, *Local People: The Struggle for Civil Rights in Mississippi* (Urbana: University of Illinois Press, 1995), 38–39.

10. Ibid., 39–40.

11. Cobb, *Most Southern Place,* 144.

12. Cook, *Segregationists,* 53.

13. Charles C. Bolton, *The Hardest Deal of All: The Battle over School Integration in Mississippi, 1870–1980* (Jackson: University Press of Mississippi, 2005), 69–70.

14. Ibid., 71–72.

15. Ibid., 25; Association of Citizens' Councils of Mississippi, Minutes of the Organizational Meeting, 1954, Z/0773.000: Association of the Citizens' Councils of Mississippi Collection, MDAH; Fred Jones, ACCM Letter, 15 October 1954, Folder 5, Box 7, Series 29, John C. Stennis Collection, Congressional and Political Research Library, MSU.

16. ACCM, "The Citizens' Council," Pamphlet, 4–5, ACCM Collection, MDAH.

17. Ibid., 2–3.

18. McMillen, *Citizens' Council,* 25–33; Bartley, *Rise of Massive Resistance,* 84–85 and 104. Bartley also makes the point that Council leadership split along rural/urban lines. In cities, leadership tended to fall into the hands of working-class whites, while in the rural areas Council leaders tended to be from the planter or business class.

19. Fred Jones, ACCM Letter, 15 October 1954, Folder 5, Box 7, Series 29, John C. Stennis Collection, Congressional and Political Research Library, MSU.

20. Robert B. Patterson to All Mississippians, 8 December 1954, Subject File, Citizens' Council Collection, MDAH.

21. ACCM, "Why We Should Vote *For* the School Amendment December 21, 1954," Subject File, Citizens' Council Collection, MDAH.

22. Ibid.

23. Jones, ACCM Letter.

24. Hodding Carter III, *The South Strikes Back* (New York: Doubleday, 1959), 45.

25. Dittmer, *Local People,* 48–49.

26. John Temple Graves, "Citizens Councils Could Lose All If Klansmen Take Charge," *State Times,* February 21, 1956, Medgar Wiley and Myrlie Beasley Evers Papers, 1900–1994, Subgroup 1, Series 14, Box 3, Folder 4: News Clippings (Citizens Councils) 1955–1956, MDAH.

27. Patricia Sullivan, *Lift Every Voice: The NAACP and the Making of the Civil Rights Movement* (New York: New Press, 2009), 421–23; Bolton, *The Hardest Deal of All,* 73–75; McMillen, *Citizens' Council,* 211; Dittmer, *Local People,* 43–48; Annual Report, Mississippi State Office, National Association for the Advancement of Colored People, 1955, 4, Evers Papers, Subgroup 1, Series 6, Box 2, Folder 40: Annual Reports (NAACP–Mississippi Conference President), 1954–1957; Annual Report, 1956, 3, Evers Papers, Subgroup 1, Series 6, Box 2, Folder 40: Annual Reports (NAACP–Mississippi Conference President), 1954–1957, MDAH.

28. Ruby Hurley to Gloster B. Current, August 22, 1955; Hurley, Memorandum to Field Secretaries, September 19, 1955; *NAACP News and Action,* September 1955, 1–2, Evers Papers, Subgroup 1, Series 2, Box 2, Folder 3, NAACP Field Secretary Papers.

29. Bettye Collier-Thomas and V. P. Franklin, *My Soul Is a Witness: A Chronology of the Civil Rights Era, 1954–1965* (New York: Henry Holt, 2000), 35, 52, 59–60, 65, and 74.

30. Hodding Carter, "A Wave of Terror Threatens the South," *Look,* 22 March 1955, 32–36, Cox Papers.

31. Gene Roberts and Hank Klibanoff, *The Race Beat: The Press, the Civil Rights Struggle, and the Awakening of a Nation* (New York: Vintage, 2007), 76–77, 82; Annual Report, Mississippi State Office, National Association for the Advancement of Colored People, 1955, 5, Evers Papers, Series 6, Box 2, Folder 39: Annual Reports.

32. Ernst Borinski to Editor of *State Times*, May 29, 1955, Ernst Borinski Papers, Sub-Series 2, Box 6, Folder 77: Correspondence to *State Times*, 1954–1955, MDAH.

33. Roberts and Klibanoff, *Race Beat*, 76–80.

34. Ibid., 80–82.

35. ACCM, "Annual Report," August 1955, Annual Reports, 1–2, ACCM Collection, MSU.

36. R. B. Patterson, "We Must Strengthen and Build Our Organization for a Long, Hard Fight," in Annual Report, August 1955, 2, ACCM Collection, MSU.

37. Ibid., 4.

38. Cook, *Segregationists*, 66–68, quote on 68.

39. Dan Wakefield, "Respectable Racism," *The Nation*, 22 October 1955, 339–41, Folder 52B, Box 1, Series 1, Cox Papers.

40. James Desmond, "New Klan's Whip: Economic Terror," 22 November 1955, *Daily News*, Cox Papers.

41. McMillen, *Citizens' Council*, preface to the 2nd edition, xxiii–xxiv.

42. Delmar Dennis, Interview by Bobby DeLaughter, May 3, 1990, 6–7, Bobby De-Laughter Collection, Box 4, Folder 21: Rev. Delmar Dennis, 1 of 2, MDAH.

43. George Lewis, *Massive Resistance: The White Response to the Civil Rights Movement* (London: Hodder Arnold, 2006), 50.

44. Ibid., 51–53.

45. Ibid., 42.

46. Ibid., 42 and 44–46.

47. McMillen, *Citizens' Council*, 41–44.

48. Ibid., 50–56.

49. Ibid., 105–6; Lewis, *Massive Resistance*, 52–57.

50. McMillen, *Citizens' Council*, 59–67.

51. G. A. K. Sutton to James O. Eastland, 1950, Folder: 1950, Civil Rights, Box 34, Subseries 1, File Series 3, Eastland Papers.

52. Stanley F. Morse to James O. Eastland, 23 July 1955, Folder 1: 1955, Civil Rights, Box 34, Subseries 1, File Series 3, Eastland Papers.

53. Walter Sillers to J. B. Henderson, 14 December 1957, Folder 13, Box 5, Sillers Papers.

54. Chris Meyers Asch, *The Senator and the Sharecropper: The Freedom Struggles of James O. Eastland and Fannie Lou Hamer* (New York: New Press, 2008), 150–55.

55. McMillen, *Citizens' Council*, 116–18; Sarah H. Brown, "The Role of Elite Leadership in the Southern Defense of Segregation, 1954–1964," *Journal of Southern History* 77, No. 4 (November 2011): 832–40.

56. Jim Bissett, "The Dilemma over Moderates: School Desegregation in Alamance County, North Carolina," *Journal of Southern History* 81, No. 4 (November 2015): 890–91; Anthony J. Badger, *New Deal/New South: An Anthony Badger Reader* (Fayetteville: University of Arkansas Press, 2007), 88–89, 92–94.

57. John Kyle Day, *The Southern Manifesto: Massive Resistance and the Fight to Preserve Segregation* (Jackson: University Press of Mississippi, 2014), 69–70, 110, 133, 136–37.

58. Lewis, *Massive Resistance,* 83 and 87.

59. McMillen, *Citizens' Council,* 118–19.

60. "Our Scope and Purpose," *The Citizens' Council,* October 1956, MSU.

61. Dittmer, *Local People,* 70–73; NAACP, Press Release, 3 June 1956; C. R. Darden to Gloster B. Current, 29 September 1956; Gloster B. Current to F. H. Dunn, 27 November 1956, NAACP Microfilm Collection.

62. Southern Regional Council, "Pro-Segregation Groups in the South, 19 November 1956, Folder 15, Box 3, M-99, Citizens' Council Collection, USM.

63. For correspondence about Eastland's deal with Robert Patterson, see Folder 1, Box 35, Subseries 1, File Series 3, Eastland Papers.

64. John C. Stennis to Ellis Wright, 16 February 1956; Ellis Wright to John C. Stennis, 21 February 1956, Folder 6, Box 7, Series 29, Stennis Collection.

65. John C. Stennis to T. A. Stennis, 6 March 1956, and John C. Stennis to John Mc-Cully, 14 May 1956, Folder 10, Box 7, Series 29, Stennis Collection. Stennis's evolution on the issue of whether or not Kemper County should form its own Citizens' Council chapter is revealed in a series of letters he exchanged with friends and family at home. For the entire exchange, see Folder 10, Box 7, Series 29, Stennis Collection.

66. Bartley, *Rise of Massive Resistance,* 104. For a history of the political transition that the white primaries in Mississippi ushered in, see Stephen Cresswell's *Rednecks, Redeemers, and Race: Mississippi after Reconstruction, 1877–1917* (Jackson: University Press of Mississippi, 2006). For evidence of the political shifts that accompanied black access to the vote after 1965, see Chris Danielson's *After Freedom Summer: How Race Realigned Mississippi Politics, 1965–1986* (Gainesville: University Press of Florida, 2011).

67. The correspondence connected with the pursuit of tax-exempt status for the Educational Fund of the Citizens' Council is extensive. See Folder: 1954, Civil Rights, Box 34, Subseries 1, File Series 3, Eastland Papers.

68. Citizens' Council, "The Educational Fund of the Citizens' Councils," Pamphlet, 1956, Subject File, ACCM Collection, MDAH; McMillen, *Citizens' Council,* 38; "Why An Educational Fund Is Necessary for Victory," *The Citizens' Council,* April 1957, 4.

69. "Mississippi TV Shows Clicking for Councils," *The Citizens' Council,* August 1957, 1; Robert B. Patterson to Bruce Henderson, 9 May 1957, Folder 5, Civil Rights 1957, Box 37, Subseries 1, File Series 3, Eastland Papers; McMillen, *Citizens' Council,* 38.

70. "Council Mourns Passing of Dick Morphew," *Aspect,* Vol. IV, No. 9, Subject File, Association of Citizens' Councils of Mississippi, Z/0773.000: ACCM, 1942–1973, MDAH; Cook, *Segregationists,* 83.

71. "Mississippi TV Shows Clicking for Councils," *The Citizens' Council,* August 1957, 1.

72. "Committee on UnAmerican Activities and Its Function," *Forum,* Reel #57×1, 5 November 1957, Citizens' Council *Forum* Collection, Special Collections, Mitchell Memorial Library, Mississippi State University.

73. Ibid.

74. Robert Patterson to Bruce Henderson, 9 May 1957, Folder 5: Civil Rights 1957, Box 37, Subseries 1, File Series 3, Eastland Papers.

75. Yasuhiro Katagiri, *The Mississippi State Sovereignty Commission: Civil Rights and States' Rights* (Jackson: University Press of Mississippi, 2001), 5–7.

76. Ibid., 7–8.

77. Ibid., xxvii–xxvii and xxxiv–xxxv.

78. Joseph Crespino, *In Search of Another Country: Mississippi and the Conservative Counterrevolution* (Princeton, NJ: Princeton University Press, 2007), 26–27. In an interview conducted in 1993, former director of the MSSC Erle Johnston claimed that it was the Citizens' Council who initiated both the creation and naming of the MSSC. See Erle Johnston, Interview with Yasuhiro Katagiri, August 13, 1993, Forest, Mississippi, Civil Rights in Mississippi Digital Archives, digilib.usm.edu/cdm/ref/collection/coh/id/4035. Jenny Irons brings more nuance to the complex relationship between the Council and MSSC, particularly under J. P. Coleman's governorship; see Jenny Irons, *Reconstituting Whiteness: The Mississippi State Sovereignty Commission* (Nashville, TN: Vanderbilt University Press, 2010), 36–50.

79. Katagiri, *Mississippi State Sovereignty Commission*, 9–24.

80. Ibid., 24–27; Crespino, *In Search of Another Country*, 26–27; Irons, *Reconstituting Whiteness*, 40–43.

81. "State Sovereignty Commission," #57×7, Citizens' Council *Forum*, December 18, 1957.

82. Katagiri, *Mississippi State Sovereignty Commission*, 27; Robert B. Patterson to James P. Coleman, July 25, 1957, James P. Coleman Papers, Series 5, Box 12, Folder 6, MDAH; Coleman to Patterson, July 26, 1957, Coleman Papers, Series 5, Folder 6.

83. Nash, *The Conservative Intellectual Movement*, 16–18.

84. Frank Chodorov, "Civil Rights Versus Natural Rights," *Human Events* 14, No. 13, 30 March 1957, 1–3.

85. William F. Buckley, *National Review*, Vol. 1, No. 1, 5–6.

86. Clinton Rossiter, *Conservatism in America* (New York: Knopf, 1956), 2, 9, and 12.

87. Bartley, *Rise of Massive Resistance*, 237–39.

CHAPTER THREE

Note to chapter epigraph: Hodding Carter III, *The South Strikes Back* (New York: Doubleday, 1959), 19.

1. John R. Salter Jr., *Jackson, Mississippi: An American Chronicle of Struggle and Schism* (Lincoln: University of Nebraska Press, 2011), 11–14.

2. William J. Simmons, Confidential Communication No. 4 to Members of Jackson States' Rights Association, 29 April 1955, Folder 1: 1955, Civil Rights, Box 34, Subseries 1, File Series 3, Eastland Papers.

3. Zack J. Van Landingham, Memo to Director, Mississippi State Sovereignty Commission, September 23, 1959, SCR ID #1–15–0–9–1–1–1, MDAH, mdah.state.ms.us/arrec/digital_archives/sovcom/result.php?image=images/png/cd01/000601.png&otherstuff=1|15|0|9|1|1|1|592|.

4. Ronald A. Goodbread, "In Search of the Historical Millsaps," Founders' Day Address, February 18, 1983, Millsaps College, Jackson, MS; David M. Key, "A Historical Sketch of Millsaps College," *Millsaps College Bulletin* 30, No. 4 (December 1946); W. Charles Sallis and Suzanne Marrs, "History of Millsaps," Staff Orientation Address, n.d., Millsaps College Archives, Administrative Records, A 2 8 Dean's Office, Box 3, Folder 11, Millsaps College Archives, Millsaps-Wilson Library, Millsaps College, Jackson, MS.

5. Millsaps Christian Council, "Interdenominational Discussion Groups," Program, Folder 48, Box 1, Series 1, Cox Papers.

6. Zack J. Van Landingham, Memo to Director, State Sovereignty Commission, October 9, 1958, SCR ID #1–3–0–1–1–1–1, MDAH, mdah.state.ms.us/arrec/digital_archives/sovcom/result.php?image=images/png/cd01/000127.png&otherstuff=1|3|0|1|1|1|1|125|.

7. Joseph Crespino, *In Search of Another Country: Mississippi and the Conservative Counterrevolution* (Princeton, NJ: Princeton University Press, 2007), 62–63.

8. "Asks Explanation, Council Head Says Public Concerned," *State Times,* 9 March 1958, 1A and 12A, Folder 48, Box 1, Series 1, Cox Papers; Ellis W. Wright to Dr. H. Ellis Finger Jr., March 7, 1958, Administrative Records: President H. E. Finger, A 1.4, Box 24, Folder: Controversy on Christian Council Program, March 1958 (Official Communications), Millsaps College Archives.

9. "'Unfortunate Coverage,' College Head Explains Talks," *State Times,* March 9, 1958, 1A and 12A, Folder 48, Box 1, Series 1, Cox Papers; H. E. Finger Jr. to Prospective Applicants' Parents, March 12, 1958; Finger to Pastors and District Superintendents, March 12, 1958; and Finger to Parents of Millsaps College Students, March 12, 1958, Administrative Records: President H. E. Finger, A 1.4, Box 24, Folder: Controversy on Christian Council Program, March 1958 (Official Communications).

10. Citizens' Council *Forum,* Reel #58×10, 9 March 1958, Citizens' Council *Forum* Collection; William J. Simmons to Dr. H. Ellis Finger Jr., March 9, 1958, Administrative Records: President H. E. Finger, A 1.4, Box 24, Folder: Controversy On Christian Council Program, March 1958 (Official Communications).

11. Tom Ethridge, "Mississippi Notebook," *Clarion-Ledger,* March 10, 1958, 10, Folder 48, Box 1, Series 1, Cox Papers.

12. Ed Upchurch, "Millsaps Supporter's Revival Called Off," *State Times,* 13 March 1958, 1A, Folder 48, Box 1, Series 1, Cox Papers; "Revival Plans at Durant Church Cancelled by Official Board after Publication of Letter," *Lexington Advertiser,* 13 March 1958, 1, Folder 48, Box 1, Series 1, Cox Papers.

13. United Press, "'Fanned Racial Fires,' Campus Editor Gets His Job Back after Firing," April 18, 1958, Folder 48, Box 1, Series 1, Cox Papers.

14. Hodding Carter Jr. "Ellis Wright and Bill of Rights," *New South,* May 1958, 8–9, Folder 48, Box 1, Series 1, Cox Papers.

15. Hazel Brannon Smith, "Through Hazel Eyes," *Lexington Advertiser,* March 13, 1958, Folder 48, Box 1, Series 1, Cox Papers.

16. L. G. Patterson to *State Times,* March 13, 1958, Folder 48, Box 1, Series 1, Cox Papers.

17. Both Hazel Brannon Smith and Hodding Carter Jr. were openly supportive of segregation, and each of their editorials underscores that fact. L. G. Patterson's letter revealed some confusion about why Council members were so paranoid about dissent when clearly segregation was morally right.

18. "Segregationist Policy Set," *Commercial Appeal,* March 19, 1958, Folder 48, Box 1, Series 1, Cox Papers; Board of Trustees, Statement to the Friends of Millsaps College, Administrative Records: President H. E. Finger, A 1.4, Box 24, Folder: Controversy on Christian Council Program, March 1958 (Official Communication).

19. Erle Johnston, *Mississippi's Defiant Years, 1953–1973: An Interpretive Documentary with Personal Experiences* (Forest, MS: Lake Harbor Publishers, 1990), 78; Crespino, *In Search of Another Country,* 55.

20. Jimmy Morrow, "American Legions' Support of a Resolution in Legislature Concerning an Investigation of the NAACP," Citizens' Council *Forum,* Reel #58×11, March 17, 1958.

21. Johnston, *Mississippi's Defiant Years,* 78–79.

22. "Mississippi Editors, Wisdom of Giving Funds to Councils Is Questioned," 27 March 1958, Folder 22, Box 1, Series 1, Cox Papers.

23. United Press, "At NAACP Rally, Promises to Blast Donations," *State Times,* 31 March 1958, 5A, Folder 22, Box 1, Series 1, Cox Papers.

24. "Council Bill Tightens Spending Freedom," March 27, 1958, Folder 34, Box 1, Series 1, Cox Papers.

25. Morrow, "American Legions' Support," *Forum;* Russell D. Moore III and Webb Overstreet Jr., "State's Election Laws, Suit Filed in Jefferson Davis County," March 23, 1958, Reel #58×12; Halla May Pattison Turner, "5th Circuit Court of Appeals Cases on Integration, New Orleans Schools, Transportation System, Public Parks, Louisiana Universities, and Voting," March 30, 1958, Reel #58×13; William J. Simmons, "1st Anniversary of the Forum," April 6, 1958, Reel #58×14.

26. Moore and Overstreet, "State's Election Laws."

27. Sara McCorkle, "Women's Place in Citizens' Council," #58×1, January 1, 1958, Citizens' Council *Forum;* McCorkle, "Speeches throughout the State on Segregation," #58×15, April 14, 1958, Citizens' Council *Forum;* Neil McMillen, *The Citizens' Council: Organized Resistance to the Second Reconstruction, 1954–64,* 2nd edition (Urbana: University of Illinois Press, 1994), 240–41.

28. The Educational Fund of the Citizens' Councils, Inc., "Statewide Scholarship Essay Contest for Mississippi High School Students, 1958–1959," Pamphlet, 1958, Subject File, ACCM Collection, MDAH; McCorkle, "Speeches throughout the State on Segregation," #58×15.

29. John Herbers, "Committee Ponders Fate, J. P. Calls Council Donation Bill 'First Step to Disaster,'" United Press International, April 9, 1958, Folder 34, Box 1, Series 1, Cox Papers.

30. Herbers, "Here's the Background, Council Bill Emerging as Another Partisan Issue," United Press International, March 30, 1958, Folder 22, Box 1, Series 1, Cox Papers; Herbers, "Council's Gift Bill Sharply Divides State," United Press International, March 31, 1958, Folder 34, Box 1, Series 1, Cox Papers.

31. Kirby Tyrone to James P. Coleman, April 18, 1958; Ed Walker to James P. Coleman, April 2, 1958; and W. W. Brown to James P. Coleman, April 10, 1958, James P. Coleman Papers, Series 5, Z/1877.000 S, Box 12, Folder 5.

32. G. W. Misch to James P. Coleman, April 11, 1958; Louis E. Dollarhide to James P. Coleman, April 11, 1958; Leroy P. Person to James P. Coleman, April 10, 1958; Robert E. Moore to James P. Coleman, April 17, 1958; and Ed. C. Sturdivant to James P. Coleman, April 10, 1958, Coleman Papers, Series 5, Z/ 1877.000 S, Box 12, Folder 5.

33. Louis Hollis, "Citizens' Council Survey of Jackson," Citizens' Council *Forum*, April 27, 1958, Reel #58×17; Jackson Citizens' Council, "The Eight Ifs," 1958, Subject File, Citizens' Council Publications, 1952–1960, MDAH.

34. Hollis, "Citizens' Council Survey of Jackson."

35. Robert B. Patterson to Council Chapters, November 27, 1958, Subject File, Citizens' Council 1956–1958, MDAH.

36. Elizabeth Carpenter, "House Studio Used to Make Council Films," *Arkansas Gazette*, May 11, 1959, Folder 22, Box 1, Series 1, Cox Papers.

37. Dick Morphew, "Informational and Educational Work of the Citizens' Council," May 25, 1958, Reel #58×21, Citizens' Council *Forum*.

38. William J. Simmons to James Eastland, July 21, 1958, Folder: Civil Rights 1958, Box 38, Subseries 1, File Series 3, Eastland Papers.

39. McMillen, *Citizens' Council,* 111–15.

40. Lewis, *Massive Resistance,* 51.

41. McMillen, *Citizens' Council,* 107–11.

42. Introduction, "Little Rock Incident, Use of Federal Troops," 1958, Reel #5802, Citizens' Council *Forum*.

43. Simmons to James Eastland, March 13, 1959, Folder: Civil Rights 1958, Box 38, Subseries 1, File Series 3, Eastland Papers.

44. Ibid.; Citizens' Council Forum to Broadcaster, no date, Folder: Civil Rights 1959, Box 38, Subseries 1, File Series 3, Eastland Papers.

45. Simmons to Eastland, March 13, 1959.

46. John Dittmer, *Local People: The Struggle for Civil Rights in Mississippi* (Urbana: University of Illinois Press, 1995), 83–84; Johnston, *Mississippi's Defiant Years,* 88–93; Crespino, *In Search of Another Country,* 22.

47. Robert B. Patterson to Senator, May 1, 1959, Folder 7, Box 7, Series 29, Stennis Collection.

48. Robert B. Patterson to Chapters, March 12, 1959, Subject File, ACCM Collection, MDAH.

49. Patterson to Chapters, August 20, 1959, Correspondence, 1956–1967, ACCM Collection, MSU.

50. Crespino, *In Search of Another Country*, 35–36; Carroll Gartin, "State Sovereignty Commission," Citizens' Council *Forum*, December 18, 1957, Reel #57×7.

51. McMillen, *Citizens' Council*, 326–27; Johnston, *Mississippi's Defiant Years*, 85–87.

52. Jenny Irons, *Reconstituting Whiteness: The Mississippi State Sovereignty Commission* (Nashville, TN: Vanderbilt University Press, 2010), 50; Yasuhiro Katagiri, *The Mississippi State Sovereignty Commission: Civil Rights and States' Rights* (Jackson: University Press of Mississippi, 2001), 65–66.

53. Johnston, *Mississippi's Defiant Years*, 102.

54. Oliver Emmerich, "Tax Money to Private Groups Wrong," *State Times*, July 17, 1960, 2B, Folder 22, Box 1, Series 1, Cox Papers.

55. Johnston, *Mississippi's Defiant Years*, 66–68.

56. Johnston, Interview with Yasuhiro Katagiri.

57. Index, Citizens' Council *Forum* Collection, MSU.

58. Edward J. Derwinski, "Main Concern of American People Today, Increasing Tax Burden," Citizens' Council *Forum*, February 1960, Reel #6007.

59. Robert T. Ashmore, "Effect of Civil Rights Legislation on Business, Especially in the South," Citizens' Council *Forum*, March 1960, Reel #6010.

60. F. Edward Hebert, "High-Ranking Retired Military Officers Taking Jobs with the Defense Department," Citizens' Council *Forum*, March 1960, Reel #6012.

61. D. F. B. DeBeer, "South African Race Question," Citizens' Council *Forum*, December 1960, Reel #6036.

62. D. F. B . DeBeer, "Racial Composition of South Africa," Citizens' Council *Forum*, December 1960, Reel #6037.

63. S. E. D. to William J. Simmons, September 19, 1956; William J. Simmons to Charles Griffin, October 9, 1956; Francis E. Walter to Charles Griffin, October 17, 1956; and William J. Simmons to Charles H. Griffin, October 22, 1956, John Bell Williams Papers, Subject File Correspondence, Box 10382, Series 2416, Folder: Citizens Council of Mississippi, June 1956 to December 1957, Archival Reading Room, MDAH. For a more thorough treatment of the relationship between the segregationist press in the United States and South Africa, see Zoe Hyman, "American Segregationist Ideology and White Southern Africa, 1948–1975" (PhD diss., University of Sussex, 2011); see 108–88 for focused attention to the Citizens' Council.

64. Carleton Putnam, "Supreme Court's Decision in the Brown Case/Forcing School Integration in the South," Citizens' Council *Forum*, July 1960, Reel #6028.

65. Joseph B. Fisher to Albert Jones, August 20, 1960, SCR ID# 3-37A-0-18-1-1-1 and -2-1-1, www.mdah.ms.gov/arrec/digital_archives/sovcom/result.php?image=images/png /cd04/032533.png&otherstuff=3│37│0│18│1│1│1│31982│A.

66. Carter, *The South Strikes Back*, 18–19, 206.

67. Michael Vinson Williams, *Medgar Evers: Mississippi Martyr* (Fayetteville: University of Arkansas Press, 2011), 174–80; Medgar Evers, Report to Ruby Hurley, April 13, 1960, NAACP Microfilm Collection.

68. Dittmer, *Local People*, 86–87.

69. Ibid., 180–81.

70. Ibid., 184–86.

71. William J. Simmons to Albert Jones, August 17, 1960, SCR ID # 7–0-2-86-1-1-1, mdah.state.ms.us/arrec/digital_archives/sovcom/result.php?image=images/png/cd07/055233.png&otherstuff=7│0│2│86│1│1│1│54476│.

72. Malcolm S. Dale to Albert Jones, December 10, 1960, SCR ID# 7–0-2-20-2-1-1, mdah.state.ms.us/arrec/digital_archives/sovcom/result.php?image=images/png/cd07/055111.png&otherstuff=7│0│2│20│2│1│1│54352│.

73. *Billy Clyde Barton v. Ross R. Barnett,* et al., 226 F. Supp. 375 (1964).

74. Ibid.

75. McMillen, *Citizens' Council,* 57, 67, 80, 85, 100–101, and 52–57.

CHAPTER FOUR

Note to chapter epigraph: William J. Simmons, "A Comparison of Attitudes during Reconstruction I and Reconstruction II," Address to the Sons of Confederate Veterans, April 5, 1962, Jackson, Mississippi, MDAH.

1. Hodding Carter III, "Citadel of the Citizens Council," *New York Times Magazine,* November 12, 1961, 23, 125–27, Folder 52C, Box 1, Cox Papers.

2. "'Black Monday' Anniversary, Citizens Council Celebrates Seven Years of Segregation," *Clarion-Ledger,* May 14, 1961, 2A, Folder 34, Box 1, Series 1, Cox Papers.

3. United Press International, "Negroes 'Happy' in Mississippi, Council Told," *Memphis Press-Scimitar,* May 18, 1961, A-14, Folder 24, Box 1, Series 2, Cox Papers.

4. "Operation Mississippi Program," April 7, 1961; Edward J. Odom to Reverend, 1 February 1961; Medgar Evers to Robert Carter, March 15, 1961, NAACP Microfilm Collection; John Dittmer, *Local People: The Struggle for Civil Rights in Mississippi* (Urbana: University of Illinois Press, 1995), 87–88.

5. Medgar Evers, Phone Report to NAACP, March 28, 1961, NAACP Microfilm Collection; "Nine Jailed in 'Study-In,'" *Clarion-Ledger,* March 28, 1961, 1A and 8; Wallace Dabbs, "Jackson State College Students Stage Protest," *Clarion-Ledger,* March 29, 1961, 1A; and "Negroes Try Jail March in Jackson," *Clarion-Ledger,* March 29, 1961, 1A and 16, Reel #23799, Newspaper Microfilm Collection, MDAH.

6. "Negro Students Fined for Library 'Study-In,'" *Clarion-Ledger,* March 30, 1961, 1A and 7A, Reel #23799, Newspaper Microfilm Collection, MDAH; Dittmer, *Local People,* 88–89.

7. Dittmer, *Local People,* 91–92.

8. George Lewis, *Massive Resistance: The White Response to the Civil Rights Movement* (New York: Bloomsbury Academic, 2006), 138 and 140–41.

9. Dittmer, *Local People,* 94–96; Michael Vinson Williams, *Medgar Evers: Mississippi Martyr* (Fayetteville: University of Arkansas Press, 2011), 217–18; Raymond Arsenault, *Freedom Riders: 1961 and the Struggle for Racial Justice* (New York: Oxford University Press,

2011), 217–19; Edmund Noel, "Trip from Meridian Quiet Under Escort," *Clarion-Ledger*, May 25, 1961, 1A; Wallace Dabbs, "27 Mixers Jailed on Arrival Here," *Clarion-Ledger*, May 25, 1961, 1–2; Jerry DeLaughter, "Reception for 'Riders' Is Over in Few Minutes," *Clarion-Ledger*, May 25, 1961, 1, 16; Dabbs, "13 More Riders Are Jailed Here," *Clarion-Ledger*, June 3, 1961, 1A, 3; Charles M. Hills, "'Riders' May Take a Ride," *Clarion-Ledger*, June 4, 1961, 3B; Associated Press, "New 'Riders' Get Heavier Penalties," *Clarion-Ledger*, June 12, 1961, 1A; Noel, "Parchman Transfer of 'Riders' Okayed," *Clarion-Ledger*, June 13, 1961, 1A, 3; "45 'Riders' in Pen; Patience Advised," *Clarion-Ledger*, June 16, 1961, 1A; "More 'Riders' Transferred to Parchman," *Clarion-Ledger*, June 24, 1961, 1A, Reel #23801, Newspaper Microfilm Collection, MDAH.

10. Williams, *Medgar Evers*, 219–21; Dittmer, *Local People*, 97. One notable exception to this evaluation is Womanpower Unlimited, a group of black women in Jackson who used their connections to collect and distribute clothes, hygiene products, books, blankets, and other needs for the jailed Riders. The organization, under the leadership of Claire Collins Harvey, remained active in Jackson civil rights campaigns for the remainder of the movement. See Tiyi Morris, *Womanpower Unlimited and the Black Freedom Struggle in Mississippi* (Athens: University of Georgia Press, 2015).

11. Citizens' Council *Forum*, Press Release, July 12, 1961, SCR ID# 9–11–1-72–1-1–1,-2 –1-1,-3-1-1, mdah.ms.gov/arrec/digital_archives/sovcom/result.php?image=images/png /cd08/060980.png&otherstuff=9|11|1|72|1|1|1|60165|.

12. Joe T. Patterson, "Connection between Freedom Riders and Cuba," Citizens' Council *Forum*, June 1961, Reel #6125R.

13. Grady Gilmore, "Freedom Riders and Connection with Cuba," Citizens' Council *Forum*, June 1961, Reel #6124R.

14. Fred Jones, "Freedom Riders in Parchman," Citizens' Council *Forum*, June 1961, Reel #6126R.

15. Arsenault, *Freedom Riders*, 223–25 and 233–37; Dittmer, *Local People*, 98–99.

16. Erle Johnston, *Mississippi's Defiant Years, 1953–1973: An Interpretive Documentary with Personal Experiences* (Forest, MS: Lake Harbor Publishers, 1990), 133–35.

17. William J. Simmons to Mississippi State Sovereignty Commission, August 1, 1961, SCR ID# 7–4-0–27–1-1–1 and-2-1-1, mdah.state.ms.us/arrec/digital_archives/sovcom /result.php?image=images/png/cd08/059105.png&otherstuff=7|4|0|27|1|1|1|58304|; Simmons to Mississippi State Sovereignty Commission, September 1, 1961, SCR ID #7–4-0 –56–1-1–1 and-2-1-1, mdah.state.ms.us/arrec/digital_archives/sovcom/result.php?image =images/png/cd08/059140.png&otherstuff=7|4|0|46|1|1|1|58339|.

18. Eugene Cook, "Southern Governors Conference," Citizens' Council *Forum*, July 1961, Reel #6130; Paul B. Johnson Jr., "Results of Southern Governors Conference," Citizens' Council *Forum*, July 1961, Reel #6131; MacDonald Gallion and Joe Patterson, "Major Problems of the South," Citizens' Council *Forum*, July 1961, Reel #6132.

19. Organized resistance movements in other states never reached the heights of the Citizens' Council in Mississippi. Neil McMillen referred to the movement in South Carolina as "small and inactive by Deep South standards" but "considerably more vibrant than its counterpart in Georgia" where, by 1961, massive resistance began to transition into

"token compliance." See Neil McMillen, *The Citizens' Council: Organized Resistance to the Second Reconstruction, 1954–64,* 2nd edition (Urbana: University of Illinois Press, 1994), 80, 90. In the peripheral South, McMillen describes an environment where racial moderation was the norm, with pockets of radical resistance (akin to Deep South movements) in areas of the state where greater concentrations of black citizens resided (92). Florida and Tennessee rank lowest in their level of sustained activism following *Brown* (110). By 1959, North Carolina's most promising white resistance group, the North Carolina Defenders of States' Rights, could only count their membership in the hundreds (114). George Lewis, in *Massive Resistance,* argues that by 1960, Virginia and Arkansas were moving away from hard-line segregation tactics and confronting desegregation on a case-by-case basis. Lewis brings some nuance to McMillen's description of resistance groups, arguing that by 1960 most current state officials had been elected in the aftermath of *Brown.* Their leadership ushered in an era of "state-sponsored" massive resistance, rendering individual organizations less active because their objectives had been reached through state legislatures and executive fiat (113–14).

20. Southwide Conference of Municipal Officials Constitution, as read by Dick Morphew, "Southwide Conference of Municipal Officials," Citizens' Council *Forum,* August 1961, Reel #6135.

21. John W. Carter, "Southwide Conference of Municipal Officials," Citizens' Council *Forum,* August 1961, Reel #6135.

22. Ibid.

23. Erle Johnston, Interview with Yasuhiro Katagiri.

24. "Capitolizations, Survey Indicates Doubt on Wide Usage of 'Forum,'" *Jackson Daily News,* August 20, 1961, Folder 24, Box 1, Series 1, Cox Papers.

25. Hal C. DeCell, "Out on a Limb," *Deer Creek Pilot,* December 29, 1961, Folder 24, Box 1, Series 1, Cox Papers.

26. In an interview in 1980, Johnston explained that his role in the survey was a fact not included in his biography, *Mississippi's Defiant Years.* Because Bill Simmons had contributed a great deal to Johnston's material for the book, he did not want to embarrass him. See Johnston, Interview with Katagiri.

27. Mississippi Human Relations Council, "Mississippi: 1961 Report to the Commission on Civil Rights from the State Advisory Committee," 315–26, Jane Schutt Papers, Series 1.2, Box 1, Folder 21, MDAH; Irons, *Reconstituting Whiteness,* 51–52.

28. Erle Johnston, "The Practical Way to Maintain a Separate School System in Mississippi," Speech, Grenada High School, May 25, 1962, Folder 80: Sovereignty Commission, 1960–1977, Wilson F. "Bill" Minor Papers, MSU.

29. Ibid.

30. Ibid.

31. Johnston, *Mississippi's Defiant Years,* 140–44; Yasuhiro Katagiri, *The Mississippi State Sovereignty Commission: Civil Rights and States' Rights* (Jackson: University Press of Mississippi, 2001), 97–101.

32. Johnston, *Mississippi's Defiant Years,* 145; Katagiri, *The Mississippi State Sovereignty Commission,* 101–2.

33. Strom Thurmond, "Cold War and Fulbright Memorandum," Citizens' Council *Forum*, November 1961, Reel #6140; "Fulbright Memorandum and Muzzling the Military," Citizens' Council *Forum*, November 1961, Reel #6141; "Fulbright Memorandum," Citizens' Council *Forum*, November 1961, Reel #6145; "Communist Threat to U.S., Muzzling of Military," Citizens' Council *Forum*, November 1961, Reel #6146.

34. Joseph Crespino, *Strom Thurmond's America* (New York: Hill and Wang, 2012), 148–54.

35. Joseph Crespino, *In Search of Another Country: Mississippi and the Conservative Counterrevolution* (Princeton, NJ: Princeton University Press, 2007), 58 and 78–79.

36. For more context about Walker's contribution to the conservative coalition, see Jonathan Schoenwald, *A Time for Choosing: The Rise of Modern American Conservatism* (New York: Oxford University Press, 2001), 100–23. Schoenwald dedicates an entire chapter to the Walker case, explaining the publicity surrounding his resignation and speaking engagements as a watershed moment for conservatives. Walker's connection with the John Birch Society and segregationist groups like the Citizens' Council and the Conservative Society of America (a segregationist-sponsored group in Louisiana) forced more moderate conservatives to consider how inclusive they wished to be in their ideology, especially as they tried to draw support from the American public. They could not abandon Walker altogether because his case represented the fears from which the conservative cause drew most frequently—skepticism about the federal government's ability to lead the nation against national security threats.

37. *The Citizen* (November 1961): 38, *The Citizen* Collection, MSU; Pat Flynn, "Walker Charges Censorship Is Disarming U.S. Soldiers," *Jackson Daily News*, December 30, 1961, 1 and 12, SCR ID# 10–106–0–7–1–1–1, mdah.state.ms.us/arrec/digital_archives/sovcom/result.php?image=images/png/cd09/072777.png&otherstuff=10 | 106 | 0 | 7 | 1 | 1 | 1 | 71845 | .

38. Edwin A. Walker, "Walker's Resignation," Citizens' Council *Forum*, January 1961, Reel #6201.

39. Holmes Alexander, "Let's Choose Up Sides!" *The Citizen* (January 1962): 27–28.

40. Joseph Crespino, "Strom Thurmond's Sunbelt: Rethinking Regional Politics and the Rise of the Right," in *Sunbelt Rising: The Politics of Place, Space, and Region*, ed. Michelle Nickerson and Darren Dochuk (Philadelphia: University of Pennsylvania Press, 2011), 60–61, 70–71, and 80–81.

41. Darren Dochuk, *From Bible Belt to Sunbelt: Plain-Folk Religion, Grassroots Politics, and the Rise of Evangelical Conservatism* (New York: W. W. Norton, 2011), xv, 10–11.

42. Strom Thurmond, "Investigation of Muzzling of Military and Censorship," Citizens' Council *Forum*, January 1962, Reel #6204; Strom Thurmond, "Positive Program for American Victory in the Cold War," *Forum*, February 1962, Reel #6205; Jamie L. Whitten, "U.S. Expenditures, Loan to U.N.," *Forum*, February 1962, Reel #6206; John C. Stennis, "Senate Hearing on the Muzzling of the Military," *Forum*, March 1962, Reel #6209; Strom Thurmond, "Hearings and the Muzzling of the Military," *Forum*, March 1962, Reel #6211; Strom Thurmond, "Possibility of World Peace," *Forum*, April 1962, Reel #6214; Edward Hunter, "Communist Brainwashing," *Forum*, April 1962, Reel #6214; Strom Thurmond, "Communism in the U.S. and the Fulbright Memorandum," *Forum*, May 1962, Reel #6218; John Bell Williams, "United Nations," *Forum*, June 1962, Reel #6222.

43. James B. Utt, "Trend toward Conservatism," *Forum*, February 1962, Reel #6208; John G. Tower, "Conservative Views vs. Liberal Views (Economy)," *Forum*, March 1962, Reel #6210; Tower, "Conservative Influence in the Government," *Forum*, March 1962, Reel #6212.

44. A. Willis Robertson, "Supreme Court Decision on School Prayer," *Forum*, June 1962, Reel #6224.

45. John Dowdy, "Supreme Court's Decision on School Prayer," *Forum*, June 1962, Reel #6227.

46. Dittmer, *Local People*, 138–39; Johnston, *Mississippi's Defiant Years*, 146–54; Tommy Herrington, "Negro Brings Suit to Enter Ole Miss," *Jackson Daily News*, June 1, 1961, 1A and 14A, 1–67–1–4–1–1–1, mdah.state.ms.us/arrec/digital_archives/sovcom/result.php?image=images/png/cd01/003245.png&otherstuff=1|67|1|4|1|1|1|3147|; "Judge Delays Negro's Bid to Enter Ole Miss," *Jackson Daily News*, June 1, 1961, 1–67–1–8–1–1–1, mdah.state.ms.us/arrec/digital_archives/sovcom/result.php?image=images/png/cd01/003252.png&otherstuff=1|67|1|8|1|1|1|3152|; Kenneth Toler, "Negro Is Denied Ole Miss Entry," *Commercial Appeal*, December 14, 1961, Associated Press; "Meredith Hearing Set Today," *Clarion-Ledger*, January 9, 1962, 1–67–1–35–1–1–1, mdah.state.ms.us/arrec/digital_archives/sovcom/result.php?image=images/png/cd01/003334.png&otherstuff=1|67|1|35|1|1|1|3228|; W. C. Shoemaker, "Court Orders State Hands Off Meredith," *Jackson Daily News*, September 25, 1962, 1 and 14, 1–67–3–1–1–1–2, mdah.state.ms.us/arrec/digital_archives/sovcom/result.php?image=images/png/cd01/003749.png&otherstuff=1|67|3|1|1|1|2|94|; "Barnett Is Found in Contempt; Tuesday Deadline to Purge Self," *Times-Picayune*, September 29, 1962, Sec. 1, p. 1–2, 1–67–2–45–1–1–1, *mdah.state.ms.us/arrec/digital_archives/sovcom/result.php?image=images/png/cd01/003721.png&otherstuff=1|67|2|45|1|1|1|3611|*.

47. McMillen, *Citizens' Council*, 342–43. Erle Johnston, director of public relations for the Sovereignty Commission at the time of the Meredith crisis, believed that Governor Barnett's actions were self-motivated and in direct defiance of advice from his law partner and close advisor, W. F. Goodman Jr., and the city editor of the *Clarion-Ledger*, Gene Wirth, both of whom advised Barnett to capitulate after the court order was issued. See Erle Johnston, Interview with Yasuhiro Katagiri. In a similar vein, Bill Simmons denied any influence over Barnett's actions or the subsequent riots on the Ole Miss campus when Meredith arrived. Simmons remembered that Barnett's speech at the Ole Miss football game in Jackson was a last-minute response to the rousing welcome he got from the audience upon his arrival. Simmons described Barnett's approach to governance as "always irrepressible and often unpredictable," making it nearly impossible to affect him significantly. See William J. Simmons, Interview with Orley B. Caudill, Jackson, Mississippi, June 26, 1979, Center for Oral History and Cultural Heritage, University of Southern Mississippi, digilib.usm.edu/cdm/ref/collection/coh/id/6472. It has long been rumored, however, that it was the Citizens' Council that urged Jacksonians to surround the governor's mansion on Sunday, September 30, to prevent the federal arrest of Governor Barnett. The call allegedly came from Fred Beard, a prominent Council member and station manager for WLBT, the NBC affiliate in Jackson, in a televised editorial. An article in the *Clarion-Ledger*, however,

describes John Wright, Chair of the ACCM, calling to the crowd from Council offices to surround the mansion once they arrived. See "At Jackson," *Clarion-Ledger,* October 1, 1962, 1 and 17, Reel #23818, Newspaper Microfilm Collection, MDAH. James J. Kilpatrick, conservative spokesman and editor of the *Richmond News Leader,* attested to Bill Simmons's tacit approval of the mansion demonstration in his account of events surrounding Meredith's enrollment. See Gene Roberts and Hank Klibanoff, *The Race Beat: The Press, the Civil Rights Struggle, and the Awakening of a Nation* (New York: Vintage, 2007), 289.

48. "Patterson, Faubus Support Governor," *Clarion-Ledger,* September 28, 1962; "Governor Is Backed by Walker," *Clarion-Ledger,* September 28, 1962, 1–67–2–39–1–1–1–1, mdah .state.ms.us/arrec/digital_archives/sovcom/result.php?image=images/png/cd01/003680 .png&otherstuff=1│67│2│39│1│1│1│3571│.

49. Ross Barnett, "Doctrine of Interposition Enacted by Gov. Ross Barnett at Ole Miss," *Forum,* September 1962, Reel #6236.

50. Katagiri, *The Mississippi State Sovereignty Commission,* 110; Roberts and Klibanoff, *Race Beat,* 274–76.

51. Katagiri, *The Mississippi State Sovereignty Commission,* 114; Dittmer, *Local People,* 140–41; Johnston, *Mississippi's Defiant Years,* 157; Roberts and Klibanoff, *Race Beat,* 292.

52. "Negro at Ole Miss; Campus in Uproar," *Clarion-Ledger,* October 1, 1961, 1A and 2; Charles M. Hills, "Barnett Calls Use of Force Inflammatory," *Clarion-Ledger,* October 2, 1961, 1A and 21; "General Walker Is Arrested; In Hospital," *Clarion-Ledger,* October 2, 1961, Reel #23818, Newspaper Microfilm Collection, MDAH; Dittmer, *Local People,* 140–42.

53. Roberts and Klibanoff, *Race Beat,* 297–300.

54. Ibid., 299.

55. John C. Stennis, "Situation at the University of Mississippi," *Forum,* October 1962, Reel #6238.

56. Russell D. Moore, "Reactions to the Ole Miss Situation," *Forum,* October 1962, Reel #6239R.

57. William K. Shearer, "Local Views of Oxford Incident," *Forum,* October 1962, Reel #6240.

58. Dittmer, *Local People,* 138–39.

59. Robert B. Patterson to Dear Friend, October 24, 1962, Correspondence 1956–1967, Association of Citizens' Councils of Mississippi, Citizens' Council Collection, MSU; Patterson to Whom It May Concern, Subject File, Association of Citizens' Councils of Mississippi, z/0773.000.ACCM, 1942–1973, MDAH.

60. McMillen, *Citizens' Council,* 347.

61. Katagiri, *The Mississippi State Sovereignty Commission,* 115–21. Katagiri details the nature of the Sovereignty Commission's change in emphasis after Meredith's admission, explaining that the Speakers' Bureau adapted its standard speech, eliminating references to "negroes" and racial unity in Mississippi. In the new standard speech, Erle Johnston found it prudent to emphasize the states' rights argument even further to justify the legal nature of Mississippi's position. It also directly addressed the Oxford riots, denouncing violence in any form. See Katagiri, *The Mississippi State Sovereignty Commission,* 116–17.

62. "An Airwaves Anniversary," *The Citizen* (February 1963): 2.

63. John R. Salter Jr., "Exploratory Report RE Economic Destitution of Rural and Urban Negro Families in the Delta Region of the State of Mississippi," January 19, 1963, NAACP Microfilm Collection; John R. Salter Jr., *Jackson, Mississippi: An American Chronicle of Struggle and Schism* (Lincoln: University of Nebraska Press, 2011), 76–78.

64. Dittmer, *Local People*, 195–96.

65. Statement of Mrs. Wallis I. Schutt of Jackson, Mississippi, Chairman of the Mississippi State Advisory Committee to the United States Commission on Civil Rights, May 22, 1963, 8, Schutt Papers, Series 1.2, Box 1, Folder 12, MDAH.

66. Harrison Saunders to Rev. Murray Cox, January 2, 1960, Schutt Papers, Series 1.2, Box 1, Folder 12, MDAH. Also see R. Stewart Smith to Rev. Murray Cox, January 9, 1960; and Harrison Saunders to Rev. Murray Cox, January 15, 1960. The Schutt collection and the Council of Federated Organizations Records, Box 1, MDAH, include affidavits and depositions regarding police brutality in Mississippi.

67. Dittmer, *Local People*, 144–47.

68. Ibid., 148–57.

69. Ibid., 143–59; Johnston, *Mississippi's Defiant Years*, 171–73; Salter, *Jackson, Mississippi*, 62–66; "Mayor Vows to Maintain Order," *Clarion-Ledger*, December 14, 1962; and Bill Simpson, "'Picketers' Hearing Is Set Today," *Clarion-Ledger*, January 11, 1963, 1A, Reel #23821, Newspaper Microfilm Collection, MDAH.

70. Salter, *Jackson, Mississippi*, 73–74; "Monday is Willie Richardson Day," *Clarion-Ledger*, January 13, 1963, 6; and "Jackson Honors Great End Willie Richardson," *Clarion-Ledger*, January 15, 1963, 12, Reel # 23821, Newspaper Microfilm Collection, MDAH.

CHAPTER FIVE

Note to chapter epigraph: Supplementary Offense Report, Police Department, Jackson, MS, June 26, 1963, Evers Papers, Subgroup 4, Series 46, Box 29, Folder 2: Police Department Offense Report, Medgar W. Evers Murder, 1963–1964, MDAH.

1. Yasuhiro Katagiri, *The Mississippi State Sovereignty Commission: Civil Rights and States' Rights* (Jackson: University Press of Mississippi, 2001), 100; Erle Johnston, *Mississippi's Defiant Years, 1953–1973: An Interpretive Documentary with Personal Experiences* (Forest, MS: Lake Harbor Publishers, 1990), 140.

2. William B. Street, "Citizens' Councils' Simmons Plays Much Discussed Role in Politics of Mississippi," *The Commercial Appeal*, January 13, 1963, Folder 52D, Box 1, Series 1, Cox Papers.

3. James W. Silver, "Mississippi: Closed Society," Presidential Address to Southern Historical Association, printed in *Journal of Southern History* 30, No. 1 (February 1964): 11.

4. William F. Minor, "The Citizens' Councils—An Incredible Decade of Defiance," Book Manuscript, Minor Papers.

5. Simmons, Interview with Caudill, 38 and 43.

6. Neil McMillen concurs with this assessment of Simmons, arguing that by 1960, he

had replaced Patterson as the titled and practical leader of the organization. By then, both the Citizens' Councils of America and the state association operated out of Simmons's downtown Jackson office instead of Patterson's home, a move that likened the Council to a business, rather than a provincial political movement. See Neil McMillen, *The Citizens' Council: Organized Resistance to the Second Reconstruction, 1954–64*, 2nd edition (Urbana: University of Illinois Press, 1994), 122–24.

7. Simmons, Interview with Caudill; see McMillen, *Citizens' Council*, 122–23.

8. Simmons, Interview with Caudill.

9. James Graham Cook, *The Segregationists* (New York: Appleton-Century-Crofts, 1962), 67 and 73; Simmons, "A Comparison of Attitudes during Reconstruction I and II," 8–10 and 14.

10. Simmons, Interview with Caudill. Among these speeches and interviews, see the following: William J. Simmons, "The Race Problem Moves South," Speech to Carleton College, Northfield, Minnesota, May 15, 1962, 1–25, Box 3, Folder 52, Box 3, Association of Citizens' Councils of Mississippi Collection, 1942–1973, Z/0773.000, MDAH; Simmons, "A View from the South," Interview with the *Yale Political* (Summer 1963): 8, 20–23; Simmons, "Notes on Africa," *The Citizen* (July–August 1966): 2–14; Simmons, Interview with *Search for America*, Reel #0034, Forum Film Collection, MDAH; Cook, *Segregationists*, 73.

11. Bill Simmons described the reaction to Little Rock and Ole Miss as the only resource from which the Council could draw in the face of federal force. Simmons, Interview with Caudill, 58; Ellett Lawrence, Dear Friend Letters (3), 1963, Folder: Correspondence, 1956–1967, ACCM Collection, MSU.

12. McMillen, *Citizens' Council*, 346–47.

13. United Press International, "Oxford Minister Pleads for Peace, Repentance," *Clarion-Ledger*, October 8, 1962, 1A, Reel # 23818, Newspaper Microfilm Collection, MDAH; Carolyn Renee Dupont, *Mississippi Praying: Southern White Evangelicals and the Civil Rights Movement, 1945–1975* (New York: New York University Press, 2013), 141–45.

14. Jerry Furr, et al., "Born of Conviction," *The Mississippi Methodist Advocate*, 2 January 1963, 2, ACCM Collection, MDAH.

15. Dupont, *Mississippi Praying*, 146.

16. Ibid., 92–97; Louis Hollis, "Infiltration of Communist and Left-Wing Propaganda in Church Literature," Citizens' Council *Forum*, November 17, 1957, Reel #57 × 3; Hollis, "Infiltration of Communist and Left-Wing Propaganda in Church Literature," *Forum*, November 24, 1957, Reel #57 × 4; Dugas Shands, "Supreme Court Decisions Are Not the Law of the Land," *Forum*, January 19, 1958, Reel #58 × 3; Louis Hollis, "Subversive Material in Church Literature," *Forum*, February 2, 1958, Reel #58 × 5.

17. Joseph Crespino, *In Search of Another Country: Mississippi and the Conservative Counterrevolution* (Princeton, NJ: Princeton University Press, 2007), 60–61; Dupont, *Mississippi Praying*, 100–1, 131.

18. Crespino, *In Search of Another Country*, 57–59.

19. M. G. Lowman, "Circuit Riders, Inc.," *Forum*, August 1962, Reel #6230; M. G. Lowman, "Extent of Communist Exploitation of the Churches," *Forum*, August 1962, Reel #6231. For a more detailed treatment of Meyers Lowman and his impact on the anticom-

munist fervor that accompanied white resistance in the midst of the civil rights movement, see Yasuhiro Katagiri, *Black Freedom, White Resistance, and Red Menace: Civil Rights and Anticommunism in the Jim Crow South* (Baton Rouge: Louisiana State University Press, 2014).

20. McMillen, *Citizens' Council,* 196–97; Crespino, *In Search of Another Country,* 51.

21. Medford Evans, "A Declaration of Conscience on Racial Segregation," *Information Bulletin,* January 1963, ACCM Collection, MDAH.

22. Ibid.

23. Dupont, *Mississippi Praying,* 146.

24. Ibid., 96.

25. Armistead Selden, "Soviet Buildup in Cuba," *Forum,* February 1963, Reel #6307; Strom Thurmond, "Cuban Situation, Variance in Intelligence Reports," *Forum,* February 1963, Reel #6308; John C. Stennis, "Cuban Situation," *Forum,* March 1963, Reel #6309; August E. Johansen, "Cuban Situation," *Forum,* March 1963, Reel #6310; Milton M. Lory, "View of American Coalition on Cuban Crisis," *Forum,* March 1963, Reel #6311R; John Tower, "Cuban Situation," *Forum,* March 1963, Reel #6312; William C. Cramer, "Cuban Crisis and Florida," *Forum,* April 1963, Reel #6313; Strom Thurmond, "Raids of Cuban Exiles on Castro," *Forum,* April 1963, Reel #6314; Joe D. Waggoner, "American Views of the Cuban Crisis," *Forum,* April 1963, Reel #6315; Strom Thurmond, "Policies of the U.S. in the Cuban Situation Compared with Korea," *Forum,* April 1963, Reel #6316; Thomas Abernathy and Medford Evans, "Cuban Situation," *Forum,* May 1963, Reel #6317; Armistead Selden, "Communist Subversive Activities in Latin America," *Forum,* May 1963, Reel #6318; James Utt, "California's Views on the Cuban Crisis," *Forum,* May 1963, Reel #6319; H. R. Gross, "Investigation into Cuban Situation," *Forum,* May 1963, Reel #6320; John C. Stennis, "Interim Report on the Cuban Military Build-Up," *Forum,* June 1963, Reel #6321; Strom Thurmond, "Interim Report on Cuban Military Build-Up," *Forum,* June 1963, Reel #6322; Medford Evans, "Communist Nature of Castro's Movement," *Forum,* June 1963, Reel #6324.

26. Medford Evans, "U.S. Outlook for 1963 in the Cold War," *Forum,* January 1963, Reel #6301R; Edward Hunter, "Interview," *Forum,* January 1963, Reel #6304; Myers Lowman and John Bell Williams, "Racial Demonstrations and Communists," *Forum,* August 1963, Reel #6329; Myers Lowman, "Racial Agitation and Various Organizations," *Forum,* August 1963, Reel #6330; Myers Lowman, "Communist Exploitation of College Students," *Forum,* August 1963, Reel #6331; Myers Lowman, "Communist Use of Churches of Christ in America," *Forum,* August 1963, Reel #6332; Medford Evans, "Racial Demonstrations and Test-Ban Treaty," *Forum,* September 1963, Reel #6333R; Medford Evans, "August 28, March on Washington," *Forum,* September 1963, Reel #6336R.

27. William J. Simmons to Mississippi State Sovereignty Commission, April 15, 1963, SCR ID #99-30-0-121-1-1-1 through-3-1-1, mdah.state.ms.us/arrec/digital_archives/sovcom/result.php?image=images/png/cd10/075316.png&otherstuff=99|30|0|121|1|1|1|74356|.

28. Darren Dochuk, *From Bible Belt to Sunbelt: Plain-Folk Religion, Grassroots Politics, and the Rise of Evangelical Conservatism* (New York: W. W. Norton, 2012), 227–29.

29. Simmons to Mississippi State Sovereignty Commission, April 15, 1963.

30. Michael Vinson Williams, *Medgar Evers: Mississippi Martyr* (Fayetteville: University of Arkansas Press, 2011), 232–33; Dittmer, *Local People,* 159–60; John R. Salter Jr., *Jackson, Mississippi: An American Chronicle of Struggle and Schism* (Lincoln: University of Nebraska Press, 2011), 81–95.

31. Jackson NAACP Branch, North Jackson Youth Council, and Jackson Youth Council to Allen C. Thompson, May 13, 1963, NAACP Microfilm Collection.

32. Williams, *Medgar Evers,* 240–44; Salter, *Jackson, Mississippi,* 109–10 and 119–21; Medgar Evers, "I Speak as a Mississippian," Televised Speech, May 20, 1963, in *The Autobiography of Medgar Evers: A Hero's Life and Legacy Revealed through His Writings, Letters and Speeches,* ed. Myrlie Evers-Williams and Manning Marable (New York: Basic Books, 2005), 280–83.

33. Bill Simpson, "Negroes' Claim Refuted in Violence Wake Here," *Clarion-Ledger,* May 29, 1963, 1 and 19; Salter, *Jackson, Mississippi,* 132–36; Dittmer, *Local People,* 161–63; Gene Roberts and Hank Klibanoff, *The Race Beat: The Press, the Civil Rights Struggle, and the Awakening of a Nation* (New York: Vintage, 2007), 338–39.

34. Jackson Citizens' Council, "'Let Officers Handle It,' Says Council Leadership," *Clarion-Ledger,* May 30, 1963, 12.

35. "A View from the South," Interview with William J. Simmons in *Yale Political,* 8 and 20–23, University Archives, Delta State University, Cleveland, MS; "The Un-American Revolution," Panel Discussion in *The Citizen* (June 1963): 6–15.

36. "Thompson Is Considering Making Governor's Race," *Clarion-Ledger,* June 4, 1963, 20; Charles M. Hills, "Parchman Facilities Offered by Governor," *Clarion-Ledger,* June 2, 1963, 1A and 11A; "Police Detain Wilkins and Other Agitators Saturday," *Clarion-Ledger,* June 2, 1963, 1A and 12A.

37. James Saggus, "Negro Quietly Becomes Ole Miss Law Student," *Clarion-Ledger,* June 6, 1963, 1; "Carolina Racial Crisis Brings Troops to City," *Clarion-Ledger,* June 8, 1963, 1A; "500 Guardsmen Move Near Alabama Campus," *Clarion-Ledger,* June 10, 1963, 1A; "Wallace, U.S. Gird for Historic Clash," *Clarion-Ledger,* June 11, 1963, 1A; "Wallace Gives in to Federal Might," *Clarion-Ledger,* June 12, 1963, 1A; "TV Speech: Kennedy Lashes Discrimination," June 12, 1963, 1A.

38. McMillen, *Citizens' Council,* 360n; Dittmer, *Local People,* 165–66. The most comprehensive account of Medgar Evers's life and work is Michael Vinson Williams, *Medgar Evers: Mississippi Martyr* (Fayetteville: University of Arkansas Press, 2011). In it, Williams provides an in-depth analysis of Evers's final days, the work he performed, and his growing awareness of his mortality as events escalated in Jackson. See 276–84.

39. Jane Biggers, "Greenwood Shocked, Neighbors Recall Beckwith as Outspoken Marine Vet," *Clarion-Ledger,* June 24, 1963, 1A.

40. Minor, "The Citizens' Councils," 45.

41. Eudora Welty, "Where Is the Voice Coming From?" *New Yorker,* July 6, 1963, 24–25.

42. Byron De La Beckwith to the Editor, April 8, 1957, 9, DeLaughter Collection, Box 4, Folder 32, Byron De La Beckwith Writings, MDAH.

43. Supplementary Offense Report, Police Department, Jackson, Mississippi, June 14, 1963; Supplementary Offense Report, Police Department, Jackson, Mississippi,

June 21, 1963; Supplementary Offense Report, Police Department, Jackson, Mississippi, June 25, 1963; and Supplementary Offense Report, Police Department, Jackson, Mississippi, June 26, 1963, Evers Papers, Subgroup 4, Series 46, Box 29, Folder 2: Jackson Police Department Offense Report, Medgar W. Evers Murder, 1963–1964, MDAH.

44. Supplementary Offense Report, Police Department, Jackson, Mississippi, January 25, 1964, Evers Papers, Subgroup 4, Series 46, Box 29, Folder 2: Jackson Police Department Offense Report, Medgar W. Evers Murder, 1963–1964, MDAH.

45. Testimony of James Holley, Hinds County Grand Jury, December 14, 1999, De-Laughter Collection, Box 4, Folder 28, MDAH; Delmar Dennis, Interview by Bobby De-Laughter, May 3, 1990, 31–32 and 34, DeLaughter Collection, Box 4, Folder 21, Rev. Delmar Dennis, 1 of 2, MDAH; McMillen, *Citizens' Council*, 360n; Williams, *Medgar Evers*, 305–6. The Sovereignty Commission's relationship to jury selection came to light in 1989 when an investigative journalist for the *Clarion-Ledger*, Jerry Mitchell, exposed the tampering, eventually leading to Beckwith's third and final trial in 1994, which concluded with his conviction. Beckwith died in 2001. Erle Johnston's account, written in 1990, after Mitchell's article but prior to Beckwith's third indictment, denies any wrongdoing regarding the investigations, arguing that the information obtained "could have been obtained from a city directory, or through the procedure of 'voir dire.'" See Johnston, *Mississippi's Defiant Years*, 186–87; Myrlie Evers and William Peters, *For Us, the Living* (New York: Doubleday, 1967), 367–68.

46. "A View from the South," Interview with Simmons in *Yale Political*, 8 and 20–23. For text of the standard speech Simmons presented, see Folders 52 and 53, Box 3, ACCM Collection, z/0773.0000, MDAH; Richard D. Morphew, "Operation Information," Speech at Citizens' Councils of America Leadership Conference in *The Citizen* (January 1964): 17–23; W. J. Simmons, "Citizens' Council's Purpose, Increased Interest In," *Forum*, October 1963, Reel #6337R; Roy V. Harris, "Northern Interest in Race Problem," *Forum*, November 1963, Reel #6343R. No evidence seems to exist to confirm the Council's claims about membership or *Forum*'s circulation across the country.

47. Crespino, *In Search of Another Country*, 92–93; Chris Meyers Asch, *The Senator and the Sharecropper: The Freedom Struggles of James O. Eastland and Fannie Lou Hamer* (New York: New Press, 2008), 153–54.

48. McMillen, *Citizens' Council*, 245–46 and 334.

49. For a more detailed account of the CCFAF's activities, funding structure, and allies, see Sarah H. Brown, "The Role of Elite Leadership in the Southern Defense of Segregation, 1954–1964," *Journal of Southern History* 77, No. 4 (November 2011): 832–40; Crespino, *In Search of Another Country*, 92–100; Katagiri, *The Mississippi State Sovereignty Commission*, 122–25; Johnston, *Mississippi's Defiant Years*, 238–46; Loyd Wright and John C. Satterfield, "Blueprint for Total Federal Regimentation," Pamphlet for the Coordinating Committee for Fundamental American Freedoms, 1963, Folder 10, Box 2, M319, Johnston Collection, USM.

50. George Lewis, "Virginia's Northern Strategy: Southern Segregationists and the Route to National Conservatism," in *Painting Dixie Red: When, Where, Why, and How the South Became Republican*," ed. Glenn Feldman (Gainesville: University Press of Florida, 2011), 100–4; Lewis, *Massive Resistance*, 176–80.

51. John J. Synon, "Civil Rights Opposition," *Forum*, November 1963, Reel #6342; John C. Satterfield, "Civil Rights Act of 1963," *Forum*, December 1963, Reel #6345; John C. Satterfield, "Effects of CRA on Average Americans," *Forum*, December 1963, Reel #6346; John Dowdy, "Civil Rights Legislation," *Forum*, December 1963, Reel #6347R; William M. Colmer, "Civil Rights Bill," December 1963, Reel #6350; Albert Watson, "Quota System in Federal Employment Agencies," *Forum*, December 1963, Reel #6351; William Cramer, "Civil Rights Proposal," *Forum*, December 1963, Reel #6352; John Dowdy, "Proposed Civil Rights Bill," *Forum*, January 1964, Reel #6401; Robert T. Ashmore, "Civil Rights Act," *Forum*, January 1964, Reel #6402; Robert T. Ashmore, "Civil Rights Bill," *Forum*, January 1964, Reel #6403; William K. Shearer, "California's Views on the Civil Rights Act," *Forum*, January 1964, Reel #6404; Strom Thurmond, "CRA and School Prayer," *Forum*, February 1964, Reel #6405; Strom Thurmond, "Civil Rights Proposal," *Forum*, February 1964, Reel #6406; John Synon, "Proposed Civil Rights Act," *Forum*, April 1964, Reel #6413; John Bell Williams, "Civil Rights Bill," *Forum*, April 1964, Reel #6414; Ross Barnett, "Concern over CRA," *Forum*, May 1964, Reel #6417R.

52. John Synon, "Civil Rights Bill Opposition," *Forum*, November 1963, Reel #6342.

53. John Satterfield, "Civil Rights Act of 1963," *Forum*, December 1963, Reel #6345.

54. Lewis, *Massive Resistance*, 180.

55. John Satterfield to Paul Johnson, March 4, 1964, SCR ID # 6–70–0–127–1–1–1 through-5-1-1, mdah.state.ms.us/arrec/digital_archives/sovcom/result.php?image=images /png/cd07/051300.png&otherstuff=6|70|0|127|1|1|1|50574|#; Satterfield Enclosure to Paul Johnson, March 4, 1964, SCR ID #6–70–0–128–6–1–1- and-9-1-1, mdah.state.ms.us/ arrec/digital_archives/sovcom/result.php?image=images/png/cd07/051310.png&other stuff=6|70|0|128|6|1|1|50584|; mdah.state.ms.us/arrec/digital_archives/sovcom/result .php?image=images/png/cd07/051313.png&otherstuff=6|70|0|128|9|1|1|50587|.

56. Satterfield to Paul Johnson, March 4, 1964, SCR ID # 6–70–0–127–3–1–1, mdah .state.ms.us/arrec/digital_archives/sovcom/result.php?image=images/png/cd07/051302 .png&otherstuff=6|70|0|127|3|1|1|50576|#.

57. Satterfield Enclosure to Paul Johnson, March 4, 1964, SCR ID #6–70–0–128–1–1–1 through-31-1-1, mdah.state.ms.us/arrec/digital_archives/sovcom/result.php?image= images/png/cd07/051305.png&otherstuff=6|70|0|128|1|1|1|50579|#.

58. Satterfield Enclosure to Paul Johnson, March 4, 1964, SCR ID #6–70–0–128–7–1–1, mdah.state.ms.us/arrec/digital_archives/sovcom/result.php?image=images/png /cd07/051311.png&otherstuff=6|70|0|128|7|1|1|50585|#.

59. Satterfield Enclosure to Paul Johnson, March 4, 1964, SCR ID #6–70–0–128–12–1–1, mdah.state.ms.us/arrec/digital_archives/sovcom/result.php?image=images/png /cd07/051316.png&otherstuff=6|70|0|128|12|1|1|50590|#.

60. Erle Johnston, Memo to File, June 22, 1964, SCR ID #6–70–0–185–1–1–1, mdah .state.ms.us/arrec/digital_archives/sovcom/result.php?image=images/png/cd07/051492 .png&otherstuff=6|70|0|185|1|1|1|50765|.

61. Johnston, Memo to File, June 5, 1964, SCR ID # 99–36–0–26–1–1–1, mdah.state .ms.us/arrec/digital_archives/sovcom/result.php?image=images/png/cd10/076383.png& otherstuff=99|36|0|26|1|1|1|75411|; Johnston, Memo to William Burgin and John

Junkin, May 25, 1964, SCR ID # 99–36–0–38–1–1–1, mdah.state.ms.us/arrec/digital
_archives/sovcom/result.php?image=images/png/cd10/076398.png&otherstuff=
99|36|0|38|1|1|1|75426|.

62. Mississippi State Sovereignty Commission, Schedule of Payments Made to Citizens Council Forum for the Period July 1, 1960 through June 30, 1965, no date, Folder 9, Box 2, M-99, Citizens' Council Collection, USM.

63. Burke Marshall to Dan H. Shell, July 15, 1964, Folder 1, Box 3, M-99, Citizens' Council Collection, USM.

64. Americans for the Preservation of the White Race, Charter of Incorporation, SCR ID # 6–36–0–1–6–1–1, mdah.state.ms.us/arrec/digital_archives/sovcom/result.php?image =images/png/cd06/044275.png&otherstuff=6|36|0|1|6|1|1|43622|.

65. Erle Johnston, Memo to File, July 24, 1964, Folder 1, Box 3, M-99, Citizens' Council Collection, USM; Johnston, Memo to File, August 24, 1964, Folder 1, Box 3, M-99, Citizens' Council Collection, USM; Crespino, *In Search of Another Country*, 132–34.

66. Crespino, *In Search of Another Country*, 108–31.

67. "Council Urges Walkout: Jackson CC Gives Integration Protest," *Clarion-Ledger*, July 7, 1964, Folder 34, Box 1, Series 1, Cox Papers.

68. "Primos Defends Resistance, Attacks Ross Statement," *Jackson Daily News*, July 17, 1964, 2, Folder 34, Box 1, Series 1, Cox Papers.

69. Charles C. Bolton, *The Hardest Deal of All: The Battle over School Integration in Mississippi, 1870–1980* (Jackson: University Press of Mississippi, 2005), 96; United Press International, "Jackson CC Plans System of Schools," *Clarion-Ledger*, August 24, 1964, Folder 34, Box 1, Series 1, Cox Papers; United Press International, "CC Launches Drive for New Members," *Clarion-Ledger*, September 24, 1964, Folder 34, Box 1, Series 1, Cox Papers.

70. "Council School Is Opening Today," *Clarion-Ledger*, October 12, 1964; and "At Residence, 24 Pupils Attend CC School Monday," *Clarion-Ledger*, October 13, 1964, Mississippi Council on Human Relations Records, Box 17, Citizens Council Folder, MDAH; Council School Foundation, "Welcome to Council School: A Handbook of Information and School Policy," 1970, 7–8, Folder 28, Box 27, Series 2, Charles H. Griffin Collection, Congressional and Political Research Center, Mitchell Memorial Library, Mississippi State University; McMillen, *Citizens' Council*, 301.

71. Bolton, *The Hardest Deal of All*, 107.

72. McMillen, *Citizens' Council*, 301.

73. Medford Evans, "Trend of U.S. Public Opinion against Integration and the Civil Rights Movement," *Forum* #6419R, April 1964; Louis Hollis, "New Growth of Citizens' Councils," *Forum* #6424, June 1964; W. J. Simmons, "10th Anniversary of *Brown*," *Forum* #6424R, June 1964; W. J. Simmons, "Trend of Racial Disturbances in Northern Cities," *Forum* #6431, August 1964; W. J. Simmons, "School Integration in Clarksdale, Biloxi, Jackson, and Leake County," *Forum* #6434R, September 1964; Thomas Brady, "Freedom Democratic Delegation," *Forum* #6435R, September 1964; Medford Evans, "Private School Movement," *Forum* #6436R, September 1964; W. J. Simmons, "Presidential Election," *Forum* #6445R, November 1964; Medford Evans, "Long Hot Summer," *Forum* #6447R, December 1964.

74. William B. Street, "Leaders of Citizens Councils Face Lean Times," *Commercial Appeal,* October 17, 1964, Folder 11, Box 1, Cox Papers.

CHAPTER SIX

Note to chapter epigraph: David Nevin and Robert E. Bills, *The Schools that Fear Built: Segregationist Academies in the South* (Washington, DC: Acropolis Books, 1976), 19–20.

1. "White Monday in Mississippi," May 17, 1965, Reel #0038, MP 86.01, *Forum* Film Collection, MDAH.

2. Jackson Citizens' Council, *Aspect* 3:3 (April 1966): 1–2, Subject File, Citizens' Council 1962–1968, Z/0773.000: ACCM Collection, 1942–1973, MDAH; Jackson Citizens' Council, *Aspect* 4:8 (October 1966): 1–2, Subject File, Citizens' Council 1962–1968, Z/0773.000: ACCM Collection, 1942–1973, MDAH.

3. "What Is the Citizens' Council Doing?" *The Citizen* 22, No. 3 (December 1976): 28–29.

4. "What Is the Citizens' Council Doing?" *The Citizen* 22, No. 4 (January 1977): 31.

5. "What Is the Citizens' Council Doing?" *The Citizen* 22, No. 10 (July–August 1977): 21.

6. "What Is the Citizens' Council Doing?" *The Citizen* 22, No. 5 (February 1977): 13; "What Is the Citizens' Council Doing?" *The Citizen* 22, No. 6 (March 1977): 27.

7. "What Is the Citizens' Council Doing?" *The Citizen* 22, No. 6 (March 1977): 27–28.

8. "As Field Secretary, Ex-Postal Man Joins Council," *Jackson Daily News,* December 17, 1969; "Council Is Conducting Pike Membership Drive," *Clarion-Ledger,* December 24, 1968; and "Citizens Council Meet Future Cong. Griffin," *Clarion-Ledger,* May 18, 1969, Mississippi Council on Human Relations Records, Box 17, Citizens Council Folder, MDAH; "What Is the Council Doing?," *The Citizen* 21, No. 1 (October 1975): 27; "What Is the Council Doing?" *The Citizen* 21, No. 4 (January 1976): 28.

9. Charles Pearce, Interview with William J. Simmons and Wife, Bonnie Simmons, September 23, 1981, Transcript File #3, Digital File, MDAH, www.mdah.ms.gov/arrec/digital_archives/vault/projects/OHtranscripts/AU102_096183_3.pdf.

10. Charles C. Bolton, *The Hardest Deal of All: The Battle over School Integration in Mississippi, 1870–1980* (Jackson: University Press of Mississippi, 2005), 169.

11. Ibid., 174–75.

12. Pearce, Interview with Simmons.

13. Ibid.

14. Council School Foundation, "Welcome to Council School: A Handbook of Information and School Policy," 1970, 24–26, Folder 28, Box 27, Series 2, Griffith Collection.

15. Nevin and Bills, *Schools that Fear Built,* 3–4, 12–13, and 19–20.

16. Jackson Citizens' Council, "Council to Have New Home," *Aspect* 5, No. 9 (October–November 1967): 1, Subject File, Citizens' Council 1962–1968, Z/0773.000: ACCM Collection, 1942–1973, MDAH.

17. Ibid., Citizens Council Special Section, August 11, 1968, *Clarion-Ledger,* Section C;

and "Civil War General Once Owned Property," *Clarion-Ledger*, August 11, 1968, Section C, Mississippi Council on Human Relations Records, Box 17, Citizens Council Folder, MDAH.

18. "Building Dedicated in Historic Ceremony," *The Council* 13, No. 2 (November 1968): 5, 8; Robert B. Patterson, "Dedication of Citizen Council Building," August 9, 1968, 1, Box 3, Folder 47, Z0773.000/5, Citizens' Council Collection, MDAH.

19. Robert B. Patterson, "Dedication of Citizen Council Building," August 9, 1968, 1, Box 3, Folder 47, Z0773.000/5, Citizens' Council Collection, MDAH.

20. William J. Simmons, Interview with Charles Pearce, September 9, 1977, Transcript #2, Digital File, MDAH, mdah.state.ms.us/arrec/digital_archives/vault/projects/OHtran scripts/AU102_096183_2.pdf.

21. William J. Simmons to James O. Eastland, March 13, 1959, Folder Civil Rights 1959, Box 38, Subseries 1, File Series 3, Eastland Papers.

22. Joseph Crespino, *In Search of Another Country: Mississippi and the Conservative Counterrevolution* (Princeton, NJ: Princeton University Press, 2007), 98; William H. Tucker, *The Funding of Scientific Racism: Wickliffe Draper and the Pioneer Fund* (Urbana: University of Illinois Press, 2002), 126–29. Tucker's work on the Pioneer Fund's investments is outstanding for its identification of the circuitous route by which it made donations to groups that served its purposes. The path is not clear from the organization to the Council School Foundation, but the network of individuals and organizations involved as intermediaries, as well as the curious amount of monetary donations the CSF received, is convincing. The construction of the new Council headquarters is a bit ambiguous, although, in the coverage of the building's dedication, the *Clarion-Ledger* stated that the Council had taken out "a long-term bank loan" to cover the $162,000 contract with the construction firm. See *Clarion-Ledger*, August 11, 1968, Section C. It is also worth noting that when James Graham Cook interviewed Council administrations for *The Segregationists* in 1962, Council treasurer Marvin Callum mentioned an endowment initiative by which donors could bequeath land and assets to the Council in their wills. Cook mentions that his investigations found that B. C. Campbell, a Salt Lake City oil magnate, gifted the organization with 30 acres of oil land in Utah. An anonymous donor made a similar contribution to the Council shortly after. See James Graham Cook, *The Segregationists* (New York: Appleton-Century-Crofts, 1962), 99–100.

23. Tucker, *Funding of Scientific Racism*, 101–6.

24. Erle Johnston, Memo to File, June 22, 1964, SCR ID #6–70–0–185–1–1–1, mdah .state.ms.us/arrec/digital_archives/sovcom/result.php?image=images/png/cd07/051492 .png&otherstuff=6|70|0|185|1|1|1|50765|; Fund of the Founding Fathers, "Statement of Purposes and Methods," SCR ID #6–70–0–128–18–1–1 through 6–70–0–128–21–1–1, mdah.state.ms.us/arrec/digital_archives/sovcom/result.php?image=images/png/cd07 /051322.png&otherstuff=6|70|0|128|18|1|1|50596|.

25. Yasuhiro Katagiri, *The Mississippi State Sovereignty Commission: Civil Rights and States' Rights* (Jackson: University Press of Mississippi, 2001), 187–90; Crespino, *In Search of Another Country*, 44.

26. Crespino, *In Search of Another Country*, 98–99; Erle Johnston, Memo to File, 25 May

1964, SCR ID #99–36–0-38-1-1–1, mdah.state.ms.us/arrec/digital_archives/sovcom/result
.php?image=images/png/cd10/076398.png&otherstuff=99│36│0│38│1│1│1│75426│#;
Johnston, Memo to File, 5 June 1964, SCR ID #99–36–0-26-1-1–1, mdah.state.ms.us
/arrec/digital_archives/sovcom/result.php?image=images/png/cd10/076383.png&other
stuff=99│36│0│26│1│1│1│75411│#.

27. John J. Synon to William J. Simmons, December 3, 1965, Folder 1, Box 44, Subseries 1, File Series 3, Eastland Papers.

28. William J. Simmons to John J. Synon, December 6, 1965, Folder 1, Box 44, Subseries 1, File Series 3, Eastland Papers.

29. Robert Gayre, "Race Problems throughout the World," *Forum* #6544R, November 1965; Robert Gayre, "World Opinion," *Forum* #6545R, November 1965; Carleton Putnam, "Crisis in Rhodesia," *Forum* #6552, December 1965; Carleton Putnam, "Outlook for Self Government in Rhodesia," *Forum* #6601, January 1966.

30. Tucker, *Funding of Scientific Racism*, 71–75.

31. John J. Synon to E. M. Rhoodie, September 17, 1965, Folder 1, Box 44, Subseries 1, File Series 3, Eastland Papers.

32. John J. Synon to E. M. Rhoodie, September 17, 1965, Folder 1, Box 44, Subseries 1, File Series 3, Eastland Papers.

33. John J. Synon to William J. Simmons, December 3, 1965, Folder 1, Box 44, Subseries 1, File Series 3, Eastland Papers.

34. "Notes on Africa," *The Citizen* 10, No. 10 (July–August 1966): 2; William J. Simmons, "Report on a Trip to Southern Africa," *The Citizen* 10, No. 10 (July–August 1966): 4.

35. William J. Simmons, "Report on a Trip to Southern Africa," *The Citizen* 10, No. 10 (July–August 1966): 10–11; Zoe Hyman, "American Segregationist Ideology and White Southern Africa, 1948–1975" (PhD diss., University of Sussex, 2011), 168–71.

36. Hyman, "American Segregationist Ideology," 173–74.

37. Kirkpatrick Sale, *Power Shift: The Rise of the Southern Rim and Its Challenge to the Eastern Establishment* (New York: Random House, 1975), 92.

38. Sale, *Power Shift*, 91 (first quote), 100, 99 (second quote), and 104 (third quote).

39. Neil McMillen, *The Citizens' Council: Organized Resistance to the Second Reconstruction, 1954–64*, 2nd edition (Urbana: University of Illinois Press, 1994), 144.

40. San Francisco Citizens' Council to a Good American, October 1964, SCR ID #9–11–2-7-1-1–1, mdah.state.ms.us/arrec/digital_archives/sovcom/result.php?image=images
/png/cd08/061181.png&otherstuff=9│11│2│7│1│1│1│60365│#.

41. Meredith Crown to Neil McMillen, October 1, 1967, Folder 4, Box 1, M-99, Citizens' Council Collection, USM.

42. William K. Shearer, "Proposition XIV in California," *Forum* #6501R, January 1965.

43. William K. Shearer, "Proposition XIV in California," *Forum* #6502R, January 1965.

44. Daniel Martinez-HoSang, "Racial Liberalism and the Rise of the Sunbelt West: The Defeat of Fair Housing on the 1964 California Ballot," in *Sunbelt Rising: The Politics of Place, Space, and Region*, ed. Michelle Nickerson and Darren Dochuk (Philadelphia: University of Pennsylvania Press, 2011), 195, 204–5, and 210–11.

45. William K. Shearer, "Proposition XIV," *Forum* #6625, May 1965.

46. Darren Dochuk, *From Bible Belt to Sunbelt: Plain-Folk Religion, Grassroots Politics, and the Rise of Evangelical Conservatism* (New York: W. W. Norton, 2012), 274–78.

47. William J. Simmons, "Los Angeles Riots," *Forum* #6535R, September 1965; Strom Thurmond, "Causes of the L.A. Riots," *Forum* #6536, September 1965; Joe D. Waggoner, "Causes of Riots in the Large Cities," *Forum* #6538, September 1965.

48. George Lewis, *Massive Resistance: The White Response to the Civil Rights Movement* (New York: Bloomsbury Academic, 2006), 159.

49. George C. Wallace, "Maintenance of Law and Order in Selma," *Forum* #6511, March 1965.

50. George C. Wallace, "Selma Demonstrations," *Forum* #6512R, March 1965.

51. Wallace, "Maintenance of Law and Order in Selma."

52. Joe D. Waggoner, "Racial Riots," *Forum* #6539, October 1965; William J. Simmons, "Racial Disturbances in Large Cities Outside the South," *Forum* #6630, August 1966.

53. Medford Evans, "The Sheriff in the American System," *Forum* #6627, July 1966.

54. John J. Synon, "Daddybird, Riots and the Unemployed," *The Citizen* 12, No. 4 (January 1968): 20–21.

55. Editorial Opinion, "Commission on Riots," *The Citizen* 12, No. 7 (April 1968): 2.

56. William J. Simmons, "The Attack on the American System," *The Citizen* 15, No. 7 (April 1971): 10.

57. "There's Still Time to Register for 1966 CCA Conference in Scenic Chattanooga!" *The Citizen* 10, No. 3 (December 1965): 13–15; "Wallaces Will Be at CCA Conference," *The Citizen* 11, No. 4 (January 1967): 4–5; Robert B. Patterson, Speech to 14th Annual Leadership Conference, Citizens' Councils of America, August 29, 1969, Box 3, F37, Z/0773.000/5, Citizens' Council Publications, 1969–1974, MDAH; William J. Simmons, "Citizen Power," *The Citizen* 15, No. 9 (October 1970): 8.

58. Editorial Opinion, "Heart of America," *The Citizen* 15, No. 7 (April 1971): 2.

59. William J. Simmons, "The Attack on the American System," *The Citizen* 15, No. 7 (April 1971): 9.

60. William Lowndes, "Forgotten Man—1968 Style," *The Citizen* 12, No. 8 (May 1968): 14.

61. William J. Simmons, "Political and Social Implications of the 'Civil Rights' Crisis," *The Citizen* 10, No. 4 (January 1966): 18, 22.

62. McMillen, *Citizens' Council*, 58.

63. Dan T. Carter, *The Politics of Rage: George Wallace, the Origins of the New Conservatism, and the Transformation of American Politics* (New York: Simon and Schuster, 1995), 11.

64. Ibid., 12.

65. George Wallace, "Effect of Kennedy's Sending Federal Troops into Ole Miss on Future National Elections," *Forum* #6246R, November 1962.

66. George Wallace, "Wisconsin Presidential Primary," *Forum* #6415R, April 1964.

67. Charles Pearce, Interview with William J. Simmons and Wife Bonnie, September 11, 1981, 81.

68. See *The Citizen* 11, No. 9 (June 1967), *The Citizen* 11, No. 10 (July–August 1967), and *The Citizen* 11, No. 11 (September 1967); "Wallaces Will Be at CCA Conference," *The Citizen* 11, No. 4 (January 1967): 4–5; Carter, *Politics of Rage*, 296–97.

69. Robert B. Patterson, "Address at Belhaven College," October 24, 1968, Folder 47, Box 3, Z/0773.000/5, MDAH.

70. Carter, *Politics of Rage*, 298.

71. William J. Simmons, "Keynote Address to CCA Leadership Conference," *The Citizen* 13, No. 4 (January 1969): 12–13.

72. Robert B. Patterson, "Let's Get Going," *The Citizen* 13, No. 4 (January 1969): 19.

73. Kevin P. Phillips, *The Emerging Republican Majority* (New Rochelle, NY: Arlington House, 1969), 22 (quote), 36, and 286–87.

74. Sale, *Power Shift*, 106 and 109 (quote).

75. "Random Glances at the News," *The Citizen* 23, No. 7 (April 1978): 10–15.

76. Robert B. Patterson, "Black Monday in Retrospect," *The Citizen* 18, No. 8 (May 1974): 4–8.

77. William J. Simmons, "America at the Crossroads," *The Citizen* 16, No. 1 (October 1971): 5, 7.

78. "Jimmy Carter's Victory," *The Citizen* 22, No. 4 (January 1977): 2.

79. "It's Official—John Bell is a Candidate," *Jackson Daily News*, February 2, 1967, John Bell Williams Subject File, 1960–1966, MDAH; John Bell Williams, Press Release, April 26, 1967, John Bell Williams Subject File, 1967, MDAH; Charles H. Griffin to Howard Berkeley, June 27, 1967, John Bell Williams Subject Correspondence, Box 10382, Series 2416, Folder: Correspondence RE Citizens' Council, 1963–1967, MDAH.

80. "For Free Kindergartens: Council Urges Bill's Defeat," *Jackson Daily News*, January 16, 1973; W. F. Minor, "Councils Oppose Attendance Law," *Times Picayune*, December 16, 1973; "Citizens Council Poll Says Majority Agree," *Jackson Daily News*, February 20, 1973; and "Citizens' Council Raps Court Ruling on Patrol Hiring," *Clarion-Ledger*, April 7, 1974, 14A, Citizens' Council Subject File, 1969–1974, MDAH; Byron De La Beckwith, Campaign Speech for Lieutenant Governor, no date, DeLaughter Collection, Box 4, Folder 32, Byron De La Beckwith Writings, MDAH.

81. Crespino, *In Search of Another Country*, 227–28 and 234.

82. Chris Danielson, *After Freedom Summer: How Race Realigned Mississippi Politics, 1965–1986* (Gainesville: University Press of Florida, 2011), 5.

83. William J. Simmons to Bill Brock, January 16, 1980, *The Citizen* 25, No. 4 (January 1980): 21.

84. *The Citizen* 26, No. 3 (December 1980): cover; "New Hope for America," *The Citizen* 26, No. 3 (December 1980): 2.

85. George W. Shannon, "Platform Meaningless? Not to Ronald Reagan!" *The Citizen* 26, No. 4 (January 1981): 4–7.

86. Newt Gingrich, "What Is It Worth to Insure U.S. Survival?" Reprinted from Congressional Record in *The Citizen* 26, No. 7 (April 1981): 4–14, 23–31; Patrick Buchanan, "Bob Jones Critics Long on Hypocrisy," *The Citizen* 27, No. 8 (May 1982): 29, 31; George Will, "King and Irrelevance of the Civil Rights Era Today," reprinted from *Washington Post* in *The Citizen* 31, No. 7 (April 1986): 28–29.

87. "'Me-Tooism': Will Republican Liberals Drive Voters into New Third Party?" *The Citizen* 27, No. 12 (September 1982): 4–12.

88. Howard Raines, "Robert Boyd Patterson Interviewed by Author," *The Citizen* 24, No. 6 (March 1979): 16–23, esp. 22–23.

CONCLUSION

1. "Citizens Councils are with us still, but not as loudly," *Clarion-Ledger*, April 26, 1982, 3A, 10A; Jerry Mitchell, "'Progress' cited in racist council's demise," *Clarion-Ledger*, January 24, 1994, 1B, 2B.

2. William J. Simmons to Erle Johnston, November 18, 1987, Folder 9, Box 2, M319, Johnston Collection.

3. "William James Simmons Obituary," *Clarion-Ledger*, November 26, 2007.

4. Medford Evans, "Revolutionary Racism Assuaged by Council," *The Citizen* 30, No. 12 (September 1985): 29.

BIBLIOGRAPHY

MANUSCRIPT AND ARCHIVAL COLLECTIONS

Delta State University, University Archives
Walter Sillers Jr. Papers

Millsaps College Archives
Administrative Records
Millsaps College Bulletin

Mississippi Department of Archives and History

ARCHIVAL READING ROOM
Association of Citizens' Councils of Mississippi Collection
Bobby DeLaughter Collection
Brady, Thomas P. *Black Monday*. Winona: Association of Citizens' Councils of
    Mississippi, 1955
Carter, Hodding III. *The South Strikes Back*. New York: Doubleday, 1959
Citizens' Council Collection, 1954–1956
Citizens' Council Publications, 1969–1974
Citizens' Council Subject File, 1969–1974
The Citizen: Official Journal of the Citizens' Councils of America, 1961–1989
Ernst Borinski Papers
James P. Coleman Papers
Jane Schutt Papers
John Bell Williams Papers
John Bell Williams Subject Correspondence
John Bell Williams Subject File, 1960–1966
John Bell Williams Subject File, 1967
Medgar Wiley and Myrlie Beasley Evers Papers, 1900–1994

Mississippi Council on Human Relations Records

Simmons, William J. "A Comparison of Attitudes between Reconstruction I and Reconstruction II." Address to the Sons of Confederate Veterans, April 5, 1962. Jackson, MS.

Subject File, Citizens' Council, 1952–1958

Subject File, Citizens' Council Publications, 1956–1958

NEWSPAPER AND MICROFILM COLLECTION

Clarion-Ledger

Jackson Daily News

Forum Film Collection

DIGITAL COLLECTIONS

Mississippi State Sovereignty Commission Collection www.mdah.ms.gov/arrec /digital_archives/sovcom/

Sam H. Bowers Jr. Interview by Debra Spencer, January 30, 1984, Florence, MS, www.mdah.ms.gov/arrec/digital_archives/bowers/transcript.php

Mississippi State University

SPECIAL COLLECTIONS DEPARTMENT

Allen Eugene Cox Papers

Association of Citizens' Councils of Mississippi Collection

The Citizen Collection

Citizens' Council *Forum* Collection

The Citizens' Council: Official Paper of the Citizens' Councils of America

Wilson F. "Bill" Minor Papers

CONGRESSIONAL AND POLITICAL RESEARCH LIBRARY

Charles H. Griffin Collection

John C. Stennis Collection

PERIODICALS

Human Events

National Review

University of Mississippi, J. D. Williams Library, Archives and Special Collections

James O. Eastland Papers

University of Southern Mississippi, William D. McClain Library and Archives
Citizens' Council Collection
Digital Collections, Civil Rights in Mississippi Digital Archive
    Thomas P. Brady. Interview by Orley B. Caudill, March 7, 1972, Jackson, MS,
        crdl.usg.edu/export/html/usm/coh/crdl_usm_coh_mus-ohbradyt.html
        ?Welcome
    Erle Johnston. Interview by Yasuhiro Katagiri, 13 August 1993, Forest, Mis-
        sissippi, digilib.usm.edu/cdm/ref/collection/coh/id/4035
    William J. Simmons. Interview by Orley B. Caudill, June 26, 1979, Jackson,
        MS, digilib.usm.edu/cdm/ref/collection/coh/id/6472
    William J. Simmons and Bonnie Simmons. Interview by Charles Pearce, Sep-
        tember 23, 1981, catalog.mdah.state.ms.us/cgi-bin/koha/opac-detail.pl
        ?biblionumber=96183

University of Iowa Libraries
Facts Forum, Microfilm, The Right Wing Collection

BOOKS, ARTICLES, AND DISSERTATIONS

Arsenault, Raymond. *Freedom Riders: 1961 and the Struggle for Racial Justice.* New
    York: Oxford University Press, 2011.
Asch, Chris Meyers. *The Senator and the Sharecropper: The Freedom Struggles of
    James O. Eastland and Fannie Lou Hamer.* New York: New Press, 2008.
Badger, Anthony. *New Deal/New South: An Anthony Badger Reader.* Fayetteville:
    University of Arkansas Press, 2007.
Bartley, Numan V. *The Rise of Massive Resistance: Race and Politics in the South
    during the 1950's.* Baton Rouge: Louisiana State University Press, 1969.
Bell, Bernard Iddings. *Crowd Culture: An Examination of a Way of Life.* New York:
    Harper and Brothers, 1952.
Bissett, Jim. "The Dilemma over Moderates: School Desegregation in Alamance
    County, North Carolina." *Journal of Southern History* 81, No. 4 (November
    2015): 887–930.
Bolton, Charles C. *The Hardest Deal of All: The Battle over School Integration in
    Mississippi, 1870–1980.* Jackson: University Press of Mississippi, 2005.
Brown, Sarah H. "The Role of Elite Leadership in the Southern Defense of Seg-
    regation, 1954- 1964." *Journal of Southern History* 77, No. 4 (November 2011):
    827–64.

Carson, Clayborne. *In Struggle: SNCC and the Black Awakening of the 1960s.* Cambridge, MA: Harvard University Press, 1995.

Carter, Dan T. *The Politics of Rage: George Wallace, the Origins of the New Conservatism, and the Transformation of American Politics.* New York: Simon and Schuster, 1995.

Cobb, James C. *The Most Southern Place on Earth: The Mississippi Delta and the Roots of Regional Identity.* New York: Oxford University Press, 1992.

Collier-Thomas, Bettye, and V. P. Franklin. *My Soul Is a Witness: A Chronology of the Civil Rights Era, 1954–1965.* New York: Henry Holt, 2000.

Cook, James Graham. *The Segregationists.* New York: Appleton-Century-Crofts, 1962.

Crespino, Joseph. *In Search of Another Country: Mississippi and the Conservative Counterrevolution.* Princeton, NJ: Princeton University Press, 2007.

———. *Strom Thurmond's America.* New York: Hill and Wang, 2012.

———. "Strom Thurmond's Sunbelt: Rethinking Regional Politics and the Rise of the Right." In *Sunbelt Rising: The Politics of Place, Space, and Region*, edited by Michelle Nickerson and Darren Dochuk, 58–81. Philadelphia: University of Pennsylvania Press, 2011.

Cresswell, Stephen. *Rednecks, Redeemers, and Race: Mississippi after Reconstruction, 1877– 1917.* Jackson: University Press of Mississippi, 2006.

Critchlow, Donald T. *The Conservative Ascendancy: How the GOP Right Made Political History.* Cambridge, MA: Harvard University Press, 2007.

Danielson, Chris. *After Freedom Summer: How Race Realigned Mississippi Politics, 1965–1986.* Gainesville: University Press of Florida, 2011.

Day, John Kyle. *The Southern Manifesto: Massive Resistance and the Fight to Preserve Segregation.* Jackson: University Press of Mississippi, 2014.

Dittmer, John. *Local People: The Struggle for Civil Rights in Mississippi.* Urbana: University of Illinois Press, 1995.

Dochuk, Darren. *From Bible Belt to Sunbelt: Plain-Folk Religion, Grassroots Politics, and the Rise of Evangelical Conservatism.* New York: W. W. Norton, 2012.

Dupont, Carolyn Renee. *Mississippi Praying: Southern White Evangelicals and the Civil Rights Movement, 1945–1975.* New York: New York University Press, 2013.

Evers, Medgar. "I Speak as a Mississippian." In *The Autobiography of Medgar Evers: A Hero's Life and Legacy Revealed through His Writings, Letters and Speeches*, edited by Myrlie Evers-Williams and Manning Marable, 280–83. New York: Basic Books, 2005.

Evers, Myrlie, and William Peters. *For Us, the Living.* New York: Doubleday, 1967.

Feldman, Glenn. *The Irony of the Solid South: Democrats, Republicans, and Race, 1865–1944.* Tuscaloosa: University of Alabama Press, 2013.

Ferguson, Andrew. "The Boy from Yazoo City: Haley Barbour, Mississippi's Favorite Son." *Weekly Standard,* December 27, 2010, www.weeklystandard.com/articles/boy-yazoo-city_523551.html.

Frederickson, George M. *White Supremacy: A Comparative Study in American and South African History.* New York: Oxford University Press, 1981.

Frederickson, Kari. *The Dixiecrat Revolt and the End of the Solid South.* Chapel Hill: University of North Carolina Press, 2001.

Geary, Daniel, and Jennifer Sutton. "Resisting the Wind of Change: The Citizens' Councils and European Decolonization." In *The U.S. South and Europe: Transatlantic Relations in the Nineteenth and Twentieth Centuries,* edited by Cornelius A. van Minnen and Manfred Berg, 265–82. Lexington: University Press of Kentucky, 2013.

Hale, Grace Elizabeth. *Making Whiteness: The Culture of Segregation in the South, 1890–1940.* New York: Vintage Books, 1998.

Hayek, Friedrich. *The Road to Serfdom.* Chicago: University of Chicago Press, 1944.

Horne, Gerald. *Black and Red: W. E. B. DuBois and the Afro-American Response to the Cold War, 1944–1960.* New York: State University of New York Press, 1986.

Hustwit, William P. *James J. Kilpatrick: Salesman for Segregation.* Chapel Hill: University of North Carolina Press, 2013.

Hyman, Zoe. "American Segregationist Ideology and White Southern Africa, 1948–1975." PhD diss., University of Sussex, 2011.

Irons, Jenny. *Reconstituting Whiteness: The Mississippi State Sovereignty Commission.* Nashville, TN: Vanderbilt University Press, 2010.

Johnston, Erle. *Mississippi's Defiant Years, 1953–1973: An Interpretive Documentary with Personal Experiences.* Forest, MS: Lake Harbor Publishers, 1990.

Joseph, Peniel. *Waiting 'Til the Midnight Hour: A Narrative History of Black Power in America.* New York: Henry Holt, 2006.

Katagiri, Yasuhiro. *Black Freedom, White Resistance, and Red Menace: Civil Rights and Anticommunism in the Jim Crow South.* Baton Rouge: Louisiana State University Press, 2014.

———. *The Mississippi State Sovereignty Commission: Civil Rights and States' Rights.* Jackson: University Press of Mississippi, 2001.

King, Richard H. "The Struggle Against Equality: Conservative Intellectuals in the Civil Rights Era, 1954–1975." In *The Role of Ideas in the Civil Rights South,* edited by Ted Ownby, 113–36. Jackson: University Press of Mississippi, 2002.

Kruse, Kevin M. *White Flight: Atlanta and the Making of Modern Conservatism.* Princeton, NJ: Princeton University Press, 2007.

Lassiter, Matthew D. *The Silent Majority: Suburban Politics in the Sunbelt South.* Princeton, NJ: Princeton University Press, 2007.

Lewis, George. *Massive Resistance: The White Response to the Civil Rights Movement*. New York: Bloomsbury Academic, 2006.

———. "Virginia's Northern Strategy: Southern Segregationists and the Route to National Conservatism." In *Painting Dixie Red: When, Where, Why, and How the South Became Republican*, edited by Glenn Feldman. Gainesville: University Press of Florida, 2011.

Lowndes, Joseph E. *From the New Deal to the New Right: Race and the Southern Origins of Modern Conservatism*. New Haven, CT: Yale University Press, 2008.

Luckett, Robert E. Jr. *Joe T. Patterson and the White South's Dilemma: Evolving Resistance to Black Advancement*. Jackson: University Press of Mississippi, 2015.

Martinez-HoSang, Daniel. "Racial Liberalism and the Rise of the Sunbelt West: The Defeat of Fair Housing on the 1964 California Ballot." In *Sunbelt Rising: The Politics of Place, Space, and Region*, edited by Michelle Nickerson and Darren Dochuk, 188–215. Philadelphia: University of Pennsylvania Press, 2011.

McCurry, Stephanie. *Masters of Small Worlds: Yeoman Households, Gender Relations, and the Political Culture of the Antebellum South Carolina Low Country*. New York: Oxford University Press, 1995.

McGirr, Lisa. *Suburban Warriors: The Origins of the New American Right*. Princeton, NJ: Princeton University Press, 2002.

McMillen, Neil. *The Citizens' Council: Organized Resistance to the Second Reconstruction, 1954–64*, 2nd ed. Urbana: University of Illinois Press, 1994.

Morris, Tiyi. *Womanpower Unlimited and the Black Freedom Struggle in Mississippi*. Athens: University of Georgia Press, 2015.

Murphy, Paul V. *The Rebuke of History: The Southern Agrarians and American Conservative Thought*. Chapel Hill: University of North Carolina Press, 2001.

Nash, George H. *The Conservative Intellectual Movement in America Since 1945*. New York: Basic Books, 1976.

Nevin, David, and Robert E. Bills. *The Schools that Fear Built: Segregationist Academies in the South*. Washington, DC: Acropolis Books, 1976.

Nock, Albert Jay. *Our Enemy the State*. New York: William Morrow, 1935.

Noer, Thomas. "Segregationists and the World: The Foreign Policy of the White Resistance." In *Window on Freedom: Race, Civil Rights, and Foreign Affairs, 1945–1988*, edited by Brenda Gayle Plummer, 141–62. Chapel Hill: University of North Carolina Press, 2003.

Painter, Nell Irvin. *The History of White People*. New York: W. W. Norton, 2010.

Phillips, Kevin P. *The Emerging Republican Majority*. New Rochelle, NY: Arlington House, 1969.

Plummer, Brenda Gayle. *In Search of Power: African Americans in the Era of Decolonization, 1956–1974*. Cambridge: Cambridge University Press, 2013.

———. *Rising Wind: Black Americans and U.S. Foreign Affairs, 1935–1960.* Chapel Hill: University of North Carolina Press, 1996.

Roberts, Gene, and Hank Klibanoff. *The Race Beat: The Press, the Civil Rights Struggle, and the Awakening of a Nation.* New York: Vintage, 2007.

Rolph, Stephanie. "The Citizens' Council in Africa: White Supremacy in Global Perspective." *Journal of Southern History* 82, No. 3 (August 2016): 617–50.

Sale, Kirkpatrick. *Power Shift: The Rise of the Southern Rim and Its Challenge to the Eastern Establishment.* New York: Random House, 1975.

Salter, John R. Jr. *Jackson, Mississippi: An American Chronicle of Struggle and Schism.* Lincoln: University of Nebraska Press, 2011.

Schoenwald, Jonathan. *A Time for Choosing: The Rise of Modern American Conservatism.* New York: Oxford University Press, 2001.

Silver, James W. "Mississippi: Closed Society." *Journal of Southern History* 30, No. 1 (February 1964): 3–34.

Slate, Nico, ed. *Black Power beyond Borders: The Global Dimensions of the Black Power Movement.* New York: Palgrave Macmillan, 2012.

Sullivan, Patricia. *Lift Every Voice: The NAACP and the Making of the Civil Rights Movement.* New York: New Press, 2009.

———. "Southern Reformers, the New Deal, and the Movement's Foundation." In *The Civil Rights Movement,* edited by Jack E. Davis, 10–29. Malden, MA: Blackwell, 2001.

Taylor, Kristine. "Untimely Subjects: White Trash and the Making of Racial Innocence in the Postwar South." *American Quarterly* 67, No. 1 (March 2015): 55–79.

Tucker, William H. *The Funding of Scientific Racism: Wickliffe Draper and the Pioneer Fund.* Urbana: University of Illinois Press, 2002.

Viereck, Peter. *Conservatism Revisited.* New York: Collier Books, 1949.

Von Eschen, Penny M. *Race Against Empire: Black Americans and Anticolonialism, 1937–1957.* Ithaca, NY: Cornell University Press, 1997.

Ward, Jason Morgan. *Defending White Democracy: The Making of a Segregationist Movement and the Remaking of Racial Politics, 1936–1965.* Chapel Hill: University of North Carolina Press, 2011.

Watts, Trent. *One Homogeneous People: Narratives of White Southern Identity, 1890–1920.* Knoxville: University of Tennessee Press, 2010.

Webb, Clive, ed. *Massive Resistance: Southern Opposition to the Second Reconstruction.* New York: Oxford University Press, 2005.

———. *Rabble Rousers: The American Far Right in the Civil Rights Era.* Athens: University of Georgia Press, 2010.

Williams, Daniel K. *God's Own Party: The Making of the Christian Right.* New York: Oxford University Press, 2010.

Williams, Michael Vinson. *Medgar Evers: Mississippi Martyr*. Fayetteville: University of Arkansas Press, 2011.

Williamson, Joel. *The Crucible of Race: Black-White Relations in the American South since Emancipation*. New York: Oxford University Press, 1984.

INDEX

Alexander, Holmes, 113

Alexander v. Holmes, 159, 181

Americans for the Preservation of the White Race (APWR), 150–51, 152–53, 187

analysis (publication), 65

apartheid, 89–90. *See also* separate development

Ashmore, Robert T., 89

Barbour, Haley, 1

Barnett, Ross, 9–10, 69, 86–88, 93, 96, 98, 101–2, 103, 104, 105, 109, 111, 116–17, 118, 124, 126, 140, 141, 143, 145, 150, 151, 155, 161–162, 180, 181, 209n14

Barton, Billy, 95–96

Bates, Gladys Noel, 26

Beard, Fred, 60, 209n47

Beckwith, Byron De La, 41, 125, 141–44, 181, 214n45

Bell, Bernard Iddings, 16

black activism. *See* civil rights movement

Black Monday, 28–29, 30, 31, 32, 156

Booker, Simeon, 44–45, 46

Boriniski, Ernst, 45–46, 72, 73, 76

"Born of Conviction" statement, 130–35

Bowers, Sam, 31

Brady, Thomas P., 27–29, 31, 55, 61, 64, 70, 156, 161

Brown, S. E. D., 90

Brown v. Board of Education (1954), 2, 9, 18–20, 27, 65, 66, 109, 111, 155; reaction to, 27–30, 34–35, 51–52, 53, 56, 65, 81–82, 146, 163, 168, 170

Brown v. Board of Education (1955), 42, 65, 159

Buckley, William F., 66, 167

Campbell College, 94

Capitol Street boycotts, 94–95, 99, 123, 138–40

Carter, Asa, 52–53

Carter, Hodding, 44, 69, 74, 92–93, 98

Carter, Jimmy, 180

Carter, John W., 107

Carter, Lee, 107

Chodorov, Frank, 65–66

Circuit Riders, Inc. *See* Lowman, M. G.

Citizens' Council: administrative structure of, 5, 11, 61–62, 79, 157; Association of Citizens' Councils of Mississippi (ACCM), 5, 36, 40, 47, 58, 61, 66, 70, 76, 79, 84–85, 91, 96, 97, 99, 119–20, 130, 142; in California, 44, 64, 114, 118, 124, 156, 168–170, 183; *The Citizen,* 3, 4, 10, 60, 90, 91, 108, 113, 127, 135, 139–40, 157, 162, 164, 165, 171, 173–75, 177, 178–79, 180, 183, 184; *The Citizens' Council,* 48, 49–50, 57 (see also *The Citizen*); Citizens' Councils of America (CCA), 5, 8, 57, 70, 80, 83, 109, 142, 144, 151, 152–53, 157, 160–61, 162, 168, 174, 186; and civil rights movement, 3, 5, 6, 88, 92, 98–99, 118–19, 139–40, 144, 147–48, 175, 178–

Citizens' Council (*continued*)
80, 184; class identity within, 41–42, 44,
48, 52, 67, 127, 141–42, 144, 151, 196n18;
on communism, 61, 134, 135–36, 139; and
conservatism, 13, 65–67, 81, 83, 88–89,
93, 105, 107, 112–15, 118–19, 124, 126,
127–28, 134–35, 136, 145, 156, 158, 167–
70, 174–78, 180, 183–84, 185 (*see also*
conservatism); Council School Foundation, 3, 151, 152–53, 156, 158–60, 161, 162,
218n22; criticism of, 44, 45–46, 48–49,
65, 74–75, 76, 78–79, 98, 108–9, 110, 122,
201n17; and Cuban missile crisis, 135–37,
145; economic pressure of (*see* racial
terrorism); and education, 13, 35–40,
42–43, 76–78, 85, 151, 158–60, 174, 179;
Educational Fund of the Citizens' Council (EFCC), 9, 59–60, 61, 62, 64, 76–77, 85,
198n67; Engelhardt, Sam, 52; financing
of, 59–60, 61, 64, 76–77, 78, 80, 82–83,
86, 87, 93, 99, 107, 108–9, 111, 116, 120,
125–26, 130, 144, 145, 150, 157, 160, 164,
218n22; *Forum,* 9–10, 60–62, 73, 75–76,
77, 80–84, 85, 86, 87, 88–92, 93, 99, 102–
4, 105, 106, 107, 108–9, 112, 113, 114–16,
117, 118–19, 120, 125, 127–28, 130, 132,
135–37, 138, 139, 144, 145, 146, 150, 151,
153, 157, 162, 163, 164–65, 166, 168–69,
170–72, 176, 181; founding of, 2, 13, 29–
30, 31–34; ideology of, 3, 5, 7, 13, 37–38,
40, 41, 65, 67, 82, 91, 92, 110, 127, 129–30,
134–35, 144, 147–48, 162, 169–70, 171–73,
174, 178–79, 182, 183, 185; influence of,
58, 67–68, 69–70, 75–76, 86–88, 92–93,
95–96, 105, 111, 120, 126–27, 130, 131–32,
146, 151, 153, 167, 180–82; Jackson Citizens' Council, 47, 58, 60, 61, 62, 70–75,
76, 79–80, 82, 83, 86, 94, 99, 107, 113,
127, 131, 132, 139, 140, 151–52, 153, 157,
160, 166; and Ku Klux Klan, 49–51, 52,
65, 141; on law and order, 171–73, 174,
178–79; Leadership Conferences, 144,
161, 174–75, 177–78; and Medgar Evers's

murder, 141–44; membership in, 38, 77,
79–80, 85, 116, 140, 144, 157–58, 168,
196n18; and Millsaps College, 70–75, 76,
96, 131–32, 145; and Mississippi State
Sovereignty Commission (MSSC), 9,
62–64, 67, 70, 86, 87–88, 93–94, 95–96,
105, 107, 108–11, 120, 125–126, 130, 137,
163, 199n78 (*see also* Mississippi State
Sovereignty Commission); movement
in Alabama, 1, 52–53, 97, 106, 171, 176;
movement in Arkansas, 56, 206n19;
movement in Florida, 1, 43, 97, 206n19;
movement in Georgia, 1, 44, 95, 97, 106,
205n19; movement in Louisiana, 1, 44,
53, 57, 67, 97, 106; movement in Mississippi, 1, 8, 9, 10, 31–32, 33–51, 57–59, 60,
62–63, 67–68, 69–80, 82, 84–85, 92–93,
96, 98–104, 106, 109–11, 116, 118–19,
120, 124, 125, 126–27, 130–32, 134, 141–
44, 149–54, 156–57, 160–61, 180–82, 184;
movement in North Carolina, 81, 106,
185, 206n19; movement in South Carolina, 44, 86, 97, 205n19; movement in
Tennessee, 81–82, 97, 106, 185, 206n19;
movement in Virginia, 43, 53, 67, 97,
106, 146, 185, 206n19; on NAACP, 37, 47,
59, 75–76, 85; national initiatives of, 60,
61–62, 70, 80–84, 88–92, 93, 97, 108, 111,
112, 113, 125–26, 135–37, 144, 164–65,
168; and politics, 34, 59, 167, 174–75,
176–78, 180–84, 185; racial terrorism
of, 2, 5, 6, 13–14, 29, 30, 33–34, 40, 41,
42–46, 48–49, 57–58, 69–70, 106, 120–21,
142–44, 145, 152; and radical right,
91–92, 112–13, 119–20, 145, 167–68, 177,
181, 185; reputation of, 1, 11, 30, 34,
44, 48–49, 57–58, 69–70, 74–75, 78–79,
98–99, 106, 122, 128, 142, 145, 146, 150,
167; and Rhodesia, 3, 156–57, 166, 172
(*see also* Rhodesia); and school closure
amendment, 36, 38–40; South Africa, 3,
89–90, 130, 137, 156–57, 165–66, 172 (*see
also* South Africa); voting rights and,

58–59; and George C. Wallace, 3, 155, 156, 176–78, 181, 185 (*see also* Wallace, George C.); and white majority politics, 167–69, 173, 174–80, 183–84; and white moderates, 9, 11, 13, 40, 55–56, 57, 62–63, 64, 67, 73, 75, 85, 92–93, 97, 98–99, 103, 106, 134–35, 159, 185, 193n14, 201n17; women in, 76–78, 85

Civil Rights Act of 1964, 10, 132, 144–48, 149, 150–52, 153, 156

civil rights movement: after 1964, 169–70, 175, 179; historiography of, 6–7; legislation, 65, 141, 144–48, 156, 162, 168, 175, 178, 183; in Mississippi, 24–26, 41, 42, 44–46, 67, 69–70, 75–76, 86–87, 93–95, 99–102, 104–5, 110, 116–18, 120, 122–24, 130–35, 136, 137–41, 144, 145, 150–51, 205n10; prior to 1954, 23–24

Clark, Jim, 155

Coleman, James P., 55–56, 62–63, 64, 67, 68, 70, 78–79, 84, 85, 93–94, 108, 111, 193n14

Colmer, William, 61

Congress of Racial Equality (CORE), 101, 130, 124, 137, 169

conservatism, 5, 6, 8–9, 183–84, 191n9; and anticommunism, 112–14, 132–33, 135; and civil rights, 65–66, 88–89, 114, 145–48, 169–70; conservative ideology, 15–21, 28, 29–30, 65–66, 88–89, 112, 115, 136, 146–48, 169–70, 176, 177, 183–84, 207n36; conservative media, 9, 16–17, 29, 65–66, 118–19, 145, 148–49; and education, 16, 18–19, 160; and individualism, 16, 65–66, 113–14, 115, 147–48, 169; and law and order, 170–71, 176; and radical right, 113, 167, 170, 177, 207n36; relationship to segregationists, 20, 28, 29, 55, 59, 65–67, 88–89, 92, 107, 112–13, 114, 118–19, 145–48, 160, 167, 169–70, 176–77, 178, 180, 181–82, 183, 185, 187; and religion, 115, 134–35; southern strands of, 20–21, 114, 119, 136, 146–48, 167, 176–78,

182, 184, 187; Sunbelt conservatism, 114, 118–19, 133, 134–35, 136, 146, 167, 169–70, 183, 184 (*see also* Citizens' Council: and conservatism)

Coordinating Committee for Fundamental American Freedoms (CCFAF), 144–49, 163, 164

Council of Federated Organizations (COFO), 123, 210n66, 142

Courts, Gus, 45, 46

Cox, Rev. Murray, 122

Cramer, William, 136

Cuban missile crisis, 135. *See also* Citizens' Council: and Cuban missile crisis

Darden, C. R., 94

DeBeer, Rev. D. F. B., 89–90

DeCell, Hal, 63, 108

Delta Council, 25

Democratic Party, 21–22, 23, 29, 178, 180, 182

Derwinski, Edward J., 88

Dies, Martin, 61

Dixiecrats, 21–22, 23, 24, 25, 27–28, 53–54, 128, 132, 177–78, 189

Dowdy, John, 115

Draper, Wycliffe, 162

Eastland, James O., 18, 31, 53–55, 58, 59, 63, 82, 83, 132, 145

Engel v. Vitale, 115

Ethridge, Tom, 73–74

Evans, Medford, 3, 18, 132–34, 135, 139, 172, 188

Evers, Medgar, 41, 42–43, 45, 76, 93–95, 100, 116, 125, 137, 138, 140, 141–44, 181, 214n45

Facts Forum, 17–20, 65. *See also* conservatism: conservative media

Faubus, Orval, 55, 56, 117

Federation for Constitutional Government (FCG), 54–55, 57, 59, 62

Fellowship of Reconciliation, 72
Finger, Ellis, 72–73, 74, 75
Forum. See Citizens' Council: *Forum*
Franklin, Bishop Marvin, 130
Freedom Rides, 101–4, 116, 124. *See also,*
    Citizens' Council: *Forum*
Freedom Summer, 150
The Freeman, 65
Friends of Segregated Public Schools
    (FSPS), 36. *See also* Mississippi: and edu-
    cation; Citizens' Council: and education
Fund for the Republic, Inc., 63
Fund of the Founding Fathers, 163

Gallion, Macdonald, 105
Garrett, Dr. Henry, 165
Gartin, Carroll, 61, 86
Gayre, Robert, 165
Gilmore, Grady, 102, 103
Golding, E. Boyd, 61
Goldwater, Barry, 114, 136
Graves, John Temple II, 42
Green v. Connolly, 182

Hargis, Billy James, 114
Harris, Roy, 55
Harrison, Albertis, 117
Hayek, Friedrich A., 15–16
Hebert, F. Edward, 89
Henry, Aaron, 94, 100, 138
Higgs, William, 109
Hinson, Rev. J. Noel, 74
Hollis, Louis, 13, 80, 168
House Un-American Activities Committee
    (HUAC), 61, 90
Human Events, 16, 17, 65, 133
Humphrey, Hubert, 178
Hunt, H. L., 18
Hunter, Edward, 91
Hurley, Ruby, 43, 45, 94

Jackson Movement, 100–101, 205n10, 123,
    137–42

Jackson Municipal Library sit-in, 100–101
Jackson State College, 94, 100, 116, 123–
    24, 137
Jackson State University. *See* Jackson
    State College
John Birch Society, 112, 113, 207n36, 166,
    167
Johnson, Paul B., Jr., 99, 116, 148, 151,
    163
Johnston, Erle, 87–88. 104–5, 108–11, 126,
    130, 137, 145, 151, 163, 187, 188, 208n47,
    209n61, 214n45
Jones, Albert, 92, 96
Jones, Fred, 38, 40, 102, 103–4

Kennedy, Robert, 101–2, 118
King, Rev. Martin Luther, Jr., 138
Ku Klux Klan (KKK), 1, 2, 50, 150, 151, 166,
    181. *See also* Citizens' Council: and Ku
    Klux Klan

Ladner, Herbert, 61
Legal Educational Advisory Committee,
    62–63
Lee, Rev. George, 44–46, 72
Little Rock crisis, 56
Lowman, M. G., 91, 132
Lowndes, William, 175
Luburrow, W. A., 96

Mason, Dr. Gilbert, 95
massive resistance. *See* white resistance
    movements
McCorkle, Sara, 76–78, 96
McDowell, Cleveland, 140
McGill, Ralph, 95
McMilllen, Neil, 1, 3–4, 6, 11, 50, 81, 176
Meredith, James, 116–20, 209n47, 209n61,
    124, 130, 133–34, 135, 137, 142, 180
Miller, L. E., 74
Millsaps College, 128. *See also* Citizens'
    Council: Millsaps College
Minor, Bill, 141

Mississippi, 3, 18; black flight from, 24–25; black labor, 24–25, 32–33, 120–21; Delta region of, 32–33, 34, 35, 36, 42–43, 44, 120–23, 142–43; economy, 26–27, 120–21; and education, 25–27, 34–40, 42, 87, 110, 111, 131, 152–53, 158–59; Methodists in, 71, 73, 130–34; politics in, 34–35, 58, 62, 63, 78, 85–87, 180–82, 198n66. *See also* Citizens Council: Mississippi; civil rights movement: in Mississippi

Mississippi Association of Methodist Ministers and Laymen (MAMML), 132–34, 135

Mississippi Association of Teachers in Colored Schools (MATCS), 25–26

Mississippi College, 128

Mississippi Educators Association (MEA), 25, 39

Mississippi Human Relations Council (MHRC), 121–22

Mississippi State Sovereignty Commission (MSSC), 62–64, 67, 69–70, 72, 78, 87, 92, 93, 94, 95–96, 104, 109–11, 117, 120, 126, 130, 143, 145, 149–50, 151, 153, 163, 193n14, 209n61, 214n45. *See also* Citizens' Council: and Mississippi State Sovereignty Commission (MSCC)

Mississippi State University, 74

Moore, Herman, 33

Moore, Russell III, 76, 118

Morphew, Richard "Dick," 60–61, 73, 76, 80–81, 82, 88, 102, 103, 113, 136, 139, 144

Morrow, Jimmy, 75–76

National Association for the Advancement of Colored People (NAACP), 13, 23–24, 29, 34, 41, 42–43, 57, 75–76, 93–94, 95, 96, 100, 116, 137–38, 169; in Mississippi, 93–95, 100, 110, 116, 137–40, 141. *See also* Citizens' Council: on NAACP

National Civic Association, 92

National Putnam Letters Committee (NPLC), 149, 163–64

National Review, 66

Neal, Dr. Charles, 158

Nixon, Richard, 22, 175, 177, 178, 180, 181–82

Nock, Albert Jay, 15

Oakes, Donald, 157

Ole Miss. *See* University of Mississippi

Overstreet, Webb, Jr., 76

Oxford, Mississippi. *See* Meredith, James; University of Mississippi

Parchman State Penitentiary, 102, 103–4

Parker, Mack Charles, 84–85

Patterson, Joe T., 61, 70, 102, 105

Patterson, John, 117

Patterson, Robert (Tut), 3, 31–32, 35, 38–39, 47–48, 52, 55, 57, 58, 59, 60, 61–62, 64, 80, 85, 161, 178, 179, 184–85, 186, 210n6

Phillips, Kevin, 178

Pioneer Fund, 83, 162–65, 166, 172, 174, 177, 218n22. *See also* scientific racism; Weyher, Harry F.

Pittman, Bob, 108

Primos, Aleck, 152

private school movement, 152–53, 158–59, 160, 174, 181–82, 187, 188. *See also* Citizens' Council: on education; Citizens' Council: Council School Foundation

Proposition 14, 168–69, 176

Putnam, Carleton, 91, 104, 149, 163–64, 165. *See also* National Putnam Letters Committee (NPLC)

Rainach, Willie, 57

Reagan, Ronald, 167, 170, 183, 184

Republican Party, 59, 136, 146, 167, 178, 180, 181–83, 185

Rhodesia, 166, 167, 169. *See also* Citizens' Council: Rhodesia

Rhoodie, Dr. E. M., 165–66

Richardson, Willie, 123–24

Robertson, A. Willis, 115
Ross, Howard E., Jr., 152
Rossiter, Clinton, 66

Sale, Kirkpatrick, 167, 178, 184
Salter, John, 69–70, 121, 123, 138, 139, 140
Satterfield, John, 132, 145, 146, 147, 148–49
Schutt, Jane, 121, 210n66
scientific racism, 28, 29, 78, 83, 91, 129–30, 148–49, 162–66, 172–73, 174, 177, 218n22
Selma voting rights campaign, 155, 171
separate development, 166, 169, 172
Shannon, George, 4
Sharpeville Massacre, 89–90
Shearer, William K., 118–19, 168–69
Shuttlesworth, Rev. Fred, 138
Sillers, Walter, Jr., 24–25, 33, 54, 62, 63
Silver, James, 127
Simmons, Bill. *See* Simmons, William James
Simmons, W. J. *See* Simmons, William James
Simmons, William James, 3, 9, 47–48, 53, 55, 60, 62–63, 70, 73, 81, 82–83, 90, 95, 96, 98, 99, 105, 107, 109, 111, 125–30, 136, 137, 139–40, 143, 144, 158–59, 161–62, 163, 164, 166, 168, 170, 171–72, 173, 174, 175, 177–78, 179–80, 182, 187, 188, 209n47, 210n6
Smiley, Rev. Glenn, 72, 73
Smith, Lamar, 46
Smith, Robert L. T., 109
Smoot, Dan, 114. See also *Facts Forum;* conservatism: conservative media
South Africa, 89–90, 166, 169. *See also* Citizens' Council: South Africa
South African Observer, 90
Southern Christian Leadership Conference (SCLC), 138
Southern Governors Conference, 105–6
Southern Historical Association, 127

Southern Manifesto, 56
Southern Regional Council, 57–58, 63
Southwide Association of Municipal Officers, 105, 106–7
States' Rights Democratic Party. *See* Dixiecrats
Steffgan, Kent H., 168
Stennis, John, 58, 115, 118, 136
Street, William B., 126, 130
Student Nonviolent Coordinating Committee (SNCC), 101, 122, 137
Synon, John J., 4, 146, 147, 149, 163, 164–66, 172–73

Thompson, Allen C., 107, 113, 123, 138, 140, 141, 153–54
Thurmond, Strom, 22, 55, 112, 114, 170–71
Till, Emmett, 46
Tougaloo College, 69, 71–72, 75, 76, 94, 100, 123, 137, 138
Tower, John, 115, 136
Travis, Jimmy, 122

United States Commission on Civil Rights, 121, 122
University of Mississippi, 70, 95–96, 116–20, 124, 125, 130, 133–34, 135, 136, 137, 140, 142, 209n47
Utt, James B., 115, 118, 136

Viereck, Peter, 16
Virginia Commission on Constitutional Government (CCG), 146
Voluntary Committee of Christian Laymen, 132. *See also* Mississippi Association of Methodist Ministers and Laymen (MAMML)
voluntary segregation, 34, 38
Voting Rights Act of 1965, 156, 184, 187

Waggoner, Joe D., 171
Walker, Major General Edwin, 112–15, 117, 143, 207n36

Wallace, George C., 117, 140, 155–56, 170, 171, 175–76, 178, 180, 184, 185. *See also* Citizens' Council: Wallace, George C.

Watts riots, 169, 170–71

Welty, Eudora, 141–42

Weyher, Harry F., 83, 162, 164. *See also* Pioneer Fund

White, Hugh, Jr., 145

White, Hugh, Sr., 24–25, 26, 33, 34, 36, 38, 155

white moderates, 2, 9, 11, 55–56, 67, 73, 75, 81, 109–11, 131, 134, 138, 151, 153, 159, 180–81, 183, 193n14

white resistance movements, 1, 8–9, 10, 51–52, 53–54, 59, 67, 69, 81–82, 100, 106, 135, 146, 155, 205n19; anticommunism in, 28–29; historiography of, 6, 7, 11, 50, 51, 56, 186, 191n9; literature of, 22–23, 28–29; prior to 1954, 14, 21–22, 25

Whitten, Jamie, 61

Wilkins, Roy, 93–94

Williams, John Bell, 61, 80, 90, 102, 106, 113, 180–81

Winstead, Arthur, 61

Winter, William F., 181

Woolworth's counter sit-in, 139

Wright, Ellis W., Sr., 61, 72, 74, 75, 76, 132

Wright, Fielding, 22, 55

Wright, John, 99, 209n47

Yazoo City, 1, 42–43